Brain Magnet

Columbia Studies in the History of U.S. Capitalism

Columbia Studies in the History of U.S. Capitalism

Series Editors: Devin Fergus, Louis Hyman,
Bethany Moreton, and Julia Ott

Capitalism has served as an engine of growth, a source of inequality, and a catalyst for conflict in American history. While remaking our material world, capitalism's myriad forms have altered—and been shaped by—our most fundamental experiences of race, gender, sexuality, nation, and citizenship. This series takes the full measure of the complexity and significance of capitalism, placing it squarely back at the center of the American experience. By drawing insight and inspiration from a range of disciplines and alloying novel methods of social and cultural analysis with the traditions of labor and business history, our authors take history "from the bottom up" all the way to the top.

Capital of Capital: Money, Banking, and Power in New York City, 1784–2012, by Steven H. Jaffe and Jessica Lautin

From Head Shops to Whole Foods: The Rise and Fall of Activist Entrepreneurs, by Joshua Clark Davis

Creditworthy: A History of Consumer Surveillance and Financial Identity in America, by Josh Lauer

American Capitalism: New Histories, edited by Sven Beckert and Christine Desan

Buying Gay: How Physique Entrepreneurs Sparked a Movement, by David K. Johnson

City of Workers, City of Struggle: How Labor Movements Changed New York, edited by Joshua B. Freeman

Banking on Freedom: Black Women in U.S. Finance Before the New Deal, by Shennette Garrett-Scott

Threatening Property: Race, Class, and Campaigns to Legislate Jim Crow Neighborhoods, by Elizabeth A. Herbin-Triant

How the Suburbs Were Segregated: Developers and the Business of Exclusionary Housing, 1890–1960, by Paige Glotzer

Brain Magnet

Research Triangle Park
and the
Idea of the Idea Economy

Alex Sayf Cummings

Columbia University Press New York

Columbia University Press
Publishers Since 1893
New York Chichester, West Sussex
cup.columbia.edu

Library of Congress Cataloging-in-Publication Data
Names: Cummings, Alex Sayf, author.
Title: Brain magnet : Research Triangle Park and the idea of the idea economy / Alex Sayf Cummings.
Other titles: Columbia studies in the history of U.S. capitalism.
Description: New York : Columbia University Press, 2020. | Series: Columbia studies in the history of U.S. capitalism | Includes bibliographical references and index.
Identifiers: LCCN 2019047171 (print) | LCCN 2019047172 (ebook) | ISBN 9780231184908 (cloth) | ISBN 9780231184915 (paperback) | ISBN 9780231545747 (ebook)
Subjects: LCSH: Research Triangle Park (N.C.)—History. | Knowledge economy—North Carolina—Research Triangle—History. | Technology—Research—North Carolina—Research Triangle—History.
Classification: LCC HC79.I55 C87 2020 (print) | LCC HC79.I55 (ebook) | DDC 338.4/7609756—dc23
LC record available at https://lccn.loc.gov/2019047171
LC ebook record available at https://lccn.loc.gov/2019047172

Columbia University Press books are printed on permanent and durable acid-free paper.
Printed in the United States of America

Cover image: American Association of Textile Chemists and Colorists (AATCC) Technical Center, Research Triangle Park, North Carolina
Cover design: Lisa Hamm

For Saira

Because we are the last, best hope for this nation's future.
We are the creative economy.
And we will prevail!

—Gary Shteyngart, *Super Sad True Love Story*

Contents

Acknowledgments

This story originated in an idea for a dissertation topic and then became the dreaded "second book." I have complained a great deal. To those who somehow put up with this, I feel immeasurable gratitude.

I cannot thank my PhD advisers, Betsy Blackmar and Barbara Fields, enough for always sticking with me and always asking tough questions when my ideas were not good. I've had the great fortune to benefit from the insight of numerous respected scholars, including Ed Balleisen, Peter Coclanis, David Farber, Bill Graves, Margaret Pugh O'Mara, Elizabeth Tandy Shermer, Bryant Simon, and Siva Vaidhyanathan. As editors, both Susan Ferber and Joseph Parsons nurtured this project before it was even a real thing, and both Bridget Flannery-McCoy and Stephen Wesley at Columbia University Press offered stalwart support and thoughtful guidance that went a long way toward strengthening the manuscript once it was. The series editors, Devin Fergus, Louis Hyman, Bethany Moreton, and Julia Ott, have also been tremendously helpful.

Many librarians and archivists gave their time to this book at critical junctures, most notably Lynn Richardson at the Durham County Library, Jason Tomberlin at the University of North Carolina at Chapel Hill, and Matthew "Not Matthew" Farrell at Duke University. Eileen McGrath interrupted her retirement to help me build a picture of how the Triangle has been portrayed in fiction. ("If this book ever gets finished," I told Eileen in 2016, "expect to see your name in big, **bold**, *italic*, flashing letters in the Acknowledgments." I tried.)

An incredible array of interviewees made this project possible, including Nazeeh Z. Abdul-Hakeem, Saima Afzal, Mayor Bill Bell, Jeffrey Billman, Jay Bigelow, Buckley Crist, Sol Ellis, Representative Nick Galifianakis, Bob Geolas, Ferrel Guillory, Geoffrey Harpham, Tyran Hill, Farooq and Zubaida Mazhar, David Menconi, Jerry Miller, Bill Mitchell, Smita Patel, Sarah Taber, Chuck Till, Kristie VanAuken, and Tom Wenger. The project was also generously supported with real money by the North Caroliniana Society, the American Council of Learned Societies, the Mellon Foundation, and the College of Arts and Sciences at Georgia State University.

In the end, my friends have suffered the most. My colleagues Rob Baker, Marni Davis, Matt Lasner, Jared Poley, Jeffrey Trask, and Kate Wilson have been endlessly helpful, as have my dearest friends and collaborators, Joel Suarez, Romeo Guzmán, Aimee Castenell, Jeena Patel, Tyler Singh, Tanya Martinez, Michelle Lacoss, R. Mike Burr, Mary Rolinson, Christopher Staaf, Ryan Prechter, and Stanley Thangaraj. My parents, Andy and Sandy Shepherd and Taher and Crystal Zarti, have sustained me with their perpetual love and confidence in my questionable abilities.

But more than anyone, Saira Mazhar was there the entire way, always present with the greatest patience and insight—always, to steal from the novelist Edwin O'Connor, "listening, rejoicing, consoling, advising, exhorting, tempering, laughing, loving, living."

Brain Magnet

Preface

RTP DONUTS

Farooq and Zubaida Mazhar got their first taste of America in 1978. It was the poor, tiny town of Ahoskie in eastern North Carolina, where Farooq's brother Iqbal had started practicing as an eye doctor not long before. Their American odyssey included a cross-country road trip with the extended family that took them from the Carolinas to California and ended with an RV that burst into flames in Salinas, Kansas. (Thankfully, everyone survived.)

Farooq and Zubaida hailed from Karachi, the vast Pakistani metropolis on the shores of the Arabian Sea. The couple brought their growing family to Chicago in 1985, where Farooq's other brother, Masood, lived, and started a business selling women's handbags, jewelry, and various tchotckes from South Asia. But the bitter cold of Chicago winters turned out to be too much for the family, who were accustomed to the practically sliceable heat and humidity of Karachi, and so they returned home.

Life brought them back to North Carolina again and again, though, in the 1980s—yearly, in fact. More than anything, the Mazhars wanted to find a better life for their three children that was far from the political turmoil and violence of their home city. A safe, quiet home, education in American universities—these were the hopes that led the couple to leave a relatively comfortable life and a successful business in Pakistan for the leafy suburbs around Research Triangle Park (RTP), the high-tech mecca near Durham, North Carolina. There, companies such as IBM and Nortel employed thousands amid scrawny pine trees and masses of ungovernable kudzu.

They left it all to wake up at 3:00 a.m. and make doughnuts in a small shop—aptly dubbed RTP Donuts—at the intersection of Highways 54 and 55, a stone's throw from the research park. The store supplied sugary goods for the in-house cafeterias of companies such as pharmaceutical giant Glaxo, and their walk-in traffic came mostly from workers in RTP, which had no dining or retail establishments of its own thanks to strict zoning. For several years the Mazhars split their time between Durham and Karachi, doing arduous, low-wage labor so they could be with their children, who were studying at nearby Duke University and North Carolina State University.

But the Mazhars soon soured on the doughnut trade. The hours were long and the profits nonexistent, and they had to rely on others for doughnut-making expertise—primarily, an Eritrean immigrant named Danny, who sometimes left them in the lurch. ("It's not easy making doughnuts," Farooq later recalled. "I basically thought you put something in the machine at one end and at the other end the doughnut comes out. It wasn't anything like that.")[1]

The schools and universities of the Research Triangle—the greater metropolitan area that encompasses Raleigh, Durham, and Chapel Hill—brought the Mazhars to North Carolina. RTP itself brought them to the doughnut shop. One of their daughters, Saira, attended the University of North Carolina at Charlotte, where we met and later married.

This story is not of merely personal or sentimental significance, I hope. Rather, it is the tale of one family swept up in the centripetal forces that brought scientists and engineers, academics and artists, immigrants and hayseeds to the Triangle in the late twentieth century. The emergence of a high-tech economy in Raleigh-Durham changed the face of North Carolina, in terms of plain dollars and cents. Software engineers employed in

RTP made far more money than workers in furniture or tobacco or textiles, the state's traditional industries, generating greater tax revenue, lifting property values, and spawning other jobs and enterprises (such as the doughnut shop). It also brought people from the hinterland of North Carolina, from across the United States and, indeed, the world to a place that was once among the nation's poorest, sleepiest backwaters.

I remember visiting the Research Triangle as a child, when my grandfather needed medical treatment at Duke because of exposure to toxic chemicals at the plastics plant in Charlotte, where he worked. I was struck by the relative ethnic diversity on display as white, black, Latino, and Asian customers idled in line at a McDonald's. It was not exactly Queens, but it was still a far cry from the small textile town where I grew up. The Triangle was the land of hospitals, universities, technology—an Emerald City of sorts, or a "City of Medicine," in Durham's canny self-description.

I always wondered why this place had better jobs and opportunities than other stretches of America, whether in rural North Carolina or Indiana or West Virginia, where people scraped by in factories, grocery stores, and gas stations. The central question of history as a discipline, of course, is "when": why did things change when they did? The central question of geography is "where": why did this happen here, and not there? This book attempts to answer both, by putting the familiar image of the information or knowledge economy in a different relief.

A NEW GENEALOGY OF THE FUTURE

This book seeks to interrogate the idea of the knowledge economy itself—a phrase so shopworn and mundane that it hardly seems to merit a first thought, let alone a second. Barely a day goes by when someone on National Public Radio (NPR) does not refer to "today's knowledge-based economy." That the United States and the rest of the world's most advanced nations have moved on to economies driven by information, not manufacturing, is broadly taken for granted. Thanks to new technologies—whether automation or the Internet or other telecommunications—the basic structure of American capitalism changed in the late twentieth century, placing knowledge and the workers who have it at the forefront of economic change. The transition feels natural, inevitable, inexorable.

But what if the information economy was not the result of a natural progression, one that pursued its own internal economic and technological logic? What if it was contrived, created intentionally by planners, politicians, and public policy?

My first book, *Democracy of Sound*, explored the shift toward a postindustrial economy through changing ideas about intellectual property law—specifically the legal status of recorded sound, which was not protected by copyright in the United States until 1972 (much later than in most developed nations). The story of music piracy revealed how Americans first thought of copyright as a monopoly power, necessary but limited, in the time of the Progressive Era and New Deal; yet businesspeople, jurists, and legislators increasingly saw stronger and more expansive intellectual property rights as vital to the nation's economic health from the 1970s forward, as deindustrialization reshaped the economic landscape. Thinkers such as Peter Drucker and Daniel Bell sketched out the intellectual framework of a postindustrial economy, and lawmakers responded by tailoring policy to the needs of industries such as biotechnology, entertainment, fashion, and software—fields that were about ideas and creativity, not "making stuff."[2]

Brain Magnet examines this same transition from a different angle of vision—looking not at intellectual property per se but at the places where it is made. It is a story of local economic development, particularly the creation of a high-tech enclave in what was once one of the poorest and least educated states in the Jim Crow South. Rather than focusing on law and music, this book considers how local leaders in academia, business, and politics set out to imagine a new and different kind of economy beginning in the 1950s. Yes, it is a story of elites—bankers, professors, governors—but even these high-flying figures were ultimately small in the grand scheme of American capitalism's transformation in the late twentieth century. It is about the unlikely efforts of local leaders to solve the thorny problem of development: delivering jobs, better wages, and more opportunities for communities that desperately needed them. Every mayor wakes up every day thinking of how she will solve basic, pragmatic problems and make things work. RTP was an unusually ambitious and remarkably coordinated effort to make an economy defined for generations by poverty and underdevelopment "work" in a different way.

In some ways, it did work. RTP is the largest research park in the United States and has attracted numerous marquee employers, such as IBM and Glaxo, that pay many of their employees high-end salaries. Triangle cities such as Raleigh, Durham, and Cary have won a reputation for an excellent quality of life, ranking among "best places" to pursue a career and raise a family in the twenty-first century.[3] The region boasted a relatively affordable cost of living—at least compared with other major metro areas in the United States—as well as mostly good schools and enough cultural stimulation, thanks in large part to local universities, to make life bearable, perhaps even pleasant, for an educated, upper-income family. It was a diligently designed outpost of the professional workforce of the future, a group that urbanist Richard Florida would eventually dub the "creative class" more than forty years after RTP's founding.[4]

Indeed, RTP was a place expressly designed for knowledge workers before that term was even introduced. It was green, pastoral, sprawling, quiet, clean—everything that a traditional city was not. It was a landscape modeled on a college campus, thought to be the ideal place for thinkers to think. Nothing was accidental or organic in RTP, except perhaps for the kudzu that assembled ominously at its borders. The park's planners and boosters not only created a template of what an environment for intellectual labor ought to look like; they also pioneered an approach to economic development that leveraged creativity, culture, and especially universities to attract advanced industries and educated workers. In RTP, not Silicon Valley, one finds a conscious and deliberate effort to build an information economy. It is also a striking and early example of urban branding, in which a new metropolitan identity appeared as if from nothing.

BRAINS, CITIES, AND THE PROBLEM OF CLASS

Brain Magnet attempts to bridge the stories of cities and the information economy, of technology and space and place. Scholars have traced the rise of a postindustrial society for more than fifty years, from Peter Drucker and Fritz Machlup's early writing on knowledge work in the 1960s to

Daniel Bell's influential work in the 1970s, sociologist Manuel Castells's *The Informational City* in 1989, and historian Margaret Pugh O'Mara's *Cities of Knowledge* in 2004.[5] The centrality of Stanford to Silicon Valley's rise and Harvard and MIT to the emergence of tech in greater Boston is well documented, but scholars such as LaDale Winling and Andrew Simpson have begun to examine the increasingly crucial role of universities in urban development across metropolitan America with the rise of the "eds and meds" economy in the late twentieth century.[6]

These scholars have worked at the intersection of urban history and the information economy, but without taking a step back to consider that economy as a deliberate cultural project in its own right. This book is, in a way, a meta-narrative of how an information economy was conceived, sketched, planned, and implemented, and the underlying assumptions about class and culture that undergirded the new creative economy. It aims to connect the intellectual and cultural history of the knowledge economy and the literature on postindustrial cities, which have mostly operated on separate, if parallel, tracks.

Certainly few historians have treated the idea of the idea economy itself, the city of knowledge, the creative city, as a subject of critical scrutiny. And few have searched for the agency and intent of the real, historical individuals who set out to build it, only half knowing what they were building. *Brain Magnet* seeks to do this by employing a distinctive method: refracting the story of broad changes in the nature of capitalism through concepts of space and place. What does the genesis of a knowledge economy look like at the founding, among possum and pine, dirt roads and gleaming, modernist laboratories? What vision did the planners of this place—the academics, bankers, business leaders, managers, politicians, secretaries, and scientists who built it—have in mind when they laid out a space for technological innovation and intellectual labor?

This is the kind of work that would come to be hegemonic—if not numerically predominant within the broader economy—in the age of Silicon Valley and HBO's *Silicon Valley*, in the time of what some critics have called "cognitive capitalism."[7] French economist Yann Moulier Boutang defined this new variant of capitalism as one "founded on the accumulation of immaterial capital, the dissemination of knowledge and the driving role of the knowledge economy."[8] More than earlier mercantile and industrial economies, it derives value from "intelligent, inventive and innovative labour, and . . . mobilises the cooperation of brains in networks," particularly toward the production of intellectual property such as copyrighted works and patents.[9] Within the broader culture, these brainy people command a valorized social and economic position. Consider the nerds in the TV series *Silicon Valley*, who are feted with riches by venture capitalists because of their idea for a powerful new algorithm, while workers of far lesser status, known as Taskers, scurry around shopping for groceries and picking up dry cleaning for the elite, all coordinated by an app. (The episode was called, fittingly, "Intellectual Property.")[10]

Indeed, knowledge work is the kind of labor most valued and prized in an economy driven by brains. Back in the 1970s, sociologist Daniel Bell spelled out the special role a new class of educated experts would assume in a changing economy. More recently, Richard Herrnstein and Charles Murray spun the same message in more sinister, if franker, terms in their controversial 1994 book, *The Bell Curve*: in a postindustrial society, the less educated and less able risked falling far behind a new "cognitive elite." Later commentators celebrated and teased this new class of tech bros and bobos, and Richard Florida repackaged them as the essential ingredient of urban development: the "creative class."[11]

In Raleigh-Durham, we see the hazy, early outlines of this new political economy, with all the contradictions and shortcomings that come with a development strategy explicitly geared toward the interests of the affluent and educated and technologically advanced industries. High-tech, postindustrial capitalism is both more innovative and prosperous and more unequal and uneven, better planned yet more socially fragmented. In a time of the movement of young people "back to the city," gentrification, and increasing social and economic stratification, the story of the world's first designed-to-order city of ideas has much to teach us.[12]

Of course, it was not just hipsters coming back to the city in the late twentieth century and early twenty-first. Since the 1960s, people had been coming from Pakistan and Yugoslavia, Westchester and Harlem and Palo Alto to live and work in the Triangle. They were part of a great social drama that unfolded in the United States, as social and geographical mobility within the nation and new waves of immigration led to the multiethnic metropolitan landscape of the twenty-first-century United States.[13] The Triangle is not the largest or most diverse of those places by any means. But in its own Southern context, it represents a distinct version of the American Dream that is irresistible to many—green and sprawling, prosperous and unequal, with laboratories and lofts looming in the background.

RTP was the city of ideas par excellence, a wholly created place, a *Field of Dreams* for the tech economy—"If you build it, they will come." For a family like the Mazhars, the Triangle opened pathways to American prosperity, whether that meant a daughter studying film and chemistry at Duke or a weary mother delivering doughnuts at 6:00 a.m. to chemists and secretaries at Glaxo. RTP meant job opportunities that kept many graduates of universities such as the University of North Carolina from departing for greener shores, heading off "brain drain" and becoming a brain magnet instead. It resulted in the creation of many other jobs serving and supporting the knowledge workers, their families, and their employers: doughnut men and bag boys; accountants and realtors; math teachers and custodial staff. Yet a nettlesome question still lingers. Can the city of the ideas also be a city of hope—or is it destined to be only the province of a privileged few, a new cognitive elite?

Introduction

FROM TEXTILES AND TOBACCO TO THE CITY OF IDEAS

In the 1950s, North Carolina faced a nearly insurmountable problem—an economy plagued literally for centuries by low wages, poverty, structural racism, and undereducation. A handful of its leaders decided to reach for a nearly impossible solution.

Beginning in 1955, political and business elites in Raleigh and Durham set out on a quest to turn the state away from an economy based largely on agriculture, furniture, textiles, and tobacco toward a high-tech future. They were prescient, in ways that they scarcely could have realized at the time. California's Stanford Research Park had been founded only recently, in 1951—the kernel of what would become the iconic land of innovation, Silicon Valley, a term that was not coined until 1971.[1] Local, state, and federal policy makers almost everywhere across the United States eventually embraced the idea of trying to lure high-tech industries in the late twentieth century. But the small coterie of bankers, politicians, and professors who created the blueprint for North Carolina's Research Triangle Park—officially founded in 1959—foresaw the outlines of a knowledge-based, research-intensive economy in a sweeping and persistent sense that few, if any, at the time could match.

By the end of the twentieth century, Research Triangle Park (RTP) had become the largest such high-tech development in the United States. It was home to corporate giants such as IBM, Glaxo, and Cisco, as well as nonprofits and government agencies such as the National Humanities Center, the North Carolina Biotechnology Center, and the U.S. Environmental Protection Agency. In the process, from the 1950s to the early twenty-first century, it became a model case study for politicians and policy makers throughout the United States and, indeed, the world showing how to create a prosperous, high-tech economy—out of almost nothing. The journey from possums and tobacco to SAS and the drug AZT might have seemed rapid and jarring to many, but it was especially so to journalists from outside, who could not help indulging the cliché of Southern primitiveness sitting side by side with hypercapitalist modernity.[2]

North Carolina was unmistakably part of the New South in the mid-twentieth century, fastened tightly to a regime of both segregation and low wages but also possessing a business elite that desperately wanted to move the state forward—albeit, of course, on their own terms. Always hungry to boast of new jobs won, North Carolina boosters spent much of the early to mid-twentieth century persuading Northern employers to bring their mills and other enterprises to the state with the traditional promises of cheap, nonunion labor and low taxes.[3] The state, in fact, added a greater percentage of nonagricultural jobs between 1950 and 1961 than the national average, and, among its neighbors, only Georgia surpassed it on this count.[4]

But the picture was not so rosy. Certainly the state economy did not reach the dizzying heights of profit and productivity that boosters had long grown accustomed to claiming.[5] Even as the population grew, an average of 90 people left North Carolina every day. African Americans in particular were abandoning the state at an even greater rate than during the wartime boom years of the 1940s, when so many escaped the strictures of Southern segregation to search for better opportunities in other parts of the country.[6] Privately, and in their local newspapers, North Carolinians were willing to admit the obvious: the state was poor. A recession in 1954 hit its textile industry, the state's largest manufacturing sector, hard, and employees worked fewer hours as a result. In a largely rural state where many residents supplemented their meager farm income with millwork, this blow was painful.

Worse still, the industries that did exist in North Carolina were highly competitive, driving workers to mass-produce cheap and undifferentiated products for the lowest possible wage. "Industries which are characterized by a high degree of technological progress and by a limited number of suppliers normally retain a high ratio of the benefits of productivity in higher returns on capital and increased wages and salaries," Rep. Charles B. Deane, a Democrat of textile country, explained to the citizens of Greensboro in 1955.[7] The state's dominant industries, such as furniture and textiles, did not allow North Carolinians to earn greater wages by producing a higher-value, more distinctive product; wood was wood, and a sock was a sock, at least to a certain extent. The rural workers who had been pushed out of tenant farms by mechanization and the consolidation of landholdings had neither the skills nor the opportunity to earn a better wage.

Southerners have long tried to understand why their region lagged so much in terms of education, industry, and innovation. Some criticized a colonial North, which allegedly preyed on the fruits of Southern agriculture and industry while maintaining its inferior status through political mechanisms (such as the tariff, which made farm exports less competitive) and unfair trade practices (for example, freight rates that discriminated against Southern farmers). Others maintained that the inequitable heritage of slavery had retarded the development of free enterprise and capitalism in the South, while the systems of sharecropping and tenant-farming that emerged after the Civil War locked Southern workers into a nearly inescapable cycle of debt and dependency.[8]

Conversely, historian David Carlton has described North Carolina's predicament in terms of the "product cycle," suggesting that the state's lack of capital, entrepreneurship, and technology hobbled it throughout the nineteenth and twentieth centuries. Northerners developed new innovations in production and marketing and only transferred these resources to the South once they could be exploited cheaply, without a need for advanced expertise or skilled labor. The textile industry, for instance, first evolved in England, before Americans pilfered the knowhow and technology to develop their own means of mechanically spinning and knitting.

Although these processes were still prized—and though they depended on the specific knowledge of workers and entrepreneurs in the North—they remained above the Mason-Dixon Line. Only when businesses could set up factories that could operate cheaply and simply, far from home, were these industries relocated to the South. And even then, Carlton suggests, Northerners retained the expertise about marketing that enabled them to control the entire process of production.[9]

When a Greensboro contractor named Romeo Guest laid out his vision of a "Research Triangle" in 1954, he had this very problem in mind. "We expect to *hatch our new industries rather than steal them*," Guest told his secretary in November 1954.[10] Soon after, Guest wrote to the wife of Julius Cone, a Greensboro textile magnate, to elaborate. North Carolina could no longer persist in competing for the low-wage industries streaming from the North. Perhaps thinking of that year's recession, he noted that "the pace of migration has greatly slowed down and now we are sponsoring the idea of getting nationally known concerns to establish research laboratories in the triangle area formed by State, Duke and Carolina. The idea of this is that [if] we develop new products in these laboratories many of the products will be manufactured in North Carolina."[11] The Research Triangle would redefine the entire metropolitan landscape of Chapel Hill, Durham, and Raleigh, leveraging the University of North Carolina, Duke University, and North Carolina State College (later, university) as the kernel for a new economy based on research and technology.

Although Guest's idea—really, a slogan—came to fruition in the ensuing decades, with companies like IBM and Red Hat setting up shop amid the universities of central North Carolina, it remained unclear whether he achieved his original aim. Did the Research Triangle "hatch" new innovations and jobs rooted in the local economy? The evidence is hazy at best, and the Triangle has arguably generated fewer local companies (or startups) than similar tech hubs in or near Boston or San Francisco.[12] Did the Triangle help Tar Heels break their dependence on outside corporations for capital and jobs? The signs of companies such as GlaxoSmithKline and Sumitomo grace streets named after such North Carolinian elites as T. W. Alexander and Robert Hanes, yet their operations are based not even in the North but in the United Kingdom and Japan. Northern corporations are, of course, also well represented.

If the Research Triangle did not succeed by these measures, perhaps a different set of questions ought to be asked. How did the effort to build a center for research and technology change the social, economic, and physical landscape of North Carolina? Did it create higher-wage jobs, and did it stem the "brain drain" of educated North Carolinians to greater opportunities in the cities of the North and West? How did the influx of new residents who followed industries such as electronics and pharmaceuticals change the political and cultural dynamics of the state? For one measure, consider that a state that offered its resolute support to Republican candidates such as Richard Nixon, Ronald Reagan, and George W. Bush tipped ever so slightly to the Democratic Party of Barack Obama in 2008. Although political commentators indulged in characterizing the urban denizens of Charlotte and the Triangle as "wine and cheese liberals," it is by no means clear that the migration of educated, affluent, and largely white workers to the state necessarily made the electorate more liberal in its leanings. Indeed, a strongly rightward turn in state government after 2010 challenged the notion that the state's stalwart conservatism was on the wane.[13]

The story of the Research Triangle is that of a particular vision of economic change and urban development taking hold in the mid-twentieth century, which its proponents themselves did not fully understand. Without the assistance of postindustrial theorists such as Daniel Bell or Alain Touraine, bankers and educators in North Carolina intuited that the state's manufacturing base would not provide the income or security that a rising generation of workers needed. Contractors and politicians crafted an ideal of employment that demanded high levels of technology and education—as well as, it was hoped, high wages. This vision emerged haltingly, first imagining research as a supplement to manufacturing, an enhancer of productivity and products, and then conceiving of information as an end in itself. This perspective changed among North Carolina's elite almost imperceptibly, but it tracked alongside an emergent ideology in the 1960s and 1970s by which the work of scientists and other educated professionals was perceived not as one part of a portfolio of economic activity but as the only sector that really mattered. The nascent traces of the so-called Information Revolution or knowledge economy can be found among the supposedly empty piney woods of Durham and Wake Counties, where hunting clubs and trailers were cleared out to make way for the jobs of the future.[14]

INVENTING SPACE AND PLACE IN THE INFORMATION ECONOMY

This ambition to create a high-tech economy took on a distinctive spatial and urban form, which offers clues about the broader sweep of metropolitan history in America's age of sprawl and deindustrialization. Romeo Guest and his colleagues explicitly conceived of the Triangle as an in-between space, a region that encompassed the three cities—Chapel Hill, Durham, and Raleigh—that defined it. In the early years of the 1950s, boosters were rarely clear about whether the Triangle was a general area between these cities, the region as a whole, or a specific property, such as the eventual Research Triangle Park. "After seven years the question is often asked: What is the Research Triangle?" the *Greensboro Daily News* observed in 1965. "That's pardonable, even when the questioner is a North Carolinian because the Triangle is several things at once. It is an idea, a concept; a very tangible geographic area; it is a concentration of human and scientific resources aimed at the betterment of mankind."[15]

In designing the research park at the Triangle's center, planners hewed to the bucolic ideal of a campus where deep thinkers could contemplate in the quiet of a carefully cultivated nature, far from the distractions of the noisy city. As Margaret Pugh O'Mara has shown, Stanford pioneered this academic-cum-corporate ideal of the laboratory in the garden. It also belongs to a longer history of ideal planned communities, including Robert Owen's nineteenth-century New Lanark and "invented edens" such as the nuclear research villages of Oak Ridge, Tennessee, and Los Alamos, New Mexico, founded during World War II.[16]

The design of RTP placed labs in a suburban landscape of curving roads and the straight lines of modernist architecture while scattering the scientific workforce throughout the greater Triangle area. Around it grew the multipolar city of late-twentieth-century urban sprawl, in which the traditional downtown business district ringed with suburbs gave way to a new pattern: a variety of nodes of activity spread across a bigger and more dispersed landscape. In a sense, the Triangle resembles metro Atlanta or Los Angeles, stretching over school districts, towns, and counties, but it lacks a single urban core. One city did not spread out and gobble up outlying villages and neighborhoods; rather, a constellation of settlements coalesced, by equal measures of convenience and contrivance, into a common area founded on a geometrical abstraction with an industrial project at its center.

A city without a mayor or manager—but with its own post office and zip code—RTP called for new forms of governance at both the regional and local levels. On one hand, the spatial scale of the Research Triangle prompted unprecedented levels of coordination among state, county, and city planning agencies to manage development and provide services such as public transit. From the very beginning, though, the Triangle was the site of new hybrids of private and public authority. Since 1959, the nonprofit Research Triangle Foundation (RTF) has acted as a de facto government for the land that became Research Triangle Park soon after.[17] The foundation resembled the new forms of so-called special districts and business improvement districts that enabled private interests to take over some of the tasks of local government throughout the United States in the late twentieth century. RTP provides an opportunity to understand better how and why government by public-private partnership emerged.[18] University presidents, business leaders, and the governor all sat on the board that managed RTP, even though the park was nominally owned by two public colleges (North Carolina State University and the University of North Carolina at Chapel Hill) and a private one (Duke).[19]

In this way, the Research Triangle represents a postindustrial update of many classic themes of Southern history. As a sprawling quasi-city that freely mixed pastures and laboratories, the Triangle typified the "rurbanization" that David Goldfield has observed in numerous cities of the New South, where a combination of automobiles and annexation permitted urban areas to retain many of the hallmarks of the countryside.[20] The alliance of academics, bankers, industrialists, and politicians who championed the idea of the Triangle in the late 1950s represents a textbook case of the "civic elite" Blaine Brownell has found commanding the affairs of towns and cities throughout the South.[21] The subsequent rise of Cary and its main corporate patron, the SAS Institute—arguably one of the two or three largest privately held software companies in the world, with revenues of $1.68 billion and 10,110 employees in 2006—since the late 1970s reveals the old Southern mill town mentality reconfigured in a sleek new high-tech version.[22] Indeed, without the cohesive sense of shared interests, without the interconnections among these privileged North Carolinians, it appears unlikely that a project like the Research Triangle would have secured the necessary resources from either private interests or the state to succeed.

While the story of the Triangle reinforces and extends these familiar themes, it also represents a new level of urban and economic planning in the South. The region of privately run mill villages and company stores gave birth to a new and more complex work environment. It amounts to a kind of social engineering. Changes in wage levels, in-migration and out-migration, ethnic diversity, housing stock, and countless other factors were due in large part to the concerted effort of elite North Carolinians to steer the state's economy in a particular direction. Postindustrialism, in short, was not the natural outgrowth of an older capitalist manufacturing economy but, rather, the result of deliberate efforts to amend the tax code, secure state and federal subsidies, and command the resources of public and private universities in order to foster specific types of employment and enterprise. "I think you have got hold of something very important and practicable there," one of Romeo Guest's media allies, *Greensboro Daily News* editor William T. Polk, said in late 1954. "North Carolina and the South need research, perhaps more than anything else."[23] If it was research the South needed, it was research it would get—one way or another, whatever the consequences might be.

Brain Magnet tells this story by examining a series of interlocking spaces, beginning with Research Triangle Park itself—zealously designed as the ideal environment for knowledge work and a 1960s-style, modernist futurism. It looks at the work environments that followed, from the Research Triangle Institute, Burroughs Wellcome, and the National Humanities Center within the park, to SAS Institute in nearby Cary, as ideas about intellectual labor and the management of creativity evolved over the course of the late twentieth century. It goes beyond the workplace to consider what the nascent creative economy looked like in new suburbs such as Parkwood in the 1960s and 1970s, as well as the gentrifying downtowns of Durham and Raleigh of the early twenty-first century. Each locale provides a tableau of a new economy taking shape, an outline of the ideals and aspirations of its participants—whether in the ranch home or "McMansion," laboratory or executive suite, coffeeshop or coworking space.

A PARALLEL HISTORY OF THE KNOWLEDGE ECONOMY

This book is not a New South history, strictly speaking—at least not in the mold of superlative works such as Christina Greene's 2005 *Our Separate Ways* or Matthew Lassiter's 2006 *The Silent Majority*, both of which touched on the political history of the metropolitan Triangle.[24] It is not principally about issues such as desegregation or the rise of the New Right, though certainly those historical trajectories skate and streak across the background of this story of an emergent new economy. It is about the way we think about and imagine the economy, what the economy is, where the economy should go, and, above all, who matters.

Brain Magnet is in, but not of, Southern history; it is part of a different discussion, one that concerns the shift from a manufacturing-based economy to one dominated by services and information technology. Intellectuals, journalists, and policy makers struggled to define what that new economy really was for much of the late twentieth century. The Austrian American economist Fritz Machlup was among the most farsighted; his book *The Production and Distribution of Knowledge in the United States* introduced the term "information society" in 1962.[25] That same year, the young activists of the New Left recognized the decline of manufacturing as a proportion of the workforce and the increasing prominence of education, science, and technology in the economy. (At the same time, they worried about automation and the prospect of a "remote control economy.")[26] American sociologist Daniel Bell began thinking of it as "post-industrial" in the 1960s, and he and his French counterpart Alain Touraine both published books in the early 1970s that helped popularize the term. Influential management theorist Peter Drucker first wrote of the "knowledge worker" in the 1960s; economist Robert Reich's "symbolic analysts" followed in the 1990s, redefining the same set of educated, mostly professional workers. All were the forerunners of urbanist Richard Florida's concept of the "creative class," which debuted in 2002 to much acclaim.[27]

This book offers a different, parallel account of this intellectual history—one that looks out from the piney woods of rural Durham County rather than the conference panel or the editorial boardroom of the *New York Times*. It proposes that an intuitive understanding of an economy in which manufacturing was supplanted by intellectual labor developed on the ground in what was, frankly, one of the less likely places for it to happen. North Carolina boosters in the 1950s and 1960s spoke of "creativity," creative people, and brains—that is, the figure of the intellectual worker well before these ideas became a prominent part of either the academic or public discourse. And by the time deindustrialization and the emerging knowledge economy *had* become widely debated in the 1970s and 1980s, the Triangle had achieved broad recognition in the media and policy circles as a place that got the postindustrial transition right. RTP's reputation was so great by the 1980s that it was arguably better known elsewhere in the world than North Carolina itself. There is a perhaps apocryphal story, often retold, about a Japanese businessman who was told about North Carolina and responded, "Is it in the Research Triangle?"

Of course, RTP is not the paradigmatic case of the "city of knowledge," to borrow historian Margaret Pugh O'Mara's term. Scholars such as O'Mara have provided superlative studies of Silicon Valley and Massachusetts's Route 128, the quintessential American sites of high-tech innovation, while Stephen J. Pitti, Lily Geismer, and Willow Lung-Amam have undertaken careful studies of the cultural, political, and social dynamics of the communities that grew up around these tech hubs. Other cities with dynamic tech economies have begun to receive scholarly scrutiny, such as Austin, Texas, in Eliot M. Tretter's *Shadows of a Sunbelt City*. Indeed, the Triangle parallels many of the metropolitan enclaves of the affluent and educated that emerged in post–World War II America, all of which were funded directly or indirectly by the federal government. These included Orange County, California, where Cold War defense industries drew engineers and managers; the tony districts of Maryland and Northern Virginia, where employees of both government contractors such as Northrup Grumman and federal agencies such as the Food and Drug Administration built their lives; or greater Boston, where high-tech industries also spawned new, affluent suburbs.

Each of these places was remade by the movement of money, people, and technology during the Cold War.[28]

The Research Triangle, however, has received significantly less attention, apart from celebratory local histories and an informative 2011 overview of the region by University of North Carolina planning scholar William Rohe. However, it makes sense to look for the origins of the economic and technological transition of postindustrial America in a place that was not the paradigm. Many people have already written about the Bay Area or Route 128, but looking at the most typical or successful example of something simply cannot tell you about how the model evolved and diverged in places that were *not* the pinnacle of apparent success—which is to say, everywhere else.

It is especially instructive to look at a place like North Carolina, which started out at or near the bottom in terms of wealth, poverty, and technological innovation in the 1950s, and yet through assiduous effort and masterful storytelling managed to go a good distance from there. Poverty and inequality persist, of course, both within the Triangle and (especially) across the rest of the state. But how a group of academics, businesspeople, and politicians came to imagine a future economy in an unlikely place puts those very changes in the sharpest relief. In the 1960s, many intellectuals and policy makers began to intuit that an economy in which, at a minimum, manufacturing labor played a smaller role was coming. What shape that economy would take remained to be seen, but anthropologists such as Margaret Mead and activists of the New Left foresaw it.[29] It is noteworthy that a sociologist such as George Simpson or a small-town banker like Archie Davis realized this as well, often well before other intellectuals.

Those very North Carolinians were farsighted enough to anticipate, however clumsily or unintentionally, the ideas of thinkers such as Richard Florida by well over forty years. In their relentless branding of the Triangle, they spoke of the importance of creativity and the value of a stimulating intellectual environment for a nascent group of knowledge workers. They mobilized universities, museums, dance companies, and even book clubs to persuade scientists, engineers, and their families to come to the Raleigh-Durham area as early as the late 1950s. They stressed that smart people like to live near other people similar to themselves—the chemist with the linguist down the street, whose wives volunteer in the little theater or take a night class together. This was nearly fifty years before journalist Bill Bishop presented his compelling thesis in *The Big Sort*, which argues that Americans were increasingly gravitating toward communities with people who shared their political and cultural tastes.[30] This was the creative class forty-five years before *The Rise of the Creative Class*, knowledge workers sixteen years before *Coming of Post-Industrial Society*. And although the terms and buzzwords have come and gone over the years, the emphasis on creativity and the interests of a prized group of highly educated workers remained explicit throughout.

In today's age of food trucks and hipster CEOs, it is worth noting that the members of the Triangle's proto-creative class were, for the most part, "squares." Richard Florida might disdain the highbrow art and culture favored by upper-middle-class stiffs in the cities and, increasingly, suburbs of the mid- to late twentieth century, but opera and ballet were what sold in the 1960s—at least for educated outsiders who were leery of coming to sleepy towns in a seemingly remote and still backward South. The difference between the North Carolina Symphony and a Romanian-Hawaiian fusion poké bowl place might seem transparently obvious, but the difference is more superficial than it seems. The chemistry PhDs and the hip software engineers that Florida has placed in the official creative class share much in terms of education and cultural capital—as well as their role as sought-after residents, workers, and taxpayers—whether it is 1965 or 2005. The tastes simply changed.

Thus the Triangle offers a previously untold story of the origins of the information economy, of the creative city, where such ideas germinated early on and far from Boston or Palo Alto. By the 1990s and 2000s, Raleigh and Durham received lavish praise in the media as among the most creative, brainiest cities in the nation, boasting a better quality of life that frequently outranked anywhere else. The region's transformation began with an unusually intentional, conscious effort to rebrand a place, create a new economy, and attract both technologically advanced businesses and highly educated workers. It prefigured the incessant mantra of knowledge, creativity, and innovation that came to dominate discussions of urban economic policy in the early twenty-first century. RTP itself was the proving ground for a new concept of the economy that prized only brains and largely excluded the smokestacks and dirty hands of before. Yet geographer Jamie Peck has warned that this vision is an imperfect one, in a virtuoso takedown of Florida's thesis. Creativity is great—who could be against it? But "the uncreative population, one assumes, should merely look on, and learn."[31]

The Triangle's story is one of self-invention and audacious boosterism amid the high-water days of the Cold War, when federal government money was flowing into research (not just for defense but for public health, environmental protection, and other worthy causes) and one of the poorest states in the nation decided to gamble its economic future on the universities that sat at its center. In the process, boosters almost inadvertently redefined the metropolitan landscape of Chapel Hill, Durham, Raleigh, and, later, Cary as a new entity that had never existed before—"the Triangle." The knowledge economy that is so often taken for granted in the twenty-first century was born amid the possums and pine trees of North Carolina's Durham and Wake Counties. RTP might not have been a city in the strictest sense of the term, but it nevertheless gave deliberate birth to the "city of ideas."

1

Imagining the Triangle

THE UNLIKELY ORIGINS OF THE CREATIVE CITY IN THE COLD WAR SOUTH

North Carolinians got a painful psychic kick in 1955. Newspaper readers awoke to learn that the state's average weekly income had slipped to last place among the then-forty-eight states—below even its laggard neighbor to the South, the Palmetto State. Yet North Carolina was the leading manufacturing state in the Southeast and the second most populous after Florida.[1] Its population grew by 10 percent between 1950 and 1960, but such growth masked worrying trends: African Americans were leaving the state to pursue freedom and opportunity outside the Jim Crow South, while college graduates departed for the North, Midwest, and West to find jobs where they could use their degrees.

Meanwhile, federal investment in defense production and scientific research bolstered the economies of states such as California, Texas, and Florida, as the nation settled into the permanent mobilization of the Cold War. The rush to develop new means of defense, space technology, and nuclear power meant that the United States was willing to spend huge sums employing scientists and engineers and spawning whole new industries.[2] Just next door, the federal government revolutionized a lonely corner of South Carolina, where a massive nuclear facility at the Savannah River

Plant brought workers, including many scientists and engineers, to revolutionize the state's economy.[3]

It was against this backdrop that a group of elite North Carolinians in business, education, and government conceived an audacious plan to change the state's economic course. They imagined a new complex of advanced industry and scientific research flourishing among the colleges of Raleigh, Durham, and Chapel Hill—the three points of the so-called Research Triangle—where outside companies would bring better-paying jobs than traditional sectors such as textiles and furniture, importing educated outsiders and employing the state's own graduates. Incomes would rise, tax revenues would swell, and North Carolina would channel some of the largesse of what President Dwight D. Eisenhower would soon call the "military industrial complex" its way. It would be the next Silicon Valley, well before anyone had invented the term.

But how could North Carolina convince the world that a state with some of the lowest wages and poorest schools was a high-tech hub waiting to happen? Even one of the Triangle's leading proponents, University of North Carolina (UNC) sociologist George Simpson, admitted that the state suffered from a "cultural problem." Youth in the Northeast and Midwest imbibed the virtues of science and industry early on, but "our young people . . . grow up with little or no exposure to this sort of environment."[4] The Research Triangle, he told UNC faculty in 1957, aimed to foster the sort of creative milieu in which science flourished elsewhere. And it would do so by mobilizing the resources of its institutions richest in knowledge and culture: its universities.

While scientists and corporate managers were initially skeptical about relocating to North Carolina, Simpson and his allies were winning over companies such as IBM by stressing the importance of the Triangle's universities to quality of life. Central to the latter's appeal was the idea that highly educated and much-sought-after scientists and engineers would be drawn to the cultural opportunities afforded by local educational institutions—and, indeed, by virtue of living among other educated, creative people. With pamphlets and newspaper ads, they touted the state's schools, museums, golf courses, and, above all, its "climate"—not just in the sense of weather, but in terms of "academic ambience" and "intellectual stimulation."[5] In nascent form, Triangle boosters pioneered the ideas of the creative class and the creative city, mobilizing cultural resources as a means of attracting both capital investment and privileged workers.[6]

Unlike earlier campaigns for southern industrialization, the Research Triangle effort did not focus simply on cheap labor—although boosters were quick to point out, when it suited them, that the state had a "vast labor pool" of flexible, affordable workers, who could be trained on the state's dime through the new system of community colleges.[7] Most often, North Carolinian leaders sold the Triangle as a special kind of place filled with people who would be valued as neighbors and workers due to their intellectual and creative qualities. They aimed to both promote and produce a certain kind of space—one where companies such as IBM and Burroughs Wellcome would be willing to relocate from New York and where highly educated scientists would be willing to live. The "atmosphere" surrounding colleges like Duke and the cultural amenities supported by an upper-middle-class population generated a value that the Triangle's promoters in turn packaged and sold both to corporate executives and the employees they sought to hire. In the Triangle, real estate values and economic development hinged not only on infrastructure or natural resources but also on the sellable qualities of the people residing there.

By packaging the people and institutions of the Triangle area as a valuable resource, North Carolinians were able to persuade both major corporations and the federal government to bring research facilities there. But the idea of the Triangle as a "reservoir" of brains had to start somewhere—someone had to draw three arbitrary lines on a map and imagine that perceptions of social or cultural prestige could drive economic development. When Romeo Guest began circulating the phrase "research triangle" in the fall of 1954, he insisted that North Carolinians put cultural opportunities and the presence of workers with high class and educational status at the forefront of their pitch to the country at large: "We should all bear in mind that we are not selling a factory site. We are selling available engineering brains, physical research facilities and cultural living conditions."[8]

THE ORIGINS OF THE TRIANGLE

Romeo Guest was anxious about the future of North Carolina. The Greensboro contractor had inherited the family business from his father, a builder of industrial sites. Its slogan was "Serving the Industrial South," and its logo featured a city skyline encircled in a radiant glow—factories on the left, farms on the right, with the skyscrapers of the downtown business district in the center. C. M. Guest & Sons depended on the flow of new industries to the South, and Guest sensed that interest in North Carolina was flagging. "The competition for new industrial plants is becoming so keen and so competitive that it is increasingly more difficult to relocate a new plant in our State," he wrote. He also noticed that Congress was throwing federal money at military projects and scientific research, thanks to the Cold War, and North Carolina mostly missed out on this bonanza. "I have heard that MIT has research grants from the government through industry amounting to approximately $5 million per year and that California institutions are similarly loaded," Guest said.[9]

Southerners needed to look no further than Alabama for a case study of cashing in on the federal government's sudden interest in science and technology. The city of Huntsville began to change with the building of munitions plants during World War II, and it became a center for research on rocket technology following the arrival of Werner von Braun and other German scientists, who were brought to the United States in 1945 as the Americans and Soviets attempted to divvy up the scientific minds of the collapsing Nazi regime. As Guest noted, the three thousand scientists who had come to Huntsville by the mid-1950s "changed the complexion of the community." Whether this change of complexion was meant literally or figuratively, Guest believed that attracting scientific workers and federal dollars—as Huntsville, Boston, and other cities had done—would be North Carolina's path to prosperity. "Our *research triangle* is much better suited for scientists than Huntsville," he said. "We must point out our facilities both in personnel, physical and cultural to the Presidents and Research Directors of major corporations quickly while government research projects are still being handed out."[10]

So began Guest's mission to evangelize the idea of a "research area" in the middle of North Carolina. It required enlisting the support of bankers, governors, journalists, textile magnates, and university presidents and professors, who helped persuade corporations and government agencies to place scientific facilities in the state. This effort built on a long and illustrious history of Southern boosterism, in which city fathers and developers crowed about the immense business opportunities (real and imaginary) that existed in towns and counties throughout the Southeast. At the same time, though, it demonstrated a degree of cooperation across the privileged classes—from Governor Luther Hodges, a tenant farmer's son who was ardently pro-business, to deep-pocketed bankers like George Watts Hill and academics like UNC sociologist George Simpson—that was remarkable even in the context of the "commercial civic elite" that had long dominated local government in the South.[11]

The Triangle soon developed (nearly) unflagging support of not only the local Chamber of Commerce or city council but influential people at multiple levels of government and in divergent fields of endeavor, whose interests might not have always aligned. A number of professors wondered whether their universities' involvement in the Triangle campaign—which essentially promised prospective businesses access to their expertise and libraries—would really benefit the schools or the faculty. But their critical voices did little to stymie Guest's ambitious campaign.

The Triangle emerged at a time when many leaders were beginning to consider the importance of knowledge, science, and technology in the South's economic development. Boosters in High Point, a furniture center twenty miles south of Greensboro, attempted to shake off the town's low-tech image and entreat manufacturers in the growing field of electronics to locate there in 1954. But although the technology was new, the pitch was not: the local workers were docile and homogeneous. "Of especial importance is the fact that labor in the High Point area is 99.3 percent native born," Phil Clarke assured an executive at Olympic Radio and Television, in Long Island City, New York. "Labor relations are very satisfactory and work stoppages and labor disputes have seldom occurred and have never lasted for a great length of time."[12] Clarke did point to the existence of numerous schools, however, including

High Point College and Duke University, along with their distance from the city.[13]

Meanwhile, leading citizens in nearby Winston-Salem emphasized cultural and intellectual resources to a greater degree. In early 1955, Fred Linton of the Winston-Salem Chamber of Commerce sketched out a few key ideas that would become important to the Research Triangle. Like any good booster, he suggested to Guest that Winston-Salem could offer a fine alternative to Raleigh-Durham-Chapel Hill. The twin cities, after all, hosted R. J. Reynolds Tobacco Company and Bowman Gray School of Medicine, and it would soon become the home of Wake Forest College, which was relocating from the east of the state. Beyond a pitch for his home city, Linton noted that the Boston Chamber of Commerce had been promoting its own resources of "scientific talent" to prospective employers for several years, and Washington, D.C., was following suit. Raleigh or Winston-Salem could do the same. "Another possibility that has been turning over in my mind for some time with no practical result is the possibility of organizing a research organization in North Carolina with private capital to do research work on a contractual basis," Linton said. He had seen such organizations flourish in Texas and Alabama and thought the Tar Heel state could do the same.[14]

The germ of just such an idea originated with Howard Odum, a prominent sociologist at the University of North Carolina. Odum had seen the growth of government sponsorship for research during World War II and proposed in 1952 that the state set up a research center near the new Raleigh-Durham airport. That area would draw on the combined intellectual and material resources of the University of North Carolina in Chapel Hill, the Agricultural and Technical College in Greensboro, and North Carolina State College in Raleigh. Although leery of too much government meddling in the affairs of scholarship, Odum believed more could be done to harness North Carolina's academic strengths for the greater good. However, Odum passed away in 1954, before his vision could be realized.[15]

There is little evidence that either Linton or Guest was influenced by Odum's proposal, but North Carolinians in the early 1950s were well aware of experiments with new kinds of scientific organizations in other states and consciously looked to these as models.[16] Guest had studied at the Massachusetts Institute of Technology as a young man; witnessing the concentration of scholarly activity in Cambridge inspired him to see in Raleigh, Durham, and Chapel Hill the potential for a Charles River of the South.[17] He and his colleagues visited Birmingham, Alabama, in early 1955 to study the Southern Research Institute (SRI), a center for chemistry and biomedical research launched in 1941. Among the nation's first such centers, SRI would soon serve as a model for the early planners of Research Triangle Park.[18] Guest carried on a correspondence with the institute's leadership in the following months marked by mutual respect as well as competition. "Since returning from Birmingham after visiting your fine research institute, we have been trying to formalize our thinking in connection with our own Research Triangle in North Carolina," Romeo Guest wrote. He admitted, "The progress of the Triangle has been most interesting so far and really catches my interest to the point of my finding it difficult to turn my thinking into other channels."[19] William T. Polk of the *Greensboro Daily News* shared this enthusiasm when Guest shared the idea for the Research Triangle with the writer and editor in December 1954: "I think you have got hold of something very important and practicable here. North Carolina and the South need research, perhaps more than anything else."[20]

Thus, when Guest began to drum up support in late 1954, numerous North Carolinians had already been thinking about ways to bring higher-skilled and higher-paid jobs to the state. What later became known as the Triad—a junior competitor to the Triangle encompassing Greensboro, High Point, and Winston-Salem—could have taken the lead. Each town had its own colleges to boast about. Interestingly, Guest chose not to focus on the Greensboro area, despite its being his home base. By winning the support of Governor Hodges and key leaders at Chapel Hill, Duke, and North Carolina State College, Guest was able to fix the attention of private businesspeople, state development officials, and even faculty members on recruiting business for the Triangle. Guest contacted Hodges's office in December 1954, and by the following November, the Research Triangle Committee met to discuss what exactly the Triangle would be.[21]

FROM TRIANGLE TO PARK

In fall 1954, Luther Hartwell Hodges was new to the lieutenant governorship. The businessman had had a varied career before he pursued that office in 1952, working his way up to manage Marshall Field's textile mills in the Southeast and working on the Marshall Plan in Europe following World War II. At 52 he retired to devote his remaining years to public service and had won a spot on William Umstead's ticket for governor after a campaign that took him to gas stations across the state. Umstead, a Democrat, won handily in a state where, to this day, few Republicans have held the governor's mansion, but he was in poor health. So poor, in fact, that the political novice Hodges was thrust into the limelight when the governor passed away in November 1954. Soon after, he received a call from Romeo Guest.[22]

The new governor took up Guest's cause almost immediately, perhaps looking for some stamp to put on the economic development efforts of his administration. Hodges was anxious to attract outside investment, traveling everywhere from Chicago to the Soviet Union to sell the virtues of North Carolina. The governor later recalled in his 1962 memoir that the Triangle was "an idea that has produced a reality"—but in its early phases the idea itself was far from clear.[23] In March 1955 Hodges told the *Raleigh News & Observer* that the Triangle could compete with the international stature of MIT, which was "ringed" by labs. "Many industries . . . have located centers in the vicinity of the school in order to take advantage of M.I.T. staff and facilities," the paper reported. "The same thing could happen in North Carolina," according to Hodges. "It would bring in more Ph.D's than we've ever heard of here."[24]

To hear Hodges speak, one would think he intended only to import more people with advanced degrees. After all, the South's school systems were notoriously impoverished, and the region was short on highly educated workers. As historian James C. Cobb noted, "Research scientists were more than five times more numerous in the nation as a whole than in the South, and patents were issued to southerners at a rate less than one-third of the national average" by the end of World War II.[25] Indeed, Triangle planners would continue to speak frankly about their aim to "import" scientists who would, presumably, elevate the tax base and workforce in the state.[26]

But what, in fact, was the goal for the Triangle's early supporters? Was it simply to shift the state's recruitment efforts from attracting factories to wooing laboratories? Was it to set up a research center or institute along the lines that Howard Odum and Fred Linton had proposed? Was it to be a real estate venture? (Stanford Industrial Park, the nation's preeminent research park, had been designed to generate revenue for its parent university in California.[27]) Was the campaign meant to stimulate the birth of new industries at home, or was it to attract outside corporations to the area?

For the plan's boosters in politics and the press, these goals were not mutually exclusive. "The three institutions are rich in scientific knowledge and technological skill," a Durham paper noted in January 1955. "The plan is to utilize these facilities in attracting industrial laboratories to the area. From out of these labs new industries are expected to be born."[28]

"Hatching" new industries or luring new ones with better wages and higher demands for skill presented a fresh set of challenges.[29] Southern leaders had been bending over backwards for years to seduce Northern companies with tax incentives and offers to train workers and build facilities. Yet North Carolina's approach to attracting investment remained limited, for the most part, to promises of infrastructure, such as better roads, and the implicit guarantee of a docile, nonunion labor force, rather than offers of tax breaks. Guest sent his vice president, Russell A. McCoy, to sound out the local commissioners in Durham, Orange, and Wake Counties on the idea at the start of 1955.[30] McCoy proposed that the counties eliminate ad valorem taxes on research-intensive companies for ten years, perhaps longer.[31] Such incentives did not benefit any outside enterprise that might create jobs but, rather, signaled that local authorities prized particular *types* of jobs and investment.

Guest and his allies also attempted to finesse the national and local media into grabbing attention for their project. "You know I am interested in what you people are doing in the state of North Carolina," Frank P. Bennett of *America's Textile Reporter* assured Guest, "so you remember that if there is any way we can give the whole thing a boost that we want to do it."[32] (C. M. Guest & Sons had advertised its services in the textile industry journal before.) Guest reached out to his friend Peyton Beery in Charleston, South Carolina, to curry favor with *Business Week*, where Beery knew the managing editor, Kenneth Kramer. In June, William A. Newell contacted Kramer to spell out the group's message. "The news peg for *Business Week* . . . is two-fold: a challenge to the Charles River as the nation's research center, and a further step in the growth and development of the industrial South," said Newell, director of the Textiles School at NC State. "Add to that the rather unprecedented coordination of University research efforts and the factors that favor and stimulate this development, and you should have a story."[33]

Meanwhile, Guest sought to win the backing of academic leaders, whose cooperation was crucial given that the presence of colleges, faculty, and libraries was central to the Triangle public relations blitz. Guest told state Senator Arthur Kirkman that he had gotten the go-ahead from Duke in January, while Walter Harper and Dean Lampe of North Carolina State College had shown their interest and support the year before.[34] However, not all members of the academic community were pleased with the idea of hitching the colleges to Romeo Guest's wagon. When leaders from the three universities met in February 1955, a few voiced uneasiness with the concept of the Triangle, objecting to "wording which looked like Guest was offering their services and had the whole program in his hip pocket and could just go off and sell the program without letting the institutions have much part in saying just what they could offer"—in short, that the contractor would "get the institutions in over their heads."[35]

Notably, N. J. Demerath, a professor of sociology at UNC, expressed his misgivings to Guest two months later. "Your idea of an 'M.I.T. of North Carolina' as reported recently in the press is most intriguing," Demerath wrote. "It brings to mind, however, certain factors affecting research achievements at the University of North Carolina which may run counter to the realization of your idea as well as President Gray's goal of 'Excellence' for the University. Permit me to note briefly these tendencies to educational and research mediocrity." The professor went on to note that most faculty had little extra funding to support their research, and budgetary pressures led administrators and state officials to push professors to teach more than their "low" course load. Demerath also warned that the "humanist-documentary tradition" at Chapel Hill disdained consulting and applied research.

In short, the professor worried that the Triangle project would sap already scarce resources from the educational institutions while entangling faculty in relationships with outside interests that did not serve the mission of scholarship. After all, what did it mean for the faculty and resources of the colleges to be "available" to new industries that came to the area? "The 'Triangle Research Plan,' therefore, like the proposed North Carolina Board of Higher Education," he concluded, "may be perceived as one more administrative imposition to be tolerated or opposed unless effective communication is generated with local faculty members."[36]

Indeed, others at the universities shared Demerath's misgivings. One university official chided Guest, "Let me see, Romeo, if I really understand what it is we are talking about here, you want the professors here and all of us to be the prostitutes and you're going to be the pimp."[37] George Simpson, the UNC sociologist who was soon picked to head up the Research Triangle's "pimping" mission, addressed the issue with more characteristic circumspection. "There is always a chance that the university will be taken, inadvertently, into waters in which it has no business swimming," he observed in 1957. "It is possible some substantial freedom of action may be lost, or that some action may be forced upon the university by the pressure of circumstances." But he assured fellow faculty members that UNC President William Friday and the other university leaders were committed to resisting "anything that was detrimental to the character and the basic educational and research programs of their institutions."[38]

Despite doubts among some faculty, the Research Triangle Committee spent the next several years attempting to persuade outside corporations that the universities were a major draw for placing facilities in the general area around Raleigh, Durham, and Chapel Hill. In a July 1955 meeting, Hodges was asked why such industries had not chosen to come to North Carolina, and he guessed that a combination of "the living conditions of North Carolina people, tax rates, water sites, and the lack of available technical corps" was to blame. The group decided to compile an inventory of local resources, such as the schools' many laboratories, NC State's atomic reactor, and the area's "comparatively large number of hospitals . . . that would be attractive from the standpoints of health facilities for workers and markets for pharmaceuticals and medical equipment concerns." The inventory also would take note of "cultural opportunities" offered by the Triangle cities.[39]

The group soon appointed Simpson as its director—essentially, an itinerant pitchman for the Triangle, who would travel across the country to speak with scientists, executives, and policy makers.[40] In 1956 the professor met with the "appropriate research people" at "the Air Force, the Navy, the Army, the National Science Foundation, [and] the Atomic Energy Commission"—key among the many fonts of federal money at the height of the Cold War.[41] Meanwhile, chemist William F. Little of UNC met with representatives from Buckeye Cellulose, Chemstrand, Ortho Pharma, and Scott Paper at Chapel Hill in early 1957.[42] "All of these people showed real enthusiasm for the idea and without exception, have promised to turn over the brochure I gave them to research directors, etc.," Little reported to Simpson.[43] In fact, the men from Dow in Texas showed special interest. "It was an absolutely *glowing* letter of praise for our area," Little said. "Coming from *Texans* this is something."[44]

Still, Guest and his allies had been receiving kind words about their project for several years without realizing tangible results. Simpson began to sense that the committee needed a flagship project to build interest. As he reflected in February 1957,

> There is great value in having something concrete, something that can be mapped and walked over, to place before people. Something tangible stimulates the imagination. The necessity of doing this has been growing on me all along. I became finally convinced last week in Indianapolis, in talking to Dr. Carney, the Vice President of Eli Lilly for Research, Development and Control. He took an unusually sympathetic interest in the project, and he stated quite baldly that this would be of great value, especially in putting across the idea to non-scientific people.[45]

Simpson felt that such a project could be public or nonprofit, like the Research Triangle Committee itself, but he admitted that a for-profit venture might be more likely to succeed.[46] He envisioned raising funds to purchase a chunk of land in the middle of the Triangle, a "research campus" where companies could locate their laboratories in close proximity to one another. The Research Triangle would not be just the general area of Raleigh, Durham, and Chapel Hill but a Research Triangle *Park* where high-tech companies operated side by side.

In March 1957 Governor Hodges reached out to retired textile magnate Karl Robbins about funding land acquisition.[47] Robbins was born in Russia around 1893 and emigrated to the United States as a young child. He took over his father's store in New York and began to invest in the southern textile industry, soon becoming a major figure in North Carolina manufacturing. Robbins had sold his textile stock in 1954 and turned his interests to philanthropy, working to found the Albert Einstein College of Medicine at Yeshiva University and the Federation of Jewish Philanthropies in New York. In North Carolina he had been known for setting up playgrounds and parks in the communities where his workers lived, and the town of Hemp was renamed Robbins in his honor.[48] (This was the town where disgraced presidential candidate and former Senator John Edwards spent his oft-mentioned working-class youth.)

Robbins's interest in the Research Triangle reflected this sense of noblesse oblige. "I always wanted to find some way to help those in our industrial family who were so generous with their skills and loyalty," he said in a letter to Governor Hodges. "Through Christmas bonuses, creation of recreation facilities and steady jobs at better than standard wages, we tried to do our bit in raising the standard of living in the areas of our mills. But an effort at that level can only help the few thousand who are on the immediate payroll. So I am tremendously interested in the Research Triangle because through research you look ahead and create out of man's mind wonderful things for his future."[49] Robbins also had been inspired by an article on a "science city" then being built along the Ob River in Siberia.[50] "You see, we are having competition," Robbins told Hodges in June 1957, "but I assure you, in no way will their's [sic] be as nice as the one we plan to have in North Carolina."[51]

Doing his "bit" for North Carolina meant ponying up $1 million to purchase land around the villages of Nelson and Morrisville in southeastern

Figure 1.1 Durham banker George Watts Hill explains the Triangle map to Romeo Guest, George Simpson, and two others (*right to left*) in 1958. *Source*: Research Triangle Foundation.

Durham and northwestern Wake Counties (figure 1.1).[52] The operation would turn a profit, Robbins hoped, as the land was sold or leased to companies that set up labs there. Buying thousands of acres, though, even in a relatively rural area, was bound to draw attention, and the local press helped suppress the truth. "This is a highly explosive powder keg we are sitting on and anything can happen," Guest warned Saunders in June. "Many rumors began flying in the Nelson-Morrisville-Airport area once persons caught on to the wholesale acquisition," a local paper reported, after news of the purchases broke. "Some speculated the land was to be used for an atomic power plant or at least an atomic reactor project of some kind. Others figured the federal government wanted it for some other kind of hush-hush project."[53]

Hodges called in top figures from the press and urged them not to write about the project until the acquisitions were complete. Guest warned

Robbins in July that "the newspapers are onto our forestry man's acquisition and have guessed what it is for. The most influential man in Durham [presumably George Watts Hill] is trying his best to stop the newspapers from publishing anything. We don't know if he will succeed."[54]

Robbins's men succeeded in buying up most of the desired land, thanks in no small part to the press blackout. Guest was well aware of incidents when such efforts went awry, as when development officials in Warrenton, North Carolina, ended up paying $2,000 per acre for land that was purportedly worth $200 because the "secret" got out—the secret being that the land might be worth much more if the sellers knew a major industrial development was to be built there. "There are only a few gaps in the research park site," journalist O. Mac White reported in 1957. "These pockets are homesites which occupants didn't want to give up."[55]

With land purchased, the Triangle Committee was finally making material progress. The sales trips of Simpson and other faculty members seemed to be paying off. The committee's promotional brochure made the rounds at the chemical company Monsanto, and a vice president conveyed his interest in the Triangle in January.[56] The committee began drawing up plans for a research institute in April.[57] In a meeting at Pfizer, Dr. Robert J. Feeney told Simpson that the pharmaceutical giant was tired of its headquarters in "an undesirable area" of Brooklyn, and that they would consider moving to the Triangle.[58] Simpson also believed they had viable leads in the United States Testing Company, and Robbins was personally leaning on his friends at the Hoboken-based firm's board of directors.[59] By September the Research Triangle received favorable coverage in the *New York Times*, and Karl Robbins was "buoyant," according to Guest. "Thank you for a job exceedingly well managed," he told the governor.[60]

THE TROUBLE WITH THE TRIANGLE

The Triangle had land; it had the active support of a network of high-placed individuals in academia, finance, industry, media, and state government; and it appeared to have leads for potential tenants. However, certain flaws in Romeo Guest's design became evident as the plan moved forward. Some involved the logistics of local politics, infrastructure, and taxation, while others related to the viability of the Triangle as a for-profit real estate venture.

First, it was by no means clear how the research park would fit into the jigsaw puzzle of state and local government. Robbins spoke of a "science city"—would it be a town unto itself? It would soon have its own zip code; one could mail a letter to Research Triangle Park, North Carolina (figure 1.2). Could it turn to neighboring municipalities for water or the state for roads? Whether as a public project or for-profit enterprise, the park would have to obtain the basic resources, and laws as they existed in 1957 did not necessarily allow for a new development that straddled two counties to do so.

For instance, Simpson noted that state law permitted several counties to create a joint water and sewer authority, which they could provide with money for "preliminary" costs—presumably for surveying. This authority could then issue bonds to raise money for building water lines. However, planners were uncertain that a city could provide water to a site far from

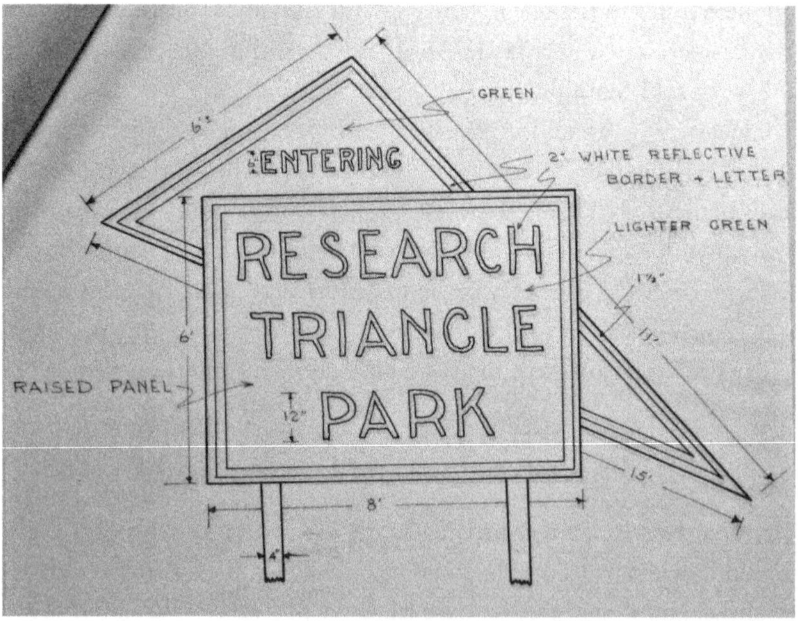

Figure 1.2 Sketch of a Research Triangle Park sign, ca. 1963. *Source*: Research Triangle Foundation.

its city limits and extending into another county, even if local officials supported it. The state legislature considered a law in May 1957 that would allow cities to provide water to areas ten miles beyond their borders, but Simpson was dubious. "Certainly any such legislation would be subject to lawsuits," he told the governor, "and probably would be of little value until the matter had been settled in the courts."[61]

Local attitudes toward the project varied throughout the Triangle. Durham's relationship with the research park was particularly vexed, from initial discussions of whether to provide it with water at reduced city rates to subsequent attempts to annex the park (and thus raise revenue) in the 1970s and 1980s.[62] Some in Chapel Hill were less thrilled. "It is not exactly clear what Gov. Hodges means by the 'scientific city' which he enthusiastically proclaims is to rise within 20 minutes' ride of Chapel Hill," the local *News Leader* commented in an editorial in 1957. The editors wished the project well but still wondered what effect a new settlement of as many as 25,000 people would have on the nearby college town. Chapel Hill "wishes to preserve its own character as a nonindustrial community centering around a major institution of learning," the article said, but the Research Triangle threatened to reorient the university's priorities, setting science and industry above its traditional emphasis on the humanities. "The growth of a city devoted wholly to scientific research so nearby will of course exert a major influence on the life of this whole area," the *News Leader* item concluded. "But this community will hope that meantime Chapel Hill's present aims and purposes will not be lost to sight, and that its ancient heritage as a seat of learning will not be overlooked."[63]

Such skepticism extended beyond the pages of the town newspaper, as the research park struggled to generate the kind of interest—and land sales—that seemed so plausible in the spring and summer of 1957. A business downturn that year left many companies reluctant to take a chance on the Triangle's as-yet-unproven potential as an ideal location for industrial laboratories. Three clients who had planned to move to the park failed to follow through.[64] A luncheon for potential investors in Charlotte in July 1958 yielded little interest, and Guest regretted having not planted any questions in the audience. Meanwhile, Pinelands was running short of funds. "I have now decided to plow into this thing full speed ahead without regard to anything except the final answer," Guest wrote in frustration to his friend Claude Q. Freeman, a Charlotte lawyer who helped recruit the city's business elite for the luncheon. "To me, the final answer is that Pinelands needs $2 million and it is up to me to get it."[65]

Robbins, in poor health by the fall of 1958, appeared to be unhappy with the direction of the project. As few companies showed interest in relocating to the area and the project's profitability was in doubt, the Research Triangle Committee realized that the project was likelier to succeed as a nonprofit venture. With the energetic support of banker Archie Davis, the committee was able to raise enough donations from wealthy North Carolinians by 1959 to buy out Robbins's shares and reorganize itself as the Research Triangle Foundation, a nonprofit that would be jointly controlled by the three universities and the state. Thus did the fledgling Research Triangle Park change from a private, commercial effort to a joint public-private partnership—albeit one without many interested tenants lined up.[66]

Clearly, businesses were not champing at the bit to relocate to the Triangle in 1958. Boosters could claim that Raleigh-Durham-Chapel Hill was an ideal area for scientific research, but skeptics would remain skeptical until corporations actually began to set up shop there. A. H. Kinzel, a chemist at Union Carbide, was not sanguine about the Triangle's prospects. Meeting with Simpson, Kinzel said that the existence of nearby research facilities was simply not a major factor when his company was deciding where to put a laboratory. Carbide would not consider the chemistry labs at Duke or UNC to be a compelling reason for locating a facility in the area, as academic research was often too slow-moving and remote from practical application to make much of a difference for the company.

> Usually, he said, the laboratory will follow the plant, and in the case of his company the plants have in recent years been located generally with reference to water supply. He pointed out the deficiencies of our area and of the South in general in the services that are necessary to support research activities, such as engineering, skilled workers for machine making and the like, the proximity of supplies, and a large skilled laboring force from which to choose. This was not the first time that this point had been made to me.[67]

Kinzel did not mince words. The chemist, Simpson recalled, "took occasion, also, to point out that in the national setting our three institutions, while quite good, did not loom especially large to such a person as he."[68] The sociologist was not offended but, in fact, took the candid words for what they were: a frank assessment of the challenges involved in persuading outsiders that a patch of piney woods between two modest-sized cities and a small college town in the South was a hotbed of scientific innovation. How could you build an "M.I.T. of North Carolina" without an MIT or Boston to go with it? If the Triangle's seeming raison d'être—its concentration of scholars and scientific resources—had only marginal utility for big business, what could be its chief selling point?

Boosters argued that geography favored the Triangle in other ways—as embodied in the rail lines, highways, rivers, and airports that criss-crossed the pages of the promotional literature. The Triangle was situated between New York, Atlanta, and Washington, D.C., at a nexus of transportation routes, including the new interstate highway system, then in its early stages of construction.[69] "The town [Chapel Hill] is twenty minutes from a regular air terminal connecting with Washington in an hour and Atlanta in one and one-half hours," Guest told the director of engineering at E. R. Squibb & Sons, a pharmaceutical firm that was itself headquartered in a college town, New Brunswick, New Jersey. Crucially, scientists and executives could catch "overnight service to New York on fast trains."[70] The research park offered direct access to the Southern and Seaboard System Railroads, and North Carolina Highway 54 converged with U.S. Highways 1, 15, and 70 in the area.[71] "The industrial scientist thus may live in an environment peculiarly suited to him and yet remain in close touch with executive offices and perhaps even production facilities located elsewhere," explained Simpson in a 1957 promotional piece in the *New York Times*.[72]

When IBM announced plans to build a research center in New York's Westchester suburbs in 1956, the company appealed to the same mix of geographical and social qualities that would define the Triangle's message. IBM officials cited Westchester's proximity to its other facilities as a top concern, just as Kinzel suggested. "The Westchester County site on which we hope to build is located midway between Poughkeepsie and New York City," president Thomas Watson said. However, a convenient location between its labs along the Hudson River was not the only consideration. "It was selected not only with an eye to accessibility but to the considerable cultural and educational opportunities in the area," Watson told the *New York World-Telegram and Sun*. "These are of great importance to scientists, whose interests individually and as a group are extremely varied."[73]

Guest anticipated this line of argument three years earlier, when he first tried to convince Squibb & Sons to come to the "research area" of Chapel Hill. "In my other work with pharmaceutical firms," Romeo Guest told Squibb's director of engineering, "I have found that the matter of location near the center of culture is very important." North Carolina's cities each had something to offer in terms of culture, but one area stood out: "It is a place where you can get plenty of workers easily and at the same time, it is a place where research chemists with doctor's degrees would be very happy because of the association with culture and extra training."[74] This approach was an attempt to sidestep strictly practical arguments about the importance of universities, libraries, and labs to an industrial firm. Instead, it focused on the appeal of the area to a company's workforce, both in practical terms—the availability of further training and graduate education—and in more diffuse terms, in the atmosphere of culture or sophistication in which "research people" would *want* to live.

G. H. Law of Union Carbide offered a contrary view from his colleague Kinzel, arguing that these less tangible factors, such as culture, could be important when businesses choose a site for a laboratory. Law told Simpson that "living conditions and cultural opportunities" were "at least as important as any other considerations" for corporations and the scientists they hoped to employ. At a time when the federal government and private industry were putting unprecedented resources into research, highly educated professionals were in short supply and high demand. "There just aren't enough good men to go around and competition is intense," Law said. "With equal opportunities and salaries at different locations the decision to accept a position is usually made on the basis of living conditions. Many of the young men we hire now are married before they leave school and their wives frequently cast the deciding vote on location."[75]

CULTURE AS "CLIMATE"

Crucial to the success of the Triangle, then, was an emphasis on the Raleigh-Durham-Chapel Hill area as a place where scientists could be happy and creative. In this sense, both the Triangle's champions and the corporations that moved there needed to present the urban landscape as valuable, rich in culture and social status. The production and sale of this new kind of space predated the discourse of "innovative milieux" and "creative" cities that came into vogue in the 1990s and 2000s.[76] North Carolinians spoke of the value of the Triangle's educational institutions and privileged workforce in terms of "climate," "atmosphere," and the ubiquitous language of "stimulation." Such rhetoric resembles the more recent trend toward emphasizing "diversity" and other qualities of neighborhoods and cities that accompanied gentrification amid the renaissance of cities such as New York and Boston in the 1990s, even though the Triangle was—at least at first—cultivated as a landscape for affluent white residents.[77]

Research Triangle Park emerged at a time of intense competition for scientists and engineers, particularly after the Russian satellite Sputnik's flight in 1957 exploded American fears of a technological lag in the race for Cold War supremacy. Companies were painfully aware that workers in new high-tech industries had to be cajoled to take a job, even with a company as powerful as IBM, and the qualities of a working and living environment soon became central to their recruiting efforts. As the federal government subsidized work on space technology and computing during the 1950s and 1960s, employers vied to recruit a scarce number of scientists and engineers with advanced degrees. "With the intense competition existing today for scientific talent, industry is finding that it must offer more than just good pay to attract the kind of people it seeks," an ad in the *New York Times* declared in 1962. If research was a new kind of industry, its workers also had new interests and demands: "When evaluating locations for new research operations, industrial concerns also look for proximity to entertainment and cultural centers."[78]

The task of the Triangle's boosters was to convince companies such as IBM that North Carolina would satisfy the desire of potential employees for good schools, entertainment, recreation, and so forth. The U.S. Chamber of

Commerce's Carl Madden said the Research Triangle was one of the places that attract "these brilliant, creative people," like "Route 128 in Massachusetts, with the facilities of Harvard and MIT," and Stanford in California. "The Research Triangle is also an outstanding area in which the industrial scientist's family may live," an ad by North Carolina's Board of Conservation and Development (BCD) announced in 1957. "To be found here are most of the advantages of a large metropolitan area, without many of the disadvantages of congestion and noise and lack of space."[79]

Beyond the standard pitch of suburban pleasures versus urban blight, the ad reassured readers in the Northeast that central North Carolina offered abundant cultural opportunities: "Each year many concert artists and groups appear here, along with many touring companies of Broadway shows, and scarcely a week passes during the fall and winter months when a speaker of national reputation does not appear somewhere in the Triangle." Such luminaries included speakers such as Ralph Bunche and Robert Frost and performers including the Ballet Russe de Monte Carlo and the Quartetto Italiano—entertainments that catered to highbrow tastes.[80] One could leave New York, in other words, without leaving Lincoln Center.

Boosters attributed these cultural amenities to the presence of scholars, students, and schools in the greater Triangle. "In Durham the flavor of fine universities blends with the tempo of diversified manufacturing set by American Tobacco Company, B. C. Remedy, Durham Hosiery, Erwin Mills, Liggett and Myers, Wright Machinery Division of Sperry Rand, and other leaders," another ad stated in 1957. "The result is a stimulating atmosphere where a productive day's work—whether it be in the factory, laboratory, office, or class room—is the accepted standard."[81] The Research Triangle Institute, a think tank that carried out projects with business and government on a contract basis, sought to woo potential employees in 1962, stating, "A stimulating environment for professional and cultural development is provided by close association with the Triangle universities: Duke, North Carolina, and North Carolina State."[82]

The Triangle's supporters at first experienced only modest success in convincing major corporations that North Carolina would satisfy the desires of potential employees for good schools, entertainment, and recreation. Simpson, Little, and company courted the likes of American

Cyanamid and Union Carbide, which sent three representatives to tour the area in July 1958.[83] The physics consulting firm ASTRA relocated from Milford, Connecticut, to Raleigh in 1958, with plans to move into RTP.[84] The first major tenant, though, was Chemstrand, a chemical firm that opted to move its facilities from Decatur, Alabama, in 1959. Ironically, in their quest to imitate the Charles River and draw business from the North, the Triangle's organizers poached a business that was thirty minutes away from Huntsville, one of the South's other scientific centers. Chemstrand hired the Wigton-Abbott Company of Plainfield, New Jersey, to build its $7.5 million site in 1959, which was dedicated three years later.[85]

When businesses decided to open facilities in or near RTP, they adopted nearly identical rhetoric (figure 1.3). Chemstrand stressed that "a principal factor in [its] decision was the stimulating research climate

Figure 1.3 A prototypical image of the white male researcher from a 1957 state promotional piece.

already established in the Triangle, with its proximity to 900 scientists at State College, Duke University, and the University of North Carolina, and to the research staff of the new Research Triangle Institute."[86] The company promised prospective mechanical engineers that the Triangle "offers excellent facilities for cultural and recreational activity." The Triangle "was chosen after a six-month study of 21 locations because: *You and your family* will enjoy living in this area where educational, cultural, recreational and residential facilities are top-notch. *You* will find intellectual stimulation in the university atmosphere which will surround Chemstrand's expanding research program."[87] Similarly, the Missile Battery Division of the Electric Storage Battery Company tried to lure engineers to the Triangle's "unusual intellectual climate" in 1960.[88]

What is this "flavor," "climate," or "atmosphere" that so "stimulated" a certain kind of worker in the 1950s and 1960s? Like many economic development efforts, which speak in terms of numbers of jobs created or feet of floor space planned by business, the Triangle's virtues could be quantified. In an early instance of national media attention, the *New York Times* observed that North Carolinians hoped to maximize the advantages of "three major universities with 2,000 faculty members, 18,000 students, libraries and laboratories."[89] The three universities were said to host "33,000 students and faculty members" in 1966.[90] That same year, a state ad boasted that the Triangle included "three of the nation's leading universities and more than 450 scientists."[91] "It's a creative community," another ad declared. "With plenty of educated men and women."[92]

Educated people were a sort of resource to be mined or consumed. Surgeon General Luther Terry described the Triangle as "reservoir of experienced consultants in nearby distinguished academic institutions" in 1965.[93] An envious Florida columnist noted the same year that North Carolina "has taken this reservoir of academic talent, created a $2 million foundation to promote and develop it, and established a Research Triangle park to attract industrial research institutions. Thus it is far ahead of states like Florida in readiness to capitalize on the most attractive adjunct to the 20th Century's technology revolution—research."[94]

The key, though, was that this "reservoir" was thought to appeal not only to management but to employees themselves. "Scientists like to live where other scientists live and where they will have the facilities they will need to carry on their work," an item in an Oregon newspaper noted, in contemplating that state's own potential as a research center.[95] A 1962 study of Boeing employees found that 80 percent of its scientific staff considered the existence of the University of Washington in Seattle a major contributor to their job satisfaction.[96] A columnist in Miami believed that the moral of the story was simple. "There is no 'which-came-first-the-chicken-or-the-egg?' argument in this story," Atlanta journalist and editor Ralph McGill opined in 1964. "The educational institutions were there. Industry and science came to them. The difference between a community making itself educationally eligible to attract modern industry and one that struggles to get a pants factory primarily is one of education."[97]

The argument for the Triangle, then, hinged on the universities and the people they employed and taught. Business leaders in New York's Hudson Valley commissioned a report by consultants at Arthur D. Little in 1967, which noted that the upstate region lacked the kind of educational programs that would attract both business and workers. "An increasing number [of women] are taking advantage of extension programs," the report said. Women who had foregone careers or advanced education to raise families increasingly looked to take advantage of nearby universities, which were more accessible in the Research Triangle than in the Hudson Valley, where few schools offered master's degree programs. "The availability of facilities to meet the educational desires of wives is often an important consideration in the choice of jobs by scientists," the Little researchers concluded.[98]

It would be too much to say that the Research Triangle succeeded entirely due to its self-promotion as an enclave for the privileged and well educated—a sort of stimulating, yet homogeneous, community. However, the idea that scientific workers would like to cluster together was as important as the notion that laboratories and industrial facilities would benefit from agglomeration economies by gathering in one area. The Triangle was both a concentration of technological and scientific infrastructure and a concentration of social capital, which was possessed by skilled workers whose training was in demand. As the geographer Blake Gumprecht observed in a rare study of college towns, these settlements are unique in "their youthful and comparatively diverse populations, their highly educated workforces, their relative absence of heavy industry, and the presence in them of cultural opportunities more typical of large cities."[99] North Carolinians helped to pioneer the sale of such traits for the purpose of regional economic development, seeking to draw both private and public investment to the "academic archipelago" that existed throughout the twenty-five-mile radius around RTP. They also, unwittingly perhaps, helped to develop a blueprint of what an information-oriented, high-tech landscape would look like: quiet, clean, with no smokestacks in sight—what geographers David Havlick and Scott Kirsch have called a "production utopia."[100]

North Carolinians in the 1950s realized that their state was facing serious economic headwinds, and in response, a handful of wealthy and well-connected citizens joined forces to chart a new course for the state's economy, one that focused on higher wages and scientific research. Romeo Guest saw that the universities of Raleigh, Durham, and Chapel Hill could serve as the springboard for some kind of high-tech development, though at first the end result was by no means clear. Leaders in academia and business pointed to the Triangle's value as a cultural center, a community of educated people that any scientist would be happy to have as neighbors.

With the menacing orb of Sputnik floating overhead and the Cold War at full tilt, the nation's scientists and engineers could be choosy about where to live, and the Triangle's boosters presented the region as ideal for footloose corporations. It was, as Simpson put it, an "environment . . . in which there are professional colleagues and a rather high cultural level," but without "the disadvantages of metropolitan congestion."[101] Boosters presented the Triangle as the ideal place for high-tech firms as well as scientists and their families to relocate, capitalizing on the prestige and cultural opportunities offered by the area's universities to launch a novel development strategy based on creativity, culture, and education.

Such was the picture that the Triangle's inventors sold to the world. But what did this utopia look like on the ground, once glass and steel began to rise from the red clay of Durham County? How did Research Triangle Park model a vision of a new economy as new jobs and new businesses came to North Carolina in the late 1950s and 1960s and a postindustrial capitalism was beginning to take shape across American society?

2

"Not a Second Ruhr"

BUILDING A POSTINDUSTRIAL ECONOMY IN THE 1960s

> Springlike Tarheel vigor was at work last week from Kitty Hawk to Cherokee, from missile plant to church pulpit, reshaping a landscape once principally adorned by loblolly pine, flue-cured tobacco and two-room farm shacks. . . . In the center of the Piedmont, engineers mapped sites for nuclear, chemical and industrial research labs in a new, 4,000-acre "Research Triangle."
>
> —"North Carolina: The South's New Leader," *Time*, May 4, 1959

Time's image of missiles among the loblolly pine marked a dramatic shift from the North Carolina of just a few years before. By the mid-1950s, prominent North Carolinians looked at the state's economic progress with dismay. Yet a savvy public relations strategy enabled boosters of Research Triangle Park to score favorable national coverage and attract a handful of tenants, such as Chemstrand (see figure 2.1). These early successes, however modest, paved the way for a major turn of fortune in 1965, when IBM and the federal government decided to place major research facilities in the park—setting RTP on a far more assured course that led to continued growth in the 1970s and beyond.

In the process, a new idea of research as an industry of its own gradually and subtly emerged. If scientific research was conceived as a way to make better use of the state's textiles and wood chips, the park soon took shape as a space for research and research alone. Were the making of knowledge and of goods two sides of the same coin, or were they completely different activities? Initially thought of as one *part* of production, "industrial research"

The sprawling multi-million dollar Chemstrand Research Center, Incorporated, is located on a 105-acre tract in a natural park setting.

Figure 2.1 An aerial view of Chemstrand's RTP facility in 1962. *Source*: United States Federal Reserve.

soon took on a separate meaning—research could be unmoored from any particular productive process and stand on its own.

Triangle boosters wished to pry scientific supremacy away from the North, but the old industrial heartland's human and technical resources, its scientists and laboratories, depended in large part on its advanced economic base. With few high-tech industries of its own, North Carolina had to persuade outside companies that their labs did not *need* to be associated with manufacturing facilities. Scientific work could be done in its own space. In fact, as Governor Terry Sanford told reporters in 1961, research was not just one part of a manufacturing process but an industry unto itself.[1]

Contradictions plagued the idea of research as its own distinct enterprise. As Sanford and his peers entreated business and government to set up labs in North Carolina, they first focused on industries with ties to the state. They saw the chemical industry as a likely candidate for the Triangle—not just because of strong biology and chemistry departments at UNC and Duke but because of the importance of chemistry to the textile industry. Chemstrand, a maker of acrylic fibers and nylons, and the American Association of Textile Chemists and Colorists (AATCC), a trade group, were among the Triangle's first tenants. Park leaders emphasized the practical value of research by such groups to the state's existing industries, in terms of making tangible and familiar products. At the same time, they struggled with the inherent difficulty of keeping production out of the park and restricting the space to purely scientific activities.

In the process, research gained a privileged status, coming to signify a particular kind of employment—professional, highly specialized, and upper middle class. It had to. Park clients wanted to set up their labs in the bucolic and serene atmosphere advertised by North Carolina's salespeople. Zoning regulations had to be rewritten, and county officials had to determine exactly what a "research district" was. Park covenants set limits on how much nonresearch employment would be allowed within RTP to ensure that the presence of working-class people and unsightly scenes of men loading and unloading trucks would not upset the ideal of the Research Triangle as a scientific enclave. But defining what made someone a research worker was not easy. At first a shimmering image of futuristic progress, science had to submit to law and regulation; what was comfortably vague in Triangle rhetoric had to become specific and, to an extent, exclusive.[2]

Planners, then, appealed to the idea of research as its own distinctive kind of work, like any other industry or trade; they saw an emergent property that results from many people in the same field working close together. In a research district, the whole would be greater than the sum of its parts, as the Research Triangle Committee said in a 1957 planning document: "A strictly research area in a park setting, will have appeal for certain types of research activities. Some of the larger companies are looking toward basic, long range research laboratories separate from production."[3]

Indeed, as planning historian Louise A. Mozingo argued in her work on "pastoral capitalism," many corporations in the 1950s sought to pivot away from their old headquarters in industrial, urban America, for the first time moving middle and upper managers to suburban estates and away from production. Such environments were thought to be especially appealing for scientists, who occupied the first research parks along Massachusetts's Route 128 and California's Stanford Industrial Park in the 1950s. Such developments aimed to foster a "campus atmosphere," since, as one developer put it, " 'Industrial' is a dirty, smoke belching word," and research parks mirrored the affluent suburbs where research workers wished to live.[4]

Boosters cultivated an image of the Triangle as just such a special, exclusive place for scientists, engineers, and executives. Industry "demands and needs a high quality area" for laboratories, RTP's Pearson Stewart told the Durham planning commission in 1959. "Research labs," he said, "don't want to be in an industrial district."[5] Stewart and his allies sought to change the zoning for the Research Triangle property in southeastern Durham county from agricultural to a "research district" in order to permit the construction of laboratories on expansive suburban lawns. Neither homes nor factories would be permitted. The following year, Research Triangle Foundation Vice President George Akers Moore averred that RTP "shall be devoted to those uses which are the breeding places of ideas for use in principal production elsewhere."[6] Here again, the goal was to import scientists and export ideas—keeping the industrial part of the industry somewhere else.[7]

THE MAKING OF KNOWLEDGE WORK IN THE 1960s

A research area, of course, needed research. The first step was to found the Research Triangle Institute (RTI), a not-for-profit think tank that was RTP's first tenant.[8] From the earliest discussions of the Triangle in 1955, boosters talked about the idea of setting up an organization staffed with scientists and engineers who would carry out research projects on contract with corporations and government agencies.[9] UNC sociologist Howard Odum had already laid out a proposal, never realized, for a research institute tied in with the area's universities in the early 1950s, and George Simpson was influenced by his colleague and mentor's ideas. The founders of RTI also looked to the successful example of the Stanford Research Institute in Palo Alto, California, and the Southern Research Institute in Birmingham, Alabama.[10] The park's flagship enterprise, then, was not a company that incorporated research into its production process; rather, it was an agency whose sole purpose was research.

In the early 1960s research in the Triangle meant using radiation to make cheaper tires, developing artificial turf for football fields, designing a bathythermograph to measure sea temperatures, and mapping gravity fields on the moon.[11] It was a world for "transistors and sterling silver and guided missiles."[12] In December 1960, Universal ECSCO announced plans to move from Downey, California, locating temporarily in Raleigh's Cameron Village, an innovative mixed-use shopping and housing development. The company did contract work for the Department of Defense on a "design and build" basis. ECSCO President Robert Swaffield acknowledged that seeing tenants come to the park encouraged him to follow through on a pledge made two years prior to come to RTP: "The rapid growth of the Research Triangle in recent months confirms our earlier decisions and we are very happy now to be an active partner in its still brighter future."[13] With the exception of defense-oriented firms such as ASTRA and ECSCO, and RTI's contract work for the Atomic Energy Commission, much work in the Triangle remained tied to ordinary things: nylon hosiery, rubber tires.

In short, research remained one ingredient in the making of everyday products for many Triangle firms. NC State and other colleges had developed strength in areas that processed the state's natural resources, with programs in biology and chemistry geared toward agriculture and forestry. (The U.S. Forest Service set up a lab in the park, taking advantage of the state's abundance of trees and long-standing timber industry.) North Carolinians made a strong case to the American Association of Textile Chemists and Colorists that the organization should leave its base in Lowell, Massachusetts, for RTP, arguing that proximity to the state's textile mills would benefit the group. Jim Shea, vice president of RTF, argued that "fifty per cent of the industry from which the AATCC draws its membership is within 150 miles of the Research Triangle."[14] Only 30 percent of the group's membership were chemists, dyers, and technicians who worked for mills, though; most were salespeople and suppliers in the industry.

In fact, the AATCC was prepared to move. Its long-running relationship with the Lowell Textile School had been mutually beneficial, as the school provided the trade group with laboratory facilities, and the organization provided the school with researchers and publicity due to its association with the trade group. However, the school morphed into the

Lowell Technological Institute in the mid-1950s, shedding its explicit ties to a diminished New England textile industry.[15] New AATCC President George Paine was determined to move the group to New York, even though the cramped, noisy conditions of the city were not well suited to developing an in-house lab for the group's use. Paine was a "confirmed northerner," according to the group's official history. As far as he was concerned, if one "crossed the Hudson River and headed South [one came] into the land of the aborigine."[16]

The Triangle's hopes were dashed in 1961 when the AATCC's Executive Commitee voted to move to New York City. RTP came in a close second among the choices, which included Philadelphia, NC State, Clemson College in South Carolina, and Washington, D.C., as potential sites for the new headquarters.[17] Rather disingenuously, Paine assured Shea that he was caught unawares by the news. "I had my bags all packed and was ready to move down to the Research Triangle," Paine said, "and when the ballots were counted, I felt like somebody who had voted for Nixon."[18] The Northeastern members won the day by arguing that New York's superior access to media, transportation, and other technical societies made it the better choice. The trade press was not impressed. "We know that our feeling is shared by a great majority of AATCC's other members in its Southern region," an item in *Textile Industries* opined, "that the Research Triangle Park was the only logical place for the new headquarters."[19] New York was too expensive, and the textile industry was shrinking in its traditional base of the Northeast.

Much of the internal debate at AATCC hinged on the relative importance of research to the organization. Some members believed that the group should focus on coordinating and administering its role as a professional group for chemists in the textile industry, contracting out whatever research it needed rather than doing it in house. New York looked like a superior location due to its direct access to the publishing industry and other professional societies headquartered there, as well as the city's convenience for business travel. However, when the decision to move to New York was announced, AATCC members revolted. Moving to the Big Apple "would have meant a drastic decrease in the size and scope of the AATCC's in-house laboratory activities," historian Mark Clark noted, and members considered research an integral part of the organization's service to the textile industry.[20]

A new vote in 1962 selected RTP as the organization's new home. The Triangle promised lower costs for rent, more space for laboratories, and a "good quality of life."[21] The key was research, which AATCC prized over New York's benefits as a center of publishing and business. North Carolina State College (later North Carolina State University) was arguably the nation's foremost institution for textile research, offering access to the same kind of intellectual and library resources that the Lowell Technological Institute previously provided.[22] The AATCC thus became one of RTP's first tenants because it saw itself as an organization whose role was to conduct research that would advance the frontiers of chemistry (see figure 2.2). It came to North Carolina to fulfill its own research mandate and to take advantage of intellectual resources at the center of the state's burgeoning textile industry.

Figure 2.2 The American Association of Textile Chemists and Colorists' headquarters in RTP. *Source*: Photo by author.

The early growth of RTP built on North Carolina's existing industrial strengths—essentially, chemical research tied to textiles—but what research would mean in the Triangle's future remained to be seen. An organization such as AATCC or RTI might not make anything in particular, instead conducting and providing research independently of any particular manufacturing enterprise. These institutions, in short, were not just "research-oriented," as Hodges described the kinds of business the Triangle wanted to attract, but research-only.

Increasingly, it was possible to imagine the Triangle as advancing the frontiers of a whole new economic sector: research. "Within this triangle research, in which the groves of academe have formed a partnership with industry," the editors of the *New York Times* said, "is itself a major industry. . . . Potentially, industrialization enlightened by humanistic research may be a strong solvent of Southern racial tensions."[23] The following year, the paper attributed the same language to Governor Terry Sanford, whom it paraphrased as saying "research was an industry in itself, with expenditures close to $13,000,000."[24] Soon, major new tenants were also echoing this message, as IBM did after deciding to relocate in RTP in 1964—a crucial turning point in the Triangle's early history. "Today's major growth industry is information handling and control," the computer giant declared, in an ad entreating workers join its new North Carolina site in 1968. "And IBM is a leader in that field."

A sense of knowledge work—research, or "information handling"—as a distinct industry was beginning to emerge in the 1960s alongside a nascent rhetoric about an "information revolution" and "postindustrial society," in both commercial advertising and academic literature.[25] A Florida newspaper still spoke of research as an "adjunct to the 20th Century's technology revolution" in 1965, but observers and supporters of the Triangle increasingly articulated a capacious sense of research as a sector in its own right.[26] The Triangle's success in winning major corporate and government clients in the mid-1960s helped escalate this discussion to a national scale.

The Federal Reserve noted in 1962,

> Research is a dynamic word. It is associated with subjects such as space exploration, nuclear physics, miracle drugs, and synthetic fibers.

> Because it is so important for our health, comfort, and, above all, our national survival, literally billions of dollars are funneled into the traditional research centers—Boston, New York City and adjacent areas in New Jersey, and the Washington-Baltimore region—but now other parts of the nation are awakening to the attractions of research. Among them is the Research Triangle in North Carolina.[27]

The Fed concluded by noting the Triangle's key importance for the state: "Its 'product' is knowledge."[28]

Less than ten years later, RTI President George Herbert conceded that the idea of research as industry "requires some explanation." Speaking at a conference on industrial innovation at Britain's University of Newcastle upon Tyne in 1971, Herbert pointed out that research meant something different to an archaeologist, a meteorologist, a businessperson, or any person on the street. He limited his own definition to the work done by people employed by business and government solely to generate new knowledge—a part of the economy that surpassed $10 billion in expenditure by the late 1950s. "Casting covetous eyes on such existing concentrations as the Boston-Cambridge complex and the San Francisco peninsula," Herbert told his British colleagues, "states and regions all began to compete vigorously for laboratories and other research-related enterprises as new sources of payrolls, plant investments, and taxes."[29] Research was not just an adjunct to business or one part of the production process. Indeed, he continued:

> The raw materials for research are imaginative and analytical scientists and engineers from a host of disciplines. The raw materials used by the "industry," therefore, are neither mined nor harvested; they are enticed and recruited. The product requires neither freight cars nor ships to reach its market.[30]

Set aside the fact that the products of research—computers, microchips, and pharmaceuticals, for instance—did in fact need trains and ships to get to consumers. Notice instead the scare quotes around *industry* and the uneasy comparisons with mining and manufacturing. Brains were the resource; Herbert understood that they must be not only mined but hunted and lured. By the early 1970s, policy makers increasingly understood research as an enterprise of its own, and RTP was among the earliest and most ambitious efforts to cultivate the ideal place for it.

COSMOPOLITAN BUT NOT URBAN: RTP AS A PLACE

At Research Triangle Park's very core is blankness. When they talk about RTP, journalists and boosters cannot resist images of modernization—possums and old shacks next to missile plants—painting a rustic old, backward South lifted into the high-tech future. ("Piedmont farm communities within the Triangle found themselves cheek-by-jowl with enclaves of Ph.D.'s and aerospace engineers," as a 1983 state history put it. "The twentieth century seemed almost to have been bypassed in a headlong plunge from the nineteenth century into the twenty-first.")[31]

But RTP also retells a frontier narrative, an old trope about finding an empty wilderness and creating a new society from scratch that Americans have recycled again and again over the centuries. Accounts of RTP's development routinely insist that there was simply nothing there—the woods where the park would soon rise were "empty acres . . . useful mostly for holding two counties together."[32]

In fact, people did live there. Locals liked to hunt turkeys in the woods, and the Durham Wildlife Club refused to give up its site to RTP until a deal was struck with IBM in the mid-1960s. (The club came out ahead, with over $100,000 and 95 acres at a new location in another corner of the park.) One family who owned three homes in the heart of the park refused to sell, while another tussled with RTP planners in 1969 when rezoning meant that they could not place a new trailer on their property for a relative to live in.[33] The past was persistent in other ways too: planners discovered early on that a slave burial ground existed on RTP land, and they had to relocate it elsewhere.[34]

Such traces of the rural past disappear in the official story of RTP. Triangle planners looked at the woods as a tabula rasa, and this sense of emptiness persists even today; with the research facilities of hundreds of employers, the park still *feels* as if there's nothing there to the casual driver passing by. That spaciousness was central to the vision of RTP, as planners aimed to create a serene and radically dispersed environment. With centralized authority and five thousand acres as their canvas, they could enforce stringent design regulations on a virtually unprecedented scale.

In fact, Research Triangle Park was both strangely typical of the South and a stark departure from the past. Like much Southern industrial development, it was the product of a paternalistic business elite—its very existence was owed to textile magnate Karl Robbins, and a broad cross-section of the state's industrial and financial leaders chipped in to save the project when its fate hung in the balance in 1959. Like the textile industry of old, the park depended significantly on outside capital and technology. And like the countless mill villages that dotted the landscape of the South, from Ranlo to Robbins, it was developed under the close scrutiny of a single authority—in this case, the Research Triangle Foundation—even if it featured labs on manicured lawns instead of tiny houses arrayed around a mill.

Yet Research Triangle Park was not a company town, in the sense that workers lived and worked in a space controlled by the boss. It could have been. Early on, Romeo Guest's "triangle" might have evolved in directions that departed sharply from the tree-lined research park surrounded by sprawling, low-density suburbs that we know today. In August 1954, Guest received a proposal from Stanley Reed, an engineer and inventor who later went on to found *Mergers & Acquisitions* magazine and dabbled in pursuits ranging from politics to opera. Reed envisioned a truly self-contained scientific city: a four-thousand-acre for-profit complex in Virginia organized around his own Reed Research Inc., encompassing both "research organizations . . . [and] residences in the $20,000 to $40,000 class for many of the personnel," as well as some manufacturing. "The whole thing would probably be fenced in and have a watchman," Reed's agent told Guest.[35]

The high-tech economy, in this vision, could have become a cloistered kind of panopticon. However, Guest rebuffed his proposal, mainly because he insisted on the project's remaining in North Carolina. Other localities also were considering the idea of combining housing and research facilities. Princeton University, for instance, planned a Center for Industrial Research—a "sanctuary for scientists"—in 1962, highlighting "the increasing difficulty of providing suitable housing and other facilities for industrial research personnel," the *New York Times* noted. The *Times* also mentioned "a similar research-and-living project" planned outside the city in Sterling Forest, New York, which would pair housing with laboratories.[36]

Research Triangle Park took a different form, in that it divorced housing from work. The park itself, though, promised tenants design controls of a type not seen even in the South's most tightly regulated mill town or subdivision. Early on, Robbins planned for uniform landscaping and rigorous controls over architectural style.[37] When RTP formally began to take shape, it mandated strict rules for any noise, odor, smoke, or vibrations emanating from a tenant's site. Firms could occupy only a tiny portion of their lots—at first 5 percent and, later, 15 percent—and structures could be built only behind generous setbacks. No manufacturing was allowed on site except for testing prototypes, although the park was forced to relax rules to accommodate IBM in 1965, as the company insisted on production being part of any facility it would build there.[38] Throughout, the emphasis was on distinguishing RTP from the landscape of traditional industry. As the Federal Reserve reported in 1962, "The Park is envisioned as an 'industrial campus,' not a second Ruhr."[39]

The Research Triangle Institute was the leading light of RTP in its early years and the institution that best embodied the postindustrial ethos of research as its own distinct enterprise. RTI had only one employee in 1959, but by 1962, more than one hundred thirty worked there. Over two thirds of the workforce were professionals, and almost half were PhDs—a high proportion for even the most science-oriented business (figure 2.3). About half of workers held degrees from local universities, although foreign scientists and engineers were robustly represented on RTI's staff.

The institute rapidly built its revenue from research contracts in the early 1960s, soon bringing in over $1 million a year, although it only went into the black by 1962. In 1964 its staff had grown to 225, and its eight divisions conducted research for the Atomic Energy Commission, NASA, and numerous other government agencies.[40]

If many of RTI's employees hailed from abroad, at least one came from Alabama. Howard G. Clark had been a chemist at Chemstrand but quit after the company announced its move to RTP. The chemist had no

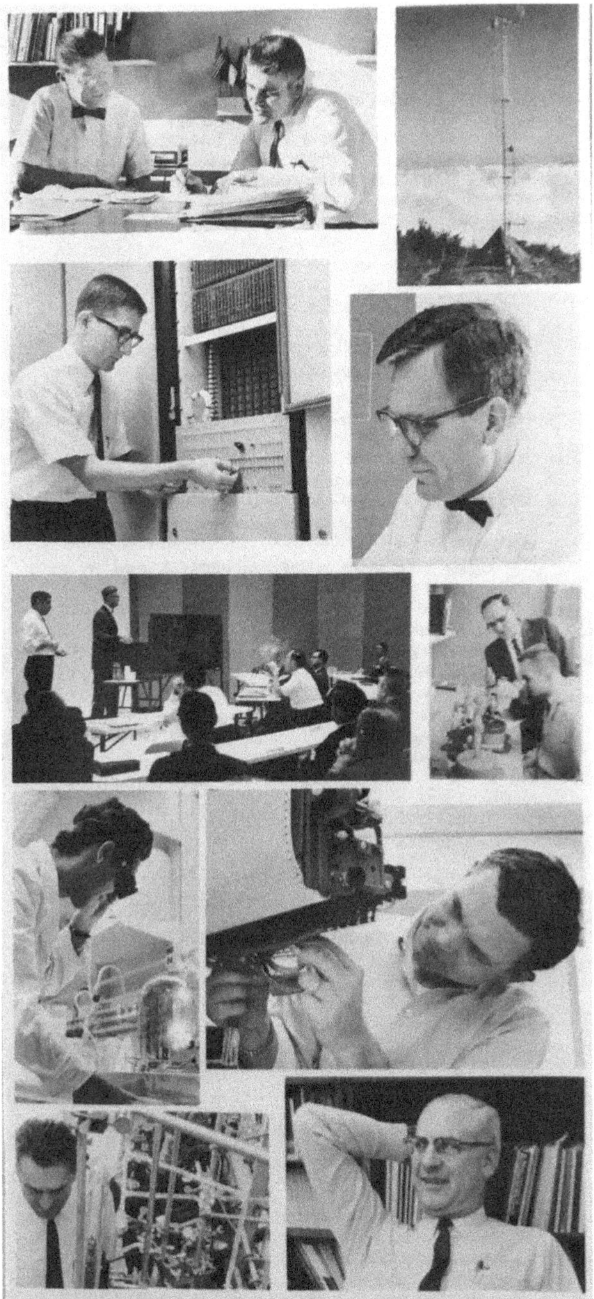

Figure 2.3 Depiction of scientific workers in a 1960s-era Research Triangle Institute promotional brochure. *Source*: Research Triangle Institute (RTI).

particular problem with relocating to North Carolina. "I did object to being told that I was required to move," he remembered. "I felt that many U.S. corporations treated their employees like cattle that could be shipped around the country at the management's whim." Clark moved instead to Florida to work as director of research at a start-up company, which turned out to be a poor choice. "The president of the company was impossible for me to deal with," Clark said. "I realized that most of my professional friends were now in North Carolina, so I swallowed my pride and telephoned for help." Friends at Chemstrand found a way for him to come back to the company, but they urged him to consider a position at the fledgling RTI instead. Clark was quickly offered a job in RTI's Dreyfus lab, and he eventually found out why: the organization could not use any of its Dreyfus Foundation funds until it had an employee on the payroll, and it was hurting for cash.[41]

Staffing the new labs proved to be a challenge, especially where recruiting top scientific talent was concerned. RTI President George Herbert was willing to go to great lengths to recruit scientists from around the world. He was particularly keen to recruit Anton Peterlin, a Yugoslav scientist who was a preeminent expert in the field of polymer science. Winning over Peterlin was no easy task, in part because his position as professor at Technische Hochschule in Munich was more prestigious than directing an obscure, fledgling laboratory in North Carolina.[42]

Herbert traveled to Munich to court the chemist, and when the Peterlins agreed to visit in January 1961, top officials from RTI and Celanese "wined and dined" the couple, attempting to sell them on the idea of relocating to North Carolina. Herbert and company even tried to dazzle Peterlin's young son and daughter with the wonders of life in America, plying them with ice cream and soda. (Daughter Tanja Peterlin insists that the ploy failed; she says she made no effort to convince her father to take the position.) Herbert liked to say it was Peterlin's first taste of grits in Charlotte that closed the deal, but other aspects of the package likely made the difference: a handsome income, the freedom to spend summers traveling in Europe, and a guarantee that Herbert would acquire a nuclear magnetic resonance spectrometer—despite the fact that Herbert did not know, at first, what the device was for or how much it would cost.[43]

Peterlin took the offer, and Herbert used the hire to create buzz in publications such as the *New York Herald-Tribune*, the *Wall Street Journal*, and *Chemical & Engineering News*.[44] Bagging such a highly regarded scientist lent credibility that Herbert craved to the uncertain new project. Clark was working in RTI's temporary lab on Bacon Street in Durham when Peterlin came on board. "I believe it created quite a scandal in Europe when Peterlin resigned his professorship at Munich to come to the backwoods of North Carolina," Clark recalls thinking. "This generated the kind of publicity that George Herbert was hoping for."[45]

RTI became a sort of minor refuge for scientists who, like Peterlin, had escaped the stifling scientific climate of Communist Eastern Europe. For instance, Petr Munk, a Prague chemist, took advantage of the relaxing regulations of Czechoslovakia's regime in the mid-1960s. He reached out to Peterlin in 1966, but a year and a half passed before the Yugoslav chemist could arrange funds for a one-year visiting position. "At the time it was unheard of that a scientist from a communist ruled country would be allowed to go for a western stay with the whole family," Munk recalled. "But I applied for it anyway and I got the permission." The Munks arrived in Durham in January 1968, greeted by lost luggage and ice.[46] Little did they know that the Prague Spring would bring a flowering of liberalism in their country within months—and a brutal Soviet invasion in August. The family waited nervously as the end of Petr's one-year appointment drew near, but Peterlin found a way for him to stay, first with a lecture tour and then with a visiting professor position at the University of Texas, which later became permanent.[47]

Peterlin's celebrity helped RTI recruit a team of accomplished scientists from the United Kingdom, Belgium, Spain, and India, and distinguished scientists soon came from Europe and Japan to deliver lectures.[48] "I was the only American-born staff member," Buckley Crist Jr. recalled. He had come from New Jersey to seek a PhD at Duke in the early 1960s, studying under Marcus Hobbs.

Upon graduation, Crist was anxious to find a job that could keep him out of the Vietnam War, which he opposed. Few positions came with a skills deferment, though, and one that did went against Crist's ethical scruples: working on chemical weapons research for the federal government.

Fortunately, he was able to obtain a postdoctoral fellowship at the Research Triangle Institute, which had an Air Force contract. The research staff was diverse, in that its scientists hailed from around the world, although very few women worked as researchers, and African Americans were employed only at menial jobs at RTI at the time. (Crist recalled the striking figure of Peterlin, who valued egalitarianism, meritocracy, and autonomy for scientists.) "It was cosmopolitan without a hint of urbanism," Crist commented.[49]

North Carolina had long boasted of its native-born workforce—code language for no immigrants or labor rabble-rousers—to lure industry, and the influx of foreign workers in RTP broke sharply with the past. In addition to Petr Munk, Peterlin brought researchers from Belgium, Germany, Italy, Japan, and Spain for one- to two-year appointments in the Dreyfus lab.[50] "It was really fun to interact with international scholars for intellectual and social reasons," Crist recalled. "And so that was kind of exciting, to see some of these famous people up close and personal."[51] The local media were quick to capitalize on the glamor of those passing through RTP. A boosterish paper enthused about the RTI's "international flavor" in 1968, depicting Peterlin and Munk alongside Dr. Davorin Dolar and Dr. Francisco J. Balta Calleja, visiting scholars from the University of Ljubljana and the University of Madrid, respectively.

Most newcomers found the Triangle area hospitable, although tensions occasionally arose. Spirited debates over the civil rights movement erupted at RTI, during which researchers from abroad chided the locals for the oppression of African Americans. An Indian scientist felt self-conscious about his skin color in what remained the Jim Crow South. The Peterlins themselves had difficulty adjusting to a new culture. "As Europeans not only my father, but our whole family had difficulty adapting to the American way of life," Tanya recalled in 2008. In fact, Peterlin nearly took a position in 1966 at the Ruder Boskovic Institute (IRB), where he would have overseen a staff of six hundred fifty at one of Yugoslavia's premier research institutions. However, the chemist worried that the same stifling culture and bureaucratic intrigue would prevail at IRB that had originally pushed him out of the Jozef Stefan Institute in the 1950s.[52] Ultimately, though, Peterlin remembered his years at RTI as the best in his scientific career.[53]

Several scientists described their early days at Dreyfus in the 1960s as "utopian." Munk recalled that the park was mostly empty then; he and Peterlin would go on brisk walks and even hunted for mushrooms in the woods of RTP.[54] "The Research Triangle Park in those days still had lots of open places," Crist recalled. "It hadn't been all built up, and we would tend to ramble for an hour or so after lunch talking with each other—sort of mobile group meetings—and you could do that without fear of being run over." The generous endowment of the Dreyfus lab also meant freedom to pursue basic research with little interference and without pressure to please contract research clients.[55] However, the money did not last forever: "We are in the squeeze for money," Peterlin admitted by 1968, and scientists soon had to devote more time to writing proposals for lucrative contracts with government and industry.[56]

By the early 1970s, many of RTI's original players had moved on. Peterlin retired in 1973, and Crist, Clark, and Munk, among others, departed for university positions.[57] But by that time, RTI was on a stable footing, and it offered a prototype of a new postindustrial economy in miniature: highly research-intensive work funded by government, foundations, and private-sector contracts that was carried out in a serene, verdant environment expressly designed for intellectual work. This model anticipated later efforts to foster innovation and creativity in work environments. Charles Landry, a leading proponent of the idea of the "creative city," observed in 2008, "Physical developments and place-making or urban design that foster communication between people . . . are likely to be a combination of quiet places and more stimulating ones, within a setting where there is greenery and great attention to aesthetics" (figure 2.4).[58]

Above all, RTI stood as proof that the park could succeed as a center for scientific research, which drew other organizations to pursue "the life of the mind" in RTP. One such group perhaps symbolized the park's anti-industrial ethos more than any other: the Foundation for Research on the Nature of Man. Founded by J. B. Rhine in 1962, who for decades had run a parapsychology lab at Duke University, the foundation purchased a plot in RTP in December 1964.[59] Although parapsychology might find little credence in the scientific world today, Rhine was well respected in the 1960s. He corresponded with the likes of Aldous Huxley and Margaret

Figure 2.4 The bucolic setting of the Research Triangle Institute in the early 1980s. *Source*: Research Triangle Institute.

Mead, major academic and business leaders sat on his advisory board, and the foundation received millions in donations in a short time.[60] Indeed, Governor Terry Sanford remarked when the move to RTP was announced that research on parapsychology would bring "international fame and recognition" to the Triangle.[61]

But at the same moment, Sanford was negotiating a deal that would keep Rhine's psychic institute out of the park—and change the fate of

RTP forever. Years of work on multiple fronts yielded two major tenants: an environmental research center, which would deepen the federal government's presence in the park, and an IBM facility that would force RTP to compromise its image as a space devoid of actual production. Rhine would soon insist on backing out of the land deal when it was revealed that zoning rules would change to accommodate IBM, as he believed the foundation's research demanded a quiet, serene environment devoid of manufacturing. To achieve the park's long-term success, though, its planners had to make a major compromise in their vision of an anti-industrial space for intellectual labor.

THE BREAKTHROUGH: 1964 AND 1965

A few weeks before his assassination in 1963, President John F. Kennedy gave a national nod to the Triangle idea. "The North Carolina site is a good one, as there is a triangle there of colleges and hospitals and medical facilities," Kennedy said. "I have indicated that would be satisfactory, if that was the judgment of Congress." After years of lobbying and courtship, North Carolina won two major projects in 1965 that ultimately set RTP on a sound course. The federal government chose the park for a major environmental health research center, and IBM selected RTP for development of a large facility. The former was the result of a long process of political horse-trading. Sanford, who was running for governor in 1960, made a politically risky endorsement of then-Senator John F. Kennedy for president, and his predecessor, Luther Hodges, accepted an appointment as Secretary of Commerce in the new Kennedy administration in 1961.[62]

Intense jockeying for the project had been going on for months in Washington, as Health Secretary Anthony Celebrezze argued for a site near other government agencies, such as the Food and Drug Administration in Maryland, and Senator Robert Byrd (D-WV) lobbied for his own state to receive the project.[63] Hodges and then-Governor Sanford worked behind the scenes to land the $25 million research center, and the existence of hospitals and universities in the Triangle was a major plank in their argument. Sanford had guaranteed the state would provide the federal government with several hundred acres in RTP for the lab free of charge.

"While the land is not a very important part of the cost," Sanford told reporters in January 1965, "for some reason that is very appealing to these agencies, and it helped a great deal to sell them on the location. Now I'm sure they wouldn't go to the wrong place in order to get free land, but it does help and we used this simply, you might say, to get their attention."[64]

In a typical instance of Johnsonian deal-making, both West Virginia and Celebrezze's home state of Ohio ultimately received smaller facilities, but the National Environmental Health Sciences Center (NEHS) ended up squarely in RTP.[65] (The NEHS was eventually renamed the National Institute of Environmental Health Sciences, or NIEHS.[66]) Although the result of pork-barrel politics, the decision also reflected the fact that policy makers during the Cold War preferred to "disperse" government facilities throughout the country to reduce the impact of a potential nuclear strike.[67] Congress had mandated that the center be no less than 50 miles from Washington, D.C.[68]

The other major victory came in the form of IBM, which announced its decision to place a major research facility in RTP in 1965—the biggest name the Triangle had landed thus far, and a deal that RTF staff had been negotiating for seven years. The Associated Press noted that IBM chose RTP for the $15 million project after "six months of secret inspections of scores of communities." Indeed, "IBM advance agents even checked on whether it was pleasant to shop in Durham, Raleigh, and Chapel Hill, the three points of the research triangle," and the Triangle was reportedly competing with Fort Lauderdale, Florida, among other sites. Of the IBM news, a Sarasota paper observed: "Bagging a big new industry for your town can be quite a coup. And it takes a lot more than luck. Figuring in it are such things as Boy Scouts, schools, beaches, hospital beds, universities and race and labor peace."[69]

Indeed, other communities were taking notice of RTP's strategy for high-tech development. As early as 1962, the *Bend Bulletin* noted that a rival paper had proposed a "research triangle" in Oregon. "It's an appealing idea, the linking of the two universities in Eugene and Corvallis and the Bureau of Mines laboratory in Albany. It does, indeed, provide a triangle not greatly different from the great research complexes in North Carolina, Massachusetts and California."[70] Papers on both sides of the political aisle rallied behind the idea, and Don Wilson, a Republican running for the state House, promised to work to develop a "local climate of support" in 1964.[71] "Here in Oregon we are fortunate in having the triangle already in place and already gaining steadily in its national reputation," *Eugene Register-Guard* declared. "What we must do now is to advertise this triangle as a triangle."[72]

Oregonians seem to have intuited the key to the Research Triangle's success as an economic development venture: public relations. Oregon already had a triangle; it just needed to advertise it as such. "The 'triangle' which includes Eugene-Springfield, Corvallis, and Albany has many attractions to offer to businesses," candidate Wilson said, "but our assets often need to be explained to those who have not had the privilege of living here."[73] The *Register-Guard* concurred, pointing to the importance of reputation and promotion in making the region a magnet for jobs. "Among the really important factors in attracting desirable industry are the presence of good schools, the reputation of a community as a pleasant place to live, and the presence in the community of people who can stimulate and communicate with the newcomers," the paper said in 1962. "We have it here in the upper Willamette Valley. Let's promote it."[74]

Of course, a triangle is just a shape. Any three points could be connected on a map by an ambitious politician or local planner. Florida's *St. Petersburg Times* in 1965 proposed that "the Suncoast will have its own 'research triangle.' That includes Mound Park Hospital, with its outstanding medical staff; Bay Pines Veterans' Hospital, in a beautiful location with plenty of space for expansion; and the University of South Florida, where a medical school and veterans' hospital are in preliminary planning stages."[75] The paper proposed that southwestern Florida capitalize on these institutions to specialize in health, particularly gerontology, and compete vigorously to receive "one of the 32 regional medical centers President Johnson has asked Congress to authorize for combating heart disease, cancer and strokes."[76]

What is most striking is the way others borrowed the exact language of the Research Triangle. "It's interesting, how these names catch on," University of North Carolina president Gordon Gray commented in 1968. "I remember here a couple of years ago the Governor of Maryland, in a speech, a message to the legislature, said, 'We need a research triangle in Maryland.' Well, he didn't even know the origin. I mean, 'research triangle' has come to have a meaning because this place has developed it somewhat successfully."[77]

Talk of triangles—and research parks more broadly—was on the policy agenda for local media, politicians, and developers throughout the United States in the 1960s. From Oregon and Florida to New York's Hudson Valley, local boosters kept score of which localities were pulling ahead in the competition to burnish their images as desirable places to live and work.[78] "Research parks, created near, or about, a university or research center, are the newest real estate developments," noted an article in the *Miami News* regarding a survey of the national and regional landscape in 1964.[79] This model of development became part of a national discourse about the direction of the economy itself, as communities wooed high-tech industries by packaging the appeal of local cultural institutions such as universities, museums, and theaters as resources to be consumed by employers and employees alike. When RTP won the site, observers in Florida bemoaned their own shortcomings in terms of "knowledge" and "research." St. Petersburg Mayor Herman Goldner said that his region needed a "knowledge center" just like North Carolina's.[80]

IBM may have prompted an outbreak of envy for RTP's knowledge center, but it actually disrupted the park's rigorous branding as a space for pure research. The computer giant was interested in RTP only if it could build a production facility, and the park's leadership was forced to compromise. Its tough zoning regulations were meant to guarantee a spacious green landscape where laboratory work would be as distinct as possible from a traditional noisy, congested industrial space, but to secure IBM's massive investment in the park and thousands of new jobs, park leaders were willing to permit a significant area for light manufacturing.[81]

The move to include real production in RTP angered some, notably J. B. Rhine. In January, the parapsychology guru fired off a letter that complained of zoning changes, particularly the announcement that another manufacturing outfit, the electronics firm Technitrol, was coming to the park. "We discovered, after purchasing the 50-acre tract in the park, that important information, well known to the RTP representative at the time of our purchase, had been withheld from us," Rhine explained; officials had been courting Technitrol well before the foundation decided to come to the park. Indeed, they assured him that no manufacturing would be allowed near the site his group had selected—even though Technitrol had been considering that very site.[82] George Akers Moore insisted that RTP meant no harm in changing the zoning in a way that brought the foundation's lot into a potential manufacturing area. After all, "the Park Board is probably more acutely conscious of the necessity to maintain the aesthetic integrity of the Park and its environs than any other group." But the ESP researcher was unmoved.[83] Through a series of tense negotiations with former Governor Hodges and other park leaders, Rhine managed to persuade RTP to take back the lot and refund the down payment.[84]

The concession to IBM and Technitrol might appear to render meaningless RTP's aspiration to so-called pure research—that is, to be more than just another industrial park. However, local leaders made it clear that the compromise was a strategic one in service to a greater goal, attempting to emphasize the intellectual element of any production that would occur in RTP. When Governor Dan K. Moore announced the arrival of Technitrol, he attempted to thread the needle of what exactly was research and what was production. "Technitrol's new facility will combine research directly with scientifically oriented production," the governor said, "so that it may achieve complete development of its over-all research activities and enable other research groups to do the same."[85] Moore also stressed that a large portion of the workforce would be engineers, despite the fact that some production would occur at the site. Similarly, the new IBM facility relied on a better-educated and more professional workforce than the traditional North Carolina factory; one of the earliest jobs it sought to fill was that of technical librarian, which required a master's of library science or a BA in engineering. At the same time, the company posted ads as far away as Spartanburg, South Carolina, seeking technicians with several years' experience working with dies, gauges, and machine tools—that is, skilled manufacturing workers.[86]

By the late 1960s, Research Triangle Park was well on its way to carving out a space for advanced industry and a new scientific workforce, even if manufacturing could not be completely divorced from research.

New industries were subsidized not only by the state of North Carolina, which volunteered land and funds, but by a major infusion of federal resources from the U.S. Forest Service, NIEHS, and, in 1971, the new Environmental Protection Agency (EPA). Expansion of RTP proceeded apace in the 1970s, as it attracted new institutes (such as the National Humanities Center) that were entirely devoted to intellectual labor. Also entering the park were major new firms (such as pharmaceutical company Burroughs Wellcome) that perfected the model of separating research from production; pills designed in the park would be popped out of a production line somewhere else—for example, at manufacturing facilities in rural eastern North Carolina.

Notably, with its growing strength in pharmaceuticals and environmental health research, the Triangle owed less to the military-industrial complex than, say, Huntsville, Alabama, or even Stanford Research Park. Although the Research Triangle Institute earned 41 percent of its income from defense contracts in 1964, and firms such as IBM did a great deal of government business,[87] North Carolina benefited from a broader expansion of government, as the American state declared war on everything from cancer to poverty to pollution. RTP developed notable strength in environmental and medical research, but its portfolio of industry did not lean entirely on a particular enterprise or industry, as Huntsville or Florida's "Space Coast" did with aerospace.

The success of RTI and the arrival of IBM and NIEHS proved that the region could attract a good share of corporate and federal resources with the right branding and zoning. Nothing succeeds like success, as the cliché goes, and these victories enabled boosters to portray North Carolina as a technological leader in order to bring other, similar projects to the Triangle. The concentration of academic resources in Raleigh, Durham, and Chapel Hill provided a rationale for the government to invest in greater infrastructure. For instance, the National Science Foundation (NSF) funded the development of the Triangle Universities Computer Center in 1966, establishing a giant computer network that connected Duke, NC State, and UNC to a mainframe in RTP. The system served thirty-three thousand students and professors, handling everything from payroll and registrations to medical research.[88]

The quest for federal largesse could turn surreal at times, as when several Tar Heel politicians suggested that the state was the best location for a lung cancer research center. In 1967, Senator Sam J. Ervin (D-NC) went before the Senate to make the case. "Today, I want to discuss an allegation which is becoming more and more frequent—that smoking is all that stands between men and immortality," Ervin began. "This proposition is being paraded before the American people with all of the pomp and certitude of Madame Curie's discovery of radium." The senator insisted that no one yet knew what caused lung cancer, but if it turned out that cigarettes were to blame, then government and business should work together to develop a better cigarette. Along with Senator Everett Jordan (D-NC) and Durham Representative Nick Galifianakis (D-NC), he proposed that Research Triangle Park would be an ideal place for such a project.[89] North Carolina was both the cause of and the solution to the problems facing the nation's lungs.

Meanwhile, the influx of both federal and private investment brought with it another infusion: scientists, engineers, managers, and their families. RTP remade the economy of a metropolitan area increasingly known as "the Triangle" in the 1960s, and the workers who followed on the heels of Petr Munk and Anton Peterlin found themselves adjusting to a new and different—as well as rapidly changing—social landscape. The growth of jobs in RTP led to the design of suburbs made very much in its own image, as a nascent class of knowledge workers sought pastoral places to raise families. But the new technoburbs, as historian Robert Fishman later called them, emerged against a backdrop of racial tension and social tumult, as even the Triangle—which zealously guarded its reputation as "progressive" and tolerant on issues of race, like the state as a whole—absorbed not only new people but fresh demands for social justice and the furious backlash of local residents who rejected them.[90]

3

Welcome to Parkwood

NEWCOMERS FIND THEIR WAY IN THE EMERGING TRIANGLE

When Bill Bell came to Durham in 1968, the city was under curfew. Martin Luther King Jr. had been shot, cities across the country burned, and Durham's civic leaders were on high alert for a similar flare-up of violence in a city that had struggled to accommodate, deflect, or stymie black political demands for years.

Born in Washington, D.C., the young engineer had grown up in Winston-Salem before leaving to study at Howard University and New York University, but he yearned to return to the South. Bell grew up hearing of Durham and its prosperous black business class, and he was determined to live there. Many newly employed workers at IBM, he soon discovered, were heading for Raleigh and Cary to settle down with their families. "You get steered to where your friends are," Bell says, with the understatement of a good politician. "And the realtors were steering [people to Raleigh and Cary, but not Durham]. But, Durham was a community that I sort of . . . I felt very comfortable in. I liked the fact that it was sort of a university town . . . [and] it was close to my job, so it was a natural for me."[1]

Durham it was. And Parkwood—a suburban development launched in 1960 with the explicit intent of housing RTP workers—seemed like the ideal location for Bell and his young family. Its first house sold in 1960, and the development's promotional literature embraced the clean, sleek futurism of the Kennedy years. Adorned with triangles and Space Age flair, brochures for the subdivision made perfectly clear that this modern suburb was to be an enclave for the affluent and educated members of a new scientific workforce.[2]

It was one, however, that did not necessarily include Bill Bell. The engineer was initially working out of a temporary IBM office in Raleigh's affluent new suburb of North Hills, but he knew he would relocate to RTP before long. Parkwood was directly adjacent to the research park, but when Bell inquired about a home, he faced resistance. The Fair Housing Act was then working its way through the knotty channels of Congress, bound for ultimate approval despite staunch opposition from conservative Democrats and Republicans alike. Although Bell did not face outright rejection from Parkwood because of his race, he could see that he was not welcome. "At that time, the community had to have a sort of a meeting to try to figure out how they were going to accept this black couple that wanted to move into Parkwood," he recalled in 2012. "And, ultimately I decided I just didn't want to move there. It wasn't a problem for me because I was at work, but my wife would have been home."[3]

Bell's remark is more ominous than it might first appear. Black families faced hostility across the United States when they moved into all-white neighborhoods—it was hardly a Southern problem. Such resistance could take the form of threats to vulnerable mothers and children, as events in the Triangle during the 1960s made all too clear. RTP's promise of social enlightenment might have been relatively uncomplicated for the scientists and engineers depicted throughout the park's promotional literature, who were almost always white and male in the 1950s and 1960s. Indeed, the Bell family's experience navigating the landscape of race in Durham reveals how the Triangle's proud veneer of progressiveness covered a far more complex picture of white anxiety and uneven opportunity, both for the black poor and upwardly mobile and even wealthy African Americans.

North Carolina boosters had worked hard to build a reputation for good race relations, even as governors such as Luther Hodges (1954–61), Terry Sanford (1961–65), and Bob Scott (1965–69) dragged their feet on integration, and many communities resisted housing desegregation during the 1960s. An image of racial progressiveness was especially important for the Triangle, which sought to woo executives and scientists who might still blanch at the thought of moving to the benighted South. The quickening pace of struggles for racial justice in the mid-1960s put the state and the Triangle's image to the test. As African Americans pushed for better public housing and access to white neighborhoods, and as university employees organized alongside white allies for better working conditions, the political landscape of the Triangle fractured along racial lines even as interracial alliances made significant breakthroughs possible, such as the 1969 election of Howard Lee as Chapel Hill mayor.

At times, Klan intimidation and the mobilization of armed forces against students and civil rights demonstrators made the Triangle look more like Alabama or Arkansas than Chapel Hill's cherished reputation as "the southern part of heaven." Progressive forces worked hard to redeem the metropolitan area from a legacy of bigotry and segregation and to burnish its liberal credentials—at times, and at least to a degree.

HOUSING FOR SCIENCE CITY

Ever since North Carolinians started discussing RTP in the mid-1950s, locals had wondered how the area would accommodate a great new influx of people. Space was not a problem—the three cities of the Triangle were broadly dispersed, and cheap land was abundant in a landscape with few natural barriers to development. The United States in the 1950s was in the midst of an orgy of homebuilding, which laid the groundwork for the sprawling, car-centric settlement pattern of most of the country that we know today. And, as geographer William Rohe noted, the Triangle was to become among the lowest-density urban areas anywhere.[4]

But early ideas of what the Triangle would be were hazy at best. Some in Chapel Hill worried that the emergence of a "scientific city" nearby would affect "its own character as a nonindustrial community centering around a major institution of learning," as the local paper put it in 1957.[5] Representatives from companies such as DuPont worried that Durham did not have enough solid middle-class housing; as one observer noted, most neighborhoods there were of either very high or low quality, reflecting Bull City's racial and class divide.[6] Meanwhile, Triangle boosters sought to ensure outsiders that the metropolitan area offered plenty of adequate housing and shopping for newcomers, pointing to developments such as Cameron Village, an award-winning project built in the late 1940s that incorporated open-air retail establishments, apartments, and single-family houses in Raleigh. It was considered the first modern shopping center between Atlanta and Washington, D.C., as well as a forerunner of mixed-use development.[7]

Developers soon seized the opportunity to build housing expressly for the scientists, engineers, and others who would work at RTP—even before the park had proven it had real momentum. The area around RTP had been sparsely populated for generations, most notably by a historic school at Lowe's Grove (founded around 1896) and the new Raleigh-Durham airport (1943) near Morrisville. Lowe's Grove was "cornbread country," as one local put it, with a school, a barber shop, and "a whistle stop on the Durham & Southern where a pasture doubled as an airstrip for the occasional barnstorming biplane."[8] With farmland going for $300 to $350 an acre, enterprising builders realized that RTP workers might not live *in* the Park, but they might very well like to live next to it, and the fittingly named Parkwood was born (figure 3.1).[9]

Developers Kavanagh & Smith heavily emphasized Parkwood's link to RTP from day one, targeting an audience of middle-class professionals. One brochure declared, "To fill the pressing needs for homes for the personnel connected with this project, in what was primarily a rural area, a revolutionary development design was employed to coordinate the new PARKWOOD into a unified community offering the greatest advantages to its residents." About a quarter of early residents worked in RTP, and the rest came from throughout the Triangle area. Kavanagh & Smith offered fourteen home designs, mostly variations on single-story or split-level ranch-style houses.[10] By twenty-first-century standards they were modest homes, although most sold for $13,000 to $16,000 early on—a substantial sum at a time when the median home value in North Carolina in 1960 was $8,000.[11]

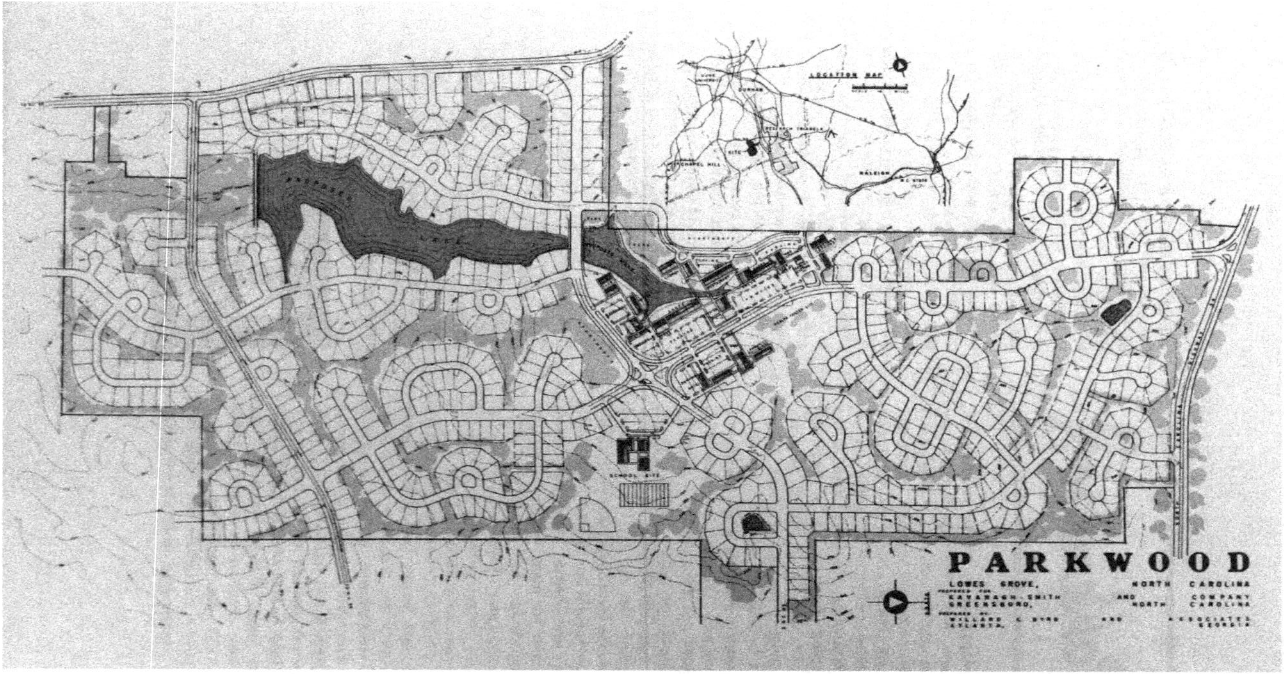

Figure 3.1 Early map of the Parkwood subdivision, adjacent to RTP. *Source*: Parkwood Homeowners Association.

Many early residents were employees of Chemstrand. Developer Roger Kavanagh had traveled to the company's Decatur, Alabama, site to win over workers who would soon be relocating to RTP. "It was a nice thing," resident Wally Lawrence recalled. "Chemstrand was a small enough company, so we all knew each other well. It helped make moving a lot easier."[12]

Parkwood was an innovation in several ways. It was not only the first housing development targeted at RTP workers but also the first homeowners association in North Carolina, offering residents the pleasure of suburban living with the tight regulations of a covenant. Parkwood lured residents with the promise of "no city taxes," along with a variety of options for "entertainment, shopping, social and cultural life," thanks to nearby Raleigh, Durham, Chapel Hill, and RTP itself.[13] It embodied "a Country Atmosphere. With City Convenience."[14] The community's first covenant mandated that no house costing less than $8,000 could be built there while setting minimum setbacks for houses and strictly forbidding any temporary structures such as barns, shacks, or tents on residents' property.[15] (Such rules prompted feisty conflict in the community, as when pharmacologist Ken Dudley resisted efforts to get him to remove his tool shed in 1969.[16]) In essence, Parkwood aimed to create a serene, highly controlled living environment much as RTP did; the spaces mirrored each other, both of them novel ways of organizing space for a middle- and upper-middle-class community, particularly in a state that had seldom seen such zealous regulation in the past.

Parkwood's innovative design, which included ample green space, winding streets, a swim club, and a modest shopping center, quickly drew attention. The *Journal of Homebuilding* named it the best residential subdivision of 1962. *Fortune* magazine took note, citing the suburb as evidence of a new trend toward cluster planning in lieu of large-lot zoning. At the time, the National Association of Home Builders considered such designs "more imaginative" and "aesthetically pleasing," journalist John McDonald wrote in 1963. "The general idea of most such plans is to 'cluster' houses on small lots, and leave open spaces for use as parks."[17] The subdivision also won a citation for excellence in community design from the Federal Housing Authority in 1964. Kavanagh declared that "ten years from now—or less—Parkwood will be the most studied and imitated community in the Southeast."[18]

Despite the good press, Parkwood was not without its problems. Friction between Kavanagh and homeowners developed early on. In the association board's earliest meetings in spring 1961, the developer's agent revealed that Kavanagh wanted to build apartments near the first section of Parkwood—a plan that the homeowners "unalterably opposed" and hoped to block at the local zoning commission.[19] The following year, the association also came out against a proposed ABC, or liquor, store in the community shopping center, and in 1966 the community unsuccessfully opposed a trailer park proposed by another developer near both Parkwood and RTP.[20] The homeowners repeatedly butted heads in the 1960s, 1970s, and 1980s with developers who wished to build a section of smaller single-family homes, Buttonwood, next door, as well as apartment and condominium developments such as Emerald Forest, across the road on Highway 54. Critics of new housing cited concerns about excessive traffic and burdens on local schools, but a fairly clear prejudice against multifamily developments and apartment dwellers in general ran through these debates—one that is familiar in the history of American suburbs.[21]

Early on, Parkwoodians also contended with inadequate water and sewage systems, a perennial problem of new suburban developments far from city infrastructure in the 1950s and 1960s.[22] The private system maintained by Kavanagh had suffered chronic problems since at least 1962. The problem was so bad by 1968 that RTP employees were bringing jugs of water home from their offices every day.[23] "One day we boiled some of the muddy water and it coagulated and turned green," one resident, a former chemistry teacher, told the press. Gloria Jimenez, an attorney and mother of two, protested frequently at meetings of the homeowners association over the issue. She and her family had moved to Parkwood from New York when her husband, an engineer, got a job at RTP. She deplored the poor condition of the community's water, drawing up a petition with hundreds of signatures to protest the situation at the State Utilities Commission. Yet, despite the dozen milk jugs of water crowding her kitchen, she still liked Parkwood. "I love it down here," she said. "It's great for children—walk to the swimming pool, walk to school . . . There's been no 'Yankee, go home,' sentiment."[24]

The community continued to draw new employees of RTP, and membership in the homeowners association grew from 37 to 350 between 1960 and 1965, after which an influx of families from IBM's huge workforce bolstered numbers even further.[25] By 1968, about 42 percent of residents in Parkwood worked in RTP, and the vast majority (80 percent) had only one family member working, suggesting that most wives and mothers stayed home.[26]

When Buckley Crist Jr. and his wife had a child, they decided to move out of the small home they rented near Duke and landed, like so many RTP workers, in Parkwood. When the Crists moved to Parkwood, they were surrounded by young families, as was the case with many parents in the suburbs of the 1960s. Most, if not all, were professionals, and many were affiliated with RTP. The Crists' neighbor across the street was a lawyer for IBM; on one side was a nurse who also worked in IBM's huge facility, and her husband, a security guard; and on the other side next door was an entrepreneur who ran a lab producing dental prostheses. In an adjacent community of townhouses, postdoctoral researchers from foreign countries often lived during their stay of a year or two in the United States.[27]

Parkwood was implicitly and effectively all-white, even if it was not bound by racist restrictive covenants that barred nonwhites from residence (figure 3.2). As late as 1979, the *Durham Morning Herald* could remark, as if in passing, "Parkwood is a white community, and its school reflects this." And local people like Al Alphin, a lawyer who worked for the developer and had lived in the community since 1962, simply stated that theirs was "a good neighborhood with good people—good, middle-class people."[28] A handful of minorities, notably Asian Americans, would join the community in the 1980s and 1990s, but earlier on, the neighborhood remained a stronghold of middle-class whiteness—in line with most affluent communities in the Triangle that saw little, if any, integration during the 1960s.[29]

Indeed, many upwardly mobile African Americans across the country were trying to break into white suburbs amid the advances of the civil rights movement. Some advocates for black equality pled for acceptance on the grounds that educated, professional African Americans were essentially as bourgeois as their white neighbors and not to be feared. "In executive-class suburbs, where income and education levels are high, open-minded elements have been making strong cases for, at the very

Figure 3.2 A vision of the good life from a Parkwood promotional brochure. *Source*: Parkwood Homeowners Association.

least, token integration," the *Chicago Defender*'s Sherwood Ross, a white pundit, urged in 1964.

> In these suburbs, where residents feel "secure," the arrival of Negro families will not harm their "prestige." Their "prestige" does not depend on anything so tenuous as a color line. The Negro move-ins would, of necessity, be of the king [sic] who could afford the homes and apartments in a suburb. These middle-income and upper-income families are culturally very much like their white counterparts.[30]

Whatever their cultural or class affinities, affluent African Americans still had to negotiate a delicate process to integrate—one that was not always easy, even in the most progressive communities. In some ways, Raleigh, Durham, and Chapel Hill were typical of struggles for integration nationwide. "One avenue of escape after World War II for middle-class African Americans in Raleigh, as throughout the country, was the acquisition of a house in a white neighborhood bordering a black area: so-called trickle-down housing," architectural historian Margaret Ruth Little wrote. "This was not the aggressive block busting so incendiary in larger cities, including Atlanta and Dallas, but a more incremental expansion of black homeownership. As white families in Raleigh's eastern core moved to the suburbs, middle-class blacks purchased their dwellings."[31] As we will see, such "trickle-down" integration was accepted in some neighborhoods more readily than in others. A pivotal incident in which a white neighbor intimidated a professional black family into leaving occurred in Rollingwood, a white community adjacent to the black middle-class suburb of Madonna Acres.

Even wealthy black executives such as John Stewart and Asa Spaulding conceded that there were limits to their own privilege. Durham's power structure might have included them as political power brokers and holders of elected office well before the Voting Rights Act of 1965—Stewart had been on the Durham City Council since 1957—but money and influence went only so far. Black elites like Stewart and Spaulding were "not apt to move into an upper-class white neighborhood of their small Southern city without resistance," Bill Surface observed in the *New York Times* in 1967, "and, even if they desired such a move and succeeded, they would risk losing Negro customers, as well as breed mistrust among poorer Negroes." However, Stewart remained optimistic that trends were running in the right direction, and young black people could lift themselves up through hard work, just as he had done. He saw the area's schools and RTP as part of that promise. "Progress goes where there's brains and water," he intoned.[32]

North Carolina might have had plenty of water, but the color line still mattered, even for the best of brains. Since *Brown v. Board of Education*, state leaders had done everything they could to skirt the edges of the 1954 ruling without actually desegregating schools. Governor Luther Hodges was keen not to appear as retrograde or inflammatory as massive resisters such as Alabama Governor George Wallace or Arkansas Governor Orval Faubus, who captured national and international attention by directly opposing federal orders to integrate schools. North Carolina's approach—a pupil assignment plan that put the onus on black parents to apply to transfer their children out of all-black schools—allowed local authorities to reject such requests on trivial grounds, bottling up pressure for integration without explicitly opposing desegregation. When Terry Sanford, a racial moderate by North Carolina standards, ran for governor in 1960s, he was forced to argue convolutedly that his approach of minimal compliance with *Brown* was the best way to avoid federal scrutiny; the hardcore segregationist stance of his opponent, I. Beverly Lake, he suggested, ultimately would lead to total desegregation.[33]

Indeed, Sanford might have been thinking of the case of Joseph Hiram Holt, whose parents tried to have him transferred from Raleigh's Ligon High School to Broughton High School. The Holts filed suit in August 1957 after Joseph was denied admission, but their objections to the process were quashed in 1959, when the Supreme Court held that the family had to exhaust all "administrative remedies" provided by the state before appealing to the federal courts.[34] Like many white observers, the *Greensboro Daily News* saw in the ruling "a promise—and a warning." It might be only a matter of time before the courts weighed in again if the application process proved to be unfair to black families. But most white Tar Heels appeared to believe that the process was, indeed, fair—and a useful way to defuse the threat of immediate integration.[35]

Integration proceeded haltingly in the numerous school systems of the Triangle—which in the 1960s included both county schools and city systems in Chapel Hill, Durham, and Raleigh—as pupil assignment succeeded, for the most part, in deterring all but token integration. The long struggle over the assignment of black students and teachers to formerly white schools even touched the neighborhood school in lily-white Parkwood, which was part of the rural and suburban Durham County Schools system. Residents voiced their "severe opposition" when the county proposed to transfer a black teacher to the Parkwood school, and superintendent Charles H. Chewning ultimately relented.[36] (Such objections would reemerge in the 1970s and again in the 1990s, when consolidation of mostly black Durham City schools and mostly white Durham County schools was proposed and eventually accomplished.)

It was at this fraught moment—in the wake of Dr. King's assassination, as riots burned American cities and white communities renewed their resistance to integration of schools and neighborhoods—that Bill Bell came to Durham. When the Bell family inquired about purchasing a home in Parkwood, they rattled the faith of residents about the future of their fledgling subdivision. Rumors circulated throughout the community about its imminent desegregation—the entry of even one black resident meant that the neighborhood had been "desegregated," of course—and the board of the homeowners association felt it had to respond to questions from nervous residents.

At a tense meeting in April 1968, members of the community board debated the risks and rewards of welcoming the Bell family. Local ministers attended, concerned about "what might be done to ease the situation for everyone." A member of the Governor's Good Neighbor Council even attended to provide advice. Gloria Jimenez argued that "the Board's duty should be to smooth the way," but other board members worried that publishing a statement on integration in the community newspaper would "invite integration" and blockbusting.[37]

The board invited Joseph Berry, a member of Greensboro's Human Relations Council (HRC), to explain how that city had coped with integration and the impact of black families moving into previously white neighborhoods. Five main fears, he explained, had gripped white homeowners as integration loomed:

1. That property values would depreciate.
2. That the neighborhood would become swamped with Negroes.
3. That the academic level of the school would be lowered.
4. That the white residents would lose social prestige from living in an integrated neighborhood.
5. Intermarriage.[38]

In Greensboro, the HRC had kept an eye on a white middle-class community where a single black family purchased a home, tracking the number of "For Sale" signs in the neighborhood. Such signs more than tripled in a single weekend. Although the HRC tried to persuade white residents not to sell, the effort was for naught. Black residents soon made up half of the community, Berry reported, and white families had lost thousands of dollars in their home value.[39]

Ultimately the board voted six to three to publish its statement urging acceptance of the Bells into the community. The acceptance came with a caveat, of course: "In accord with our charge to promote the financial welfare of the community, we, the Parkwood Board of Directors, support and urge the peaceful acceptance of any and all homeowners who elect to live in our community as long as the *actions* of those homeowners are not injurious to the welfare of the community."[40] The board resolved to "prepare Parkwood for the integration eventuality" and "take the story to all residents."[41]

When the board went public, its message to homeowners stressed that they did not face financial ruin if integration occurred. A drop in property values was not inevitable, for instance, but occurred only when white homeowners decided to flee. "With many homes on the market, prices would be depressed by the economic law of supply and demand," the board warned, "and the home owner would lose money."[42] Moreover, few black families in the Triangle could afford the $15,000 to $30,000 homes in Parkwood, meaning that the community would not be "swamped with Negroes." Indeed, the board took pains to point out that property values would remain high so long as white families did not resort to panic selling—effectively keeping most black families out. As for the schools, HRC conceded that "academic levels" had dropped in schools where black students had begun to attend, but they returned to their previous levels after a few years.[43]

The other fears were trickier to assuage, and the board resorted to an intriguing, if muddled, language of class to reassure residents. Berry had suggested that the passage of the Civil Rights Act of 1968, which forbade racial discrimination in housing, might diminish the stigma of living in an integrated neighborhood. "However, it is a real fear," the board admitted, "and he noted that housewives play a vital part in this fear." It then noted, curiously, that studies had shown that the prestige of neighborhoods in the North had actually *increased* following desegregation—so long as the community "is not primarily lower class."[44]

Intermarriage, however, remained a deep anxiety for white residents, one that the board could not explain away or massage with statistics. The community leaders instead appealed to a hazy notion of middle-classness. Interracial relationships mostly happened "at lower and higher socio-economic levels," they explained—a perverse indulgence of the poor and the rich, it seems, but not solid middle-class people like the people of Parkwood. There was little to fear, anyway, because "data suggest that middle-class Negroes fear intermarriage as much as do whites."[45]

The board appealed to residents to proceed with caution—while reading the writing on the wall. It warned that "unscrupulous real estate agents" and "radical outsiders" might try to exploit the fears of residents. After all, enterprising agents across the country had taken advantage of panic selling to buy the homes of fleeing white residents for a song, in turn selling or leasing them back to black families at extortionate rates—a practice known as *blockbusting*. White homeowners would hurt only themselves if they let fear override their better judgment, as had happened to families in Greensboro who had "escaped" to other neighborhoods, only to find those areas, too, became desegregated before long. The reference to radicals is oblique, but an earlier draft of the board's letter makes it clear that "possible organized interference" meant the Klan, which had stoked white fears in other communities by posting inflammatory fliers.[46]

In the end, Parkwoodians could only hurt themselves. "Perhaps not this month or even this year, Parkwood will eventually become at least partly integrated," the board told residents. "So will other white communities in the country. We are not looking into our crystal ball. We merely observe these facts." The law banned discrimination, and middle-class black families needed housing. "The conclusion must be clear: those Negroes who have been educated and who hold responsible positions, for which they are amply paid, can be expected to seek housing in areas like Parkwood." The community could survive as long as its middle-class character remained intact—and men like Bill Bell, drawn to the area by professional opportunities in RTP, fit the mold. He was an educated man, and, the board noted, he did not appear to be part of a "concerted effort on the part of any group to desegregate Parkwood."[47]

Parkwood might have decided to ease the way to integration, but not everyone was satisfied with the board's moderate stance. Homeowner Joseph High, for instance, was an avowed segregationist who viewed the board's report with disgust. High chided the board for seeking out the advice of ministers, the Good Neighbors Council, and the Human Relations Council:

> Since the Board of Directors of our Parkwood Association use [sic] what I presume to be general opinions of present social gospelers, and has not released the names of these envisioned prophets, I would say that no credence be given to any contemporary social reformers until they have given a lie-detector test with the results made public, before they give their dissertations of integration.[48]

He complained that bountiful evidence from Washington, D.C., Baltimore, Louisville, and other cities showed beyond doubt that the entrance of black families into a community resulted in instant ghettos, cratering property values, and white flight. Schools suffered measurable and lasting losses once black students were admitted—intellectual differences "due chiefly to heredity." Indeed, "Anyone having the temerity to suggest that integration is not harmful is either a conscious fraud," High concluded, "or subject to hallucinations." He closed his appeal by calling on neighbors to join the white supremacist Citizens Council of America.[49]

Not long after the Bell controversy, in 1969, a committee was appointed to consider the merits of incorporating as a town or pursuing annexation by the City of Durham. The community worried about the ability of the homeowners association to handle issues such as security and fire protection when turnover among residents was high and some failed to pay their dues. Becoming a town would allow a new local government to levy taxes, whereas annexation would provide city services—an improvement over the community's chronic water and sewage woes. The committee warned that the city might pay higher rates for Durham water, and incorporation might require heavier taxes to provide the desired level of services.[50] "If we desire services at the level provided by the city, we will pay city taxes and enjoy reduced water rates by voting for annexation," the committee reasoned. "We would pay somewhat more than the city tax rate, because of the inherent inefficiency of small government, and would pay the higher county water rates by voting for incorporation."[51]

Most important, the committee warned that inaction could lead to unpredictable consequences. "We may not be allowed to incorporate," it observed in its report. "Under existing laws, Durham can act to annex at any time until the community actually votes to accept the incorporation. . . . However, no action certainly means annexation eventually and the continuation of no government until that time." The committee made no recommendation but considered continuing the status quo to be "irresponsible."[52] In the end, the community pursued neither annexation nor incorporation, although it solved one big headache by connecting to Durham's city sewage system in 1979.[53] But the vexing question of Parkwood's relationship to the city would come back to haunt the community decades later.

RACE, LABOR, AND SCHOOLING IN THE CITY OF KNOWLEDGE

Bill Bell was not the only young black professional to encounter difficulty relocating to the Triangle, and his story reveals how much newcomers' fortunes varied depending on the neighborhood. Indeed, his reception in Parkwood could have been far worse, as Horace Caple would attest. Mere months after the Bells arrived in Durham, Caple brought his wife and two children from Charlotte to accept a position as assistant professor of drama at Shaw University, a traditionally black college in Raleigh that was the birthplace of the Student Nonviolent Coordinating Committee in 1960. The Caples had difficulty finding a home in the city and reluctantly opted to rent a home in the East Raleigh neighborhood of Rollingwood.

The move soon took an ugly turn. "The day we moved in here neighbors began calling us 'N– –rs," the professor told reporters. The realtor who had rented them the house received threats, "No Trespassing" signs popped up around the community, and someone strung up an effigy of Caple on a nearby tree.[54] By November, the family was gone. "It was simply too much," Caple told reporters. "My children were terrified. My life was threatened. Carloads of people drove by and shouted obscenities at us." By the time they decided to leave, the family was "all just about emotionally wrecked," Caple said. "The neighbors stood across the street and applauded when we left. We didn't say anything. We just drove away."[55]

The Caples' chief antagonist was James Lawing, a tree surgeon who took it upon himself to police the racial boundaries of his neighborhood. Lawing was among the first people tried under the 1968 Fair Housing Act, which, among other things, barred intimidation on the grounds of race. Lawing was incensed because Caple's family had allegedly moved into the home "after dark"; that they hosted members of the fair housing group HOME (Housing Opportunities Made Equal); and that Caple had not checked with the Mayor's Committee on Human Relationships before moving in. Defense attorney Irving Tucker wasted no time appealing to the racist biases of the jury. "Honestly search your conscience and ask yourself," he demanded. "Wouldn't you be afraid if a colored man moved in a few blocks from your home?"[56]

An all-white jury handed down the acquittal of James Lawing in March, even though a Raleigh policeman overheard the defendant vowing to "stomp" and "whip" Caple for moving into Rollingwood. The *Chicago Defender*'s Harry Golden deplored the ruling but took heart in the fact that the legal system showed itself capable of at least trying a white man for wronging an African American.[57]

Even as white North Carolinians were deliberating in Raleigh, nearby Chapel Hill was in turmoil. Foodworkers at the University of North Carolina campus, virtually all of whom were black, had been organizing to demand better wages, working conditions, and basic respect on the job in the spring of 1969. Despite lacking the right to bargain collectively as public employees in a resolutely antiunion state, the women who served UNC students from early in the morning until late at night went on strike with the backing of a handful of professors and the Black Student Movement. Tensions mounted when student activists were accused of "trashing" a university building. Many white North Carolinians looked on student activism and simultaneous turmoil at other campuses, such as Duke and North Carolina A&T University, with increasing derision, and Governor Dan K. Moore mobilized troops to Chapel Hill over the objections of UNC Chancellor Carlyle Sitterson. In March the foodworkers won a short-lived victory, gaining a wage increase and the use of courtesy titles—even though the university turned its on-campus dining services over to a private company and reneged on its commitments not long after.[58]

In the same tumultuous spring, as Lawing stood trial and foodworkers and students organized at UNC, a black Chapel Hillian was pursuing an audacious campaign for mayor of the college town. Howard Lee had come to the Triangle in 1965 and encountered much the same hostility as had Horace Caple and Bill Bell when Lee, his wife, and two children sought housing in the white Chapel Hill community of Colony Woods. The son of Georgia sharecroppers, Lee had studied at Georgia's Clark and Fort Valley State Colleges before coming to UNC to pursue a master's degree in social work. Before long, he was head of employee relations at Duke University. But the Lee family endured an onslaught of threatening calls from Chapel Hillians who opposed their move into a small brick home in Colony Woods. Four years later, Lee joined the fray of the local race for mayor (figure 3.3).[59]

Edwin Caldwell was deeply involved in Lee's campaign during the tumultuous spring of 1969. He, too, had encountered the limits of tolerance in the Triangle when he returned to Chapel Hill after a stint

Figure 3.3 Howard Lee campaigning for Mayor of Chapel Hill in 1969. *Source*: Howard N. Lee.

in the Army, study at Hampton University, and work at a Columbia University biochemistry lab. In 1963, he was recruited by Memorial Hospital to oversee quality control at one of its labs, but when he arrived, he learned that his application had been "held up" for unspecified reasons. "I think that they found out that I was not who they thought I ought to be," Caldwell recalled. "Too much money and the fact that I was also black. He reported that it looked like my application would be held up forever." To hedge his bets, Caldwell had previously placed an application with Chemstrand, and he ended up working there for five years before embarking on a career in local activism and politics.[60]

Caldwell committed himself to mobilizing support for Lee's campaign, which enjoyed robust backing from white faculty members at UNC as well as black activists from diverse backgrounds, including faculty and striking cafeteria workers. "We had quite a few white professors at that time working with us," Caldwell recalled. "We couldn't have done this by ourselves. We said to them that we needed to be the officers and they agreed."[61]

Even white residents unconnected with the university got involved in the campaign. Anne Barnes, a native of Gaston County, moved to Chapel Hill in 1964 when her husband took a job with the North Carolina Fund, Governor Terry Sanford's ambitious program to fight poverty. When she first expressed an interest in joining local Democratic Party politics, she was asked to bake. But then she got involved in Howard Lee's upstart campaign. "We had had the opportunity to know the Lee's [sic] through our church," she recalled in 1989. "We belonged to the same church, the Binkley Baptist Church, and I had taught Howard and Lillian's children in Sunday school and got to know them, a very lovely family." Lee had taken an active role in the community despite his antagonistic reception in 1965, focusing on issues such as zoning and integration. "So he began to talk to many of us about the possibility of helping him to run for mayor, and I thought that was a great idea," Barnes recalled. "So I became the, he has referred to me as the manager of his campaign."[62]

Lee's supporters were determined to ensure that the candidate enjoyed as much support as possible from black voters, who were newly unconstrained care of the Voting Rights Act and the melting away of Jim Crow in the community. "We had a slip of paper that we would put in their hands who they were supposed to vote for when they went in the thing," Caldwell said. "We would say, 'Look, who are you going to vote for?' 'Well you know I'm going to let the Lord.' I said, 'No, we ain't going to let the Lord choose today. You take this piece of paper, this is who you vote for. You let the Lord choose some other day.' So we pretty much told them who to vote for. We controlled things. They went in there and they came out and people were proud. You talking about South Africa and voting, people were voting in Chapel Hill and they were proud the same way."[63]

Only four years later, though, another African American in the Triangle matched Lee's feat, but on a much larger scale. Funeral director Clarence Lightner was elected the first black mayor of Raleigh in November 1973, in part on the strength of support from the new professionals who populated the city's tony northern suburbs such as North Hills, not far from RTP. Lightner was the first African American to become mayor of a large, predominantly white city in the South, riding to victory at the same time that black elected officials took office in cities across the country, including Doris Davis in Compton, California; Lyman Parks in Grand Rapids, Michigan; and Coleman Young in Detroit, Michigan.[64] Black men had served as mayors in Southern cities during the late nineteenth century, prior to the full imposition of Jim Crow, and Howard Lee had been elected mayor of the much smaller city of Chapel Hill. But Lightner's achievement remained a powerful first, coming only a month after Maynard Jackson was elected mayor of Atlanta. Lightner's feat was all the more impressive given that only 16 percent of voters were black—unlike Atlanta, where Jackson was able to pull together enough white votes along with the city's black majority to win office.[65] The *Chicago Defender* extolled Raleigh's progress to black readers:

> As steadily as any Southern city, including Atlanta, Raleigh has been moving toward a new era in racial politics. Once just another conservative Dixie town run by its Chamber of Commerce, Raleigh has become a growing city of political progressivism as thousands of educators, scientists and government officials have moved in to work in nearby universities, research centers and state and Federal offices. The city's population has almost doubled in a decade.[66]

Meanwhile, voting rights activists saw Lightner's election as part of a larger trend. Indeed, Tennessee and Virginia had twice as many black elected officials in 1973 as in 1968, and North Carolina sent ten times more black citizens to office over the same period.[67] Lightner came out on top not just in majority black districts but also in nine white precincts of the city, a victory that veteran activist John Lewis saw as symbolizing "a new trend toward political coalitions which transcend racial lines." That trend was a key goal of activists such as Lewis and Julian Bond, who sought to leverage new black voting power to support a much broader agenda of economic populism in the early 1970s.[68]

Lightner cut a mild-mannered and reassuring figure. His father was a respected Raleigh businessman who had dabbled in politics long before the breakthroughs of the civil rights era, seeking office as commissioner of public safety in 1919 but not succeeding. The younger Lightner was a football star at North Carolina College for Negros (later known as North Carolina Central University). After military service in World War II, he took over his father's mortuary business and built a distinguished, modern ranch home for his family in the middle-class black suburb of Madonna Acres in the early 1960s.[69] Lightner had been only the second black city council member, winning office in 1967, and he reminded voters that he had grown up around white people and bore no racial animosity. "We didn't go to the same schools," he said, "but when we came home we played football and basketball together."[70]

Much of Lightner's white support came from affluent voters who were not that different from him in class background. Voters in the so-called subdivision row of North Raleigh's Falls of the Neuse Road heavily favored the new mayor—at the same time, they elected a Jewish attorney and a college professor to city council. The precinct was at Raleigh's northern periphery, where "rambling farm houses and chicken coops" had been cleared to make room for pricey homes in subdivisions such as Quail Meadows and Hunting Ridge, which ranged in price from $36,000 to $100,000—a more than tidy sum at the time. Soon, shopping malls and leafy-green townhouse communities such as North Ridge were emerging in the upper reaches of Raleigh. There, managers from RTP companies and secretaries of state government agencies lived—bankers, lawyers, teachers, and scientists. "It could be suburban Atlanta, Chicago or Philadelphia," the *News & Observer* noted. It was the "New Raleigh" that "sent political analysts scrambling back to the drawing board last week to restudy the city's political equations." Voters in the New Raleigh were worried about the hasty and quickening pace of development. "Lightner seemed less oriented to the business interests in town," one middle-aged educator told the local paper.[71]

Raleigh, like the greater Triangle, had doggedly pursued economic development and in-migration for years, and the launch of RTP in 1959 brought a tide of affluent, educated newcomers to the region. Strikingly, white suburbanites lured to the Triangle could countenance voting for a black man, even if they might not appreciate his family moving in next door. Families such as the Lightners sent a new generation of leaders into politics in the wake of the civil rights breakthroughs of the 1960s, even as newcomers like Howard Lee and Bill Bell entered the political fray and won support among the scientists, engineers, and professors of the region's increasingly educated workforce and electorate.

By the early 1970s, the Triangle's vaunted liberalism could accommodate political participation and even leadership by African Americans, but it stopped short at economic justice for the working poor—not to mention significant housing integration. A few members of the black middle class, such as Howard Lee, could successfully move into white neighborhoods, albeit under serious duress, while others, including Bell and Lightner, opted instead to settle in black middle-class communities. The latter did not enjoy the immediate acceptance that their nonblack peers, such as Buckley Crist or Gloria Jimenez, received when moving to the Triangle, but the groundswell of support for leaders such as Lee and Lightner suggested that a coalition of black voters and white professionals could push the Triangle toward a more inclusive future. Lee served three terms and became a beloved local political figure, showing that a cross-race coalition could prevail in a small, liberal-leaning college town like Chapel Hill.[72]

Lightner's success suggested that a new, moderate politics of interracial cooperation could prevail in the cities of the growing Sunbelt. Yet Lightner's tenure in office was short; a bizarre scandal in which his wife,

Marguerite, was accused of shoplifting in 1974 threw a cloud over his administration. Although she was acquitted the following year, Lightner served only one term. (Some observers felt that the Lightners were targets of persecution, like other newly elected black officials and their families at the time.)[73]

Meanwhile, conflicts over schooling continued to unfold, suggesting that the relationship between black and white communities was not as rosy as local boosters or the victories of Lee and Lightner suggested. Both Durham and Raleigh saw increasingly poor and racially polarized urban school systems that were encircled by more affluent and whiter county schools in the early 1970s. The change was somewhat ironic; up until the advent of court-ordered integration, county schools in North Carolina often had been poorer than city schools and at times had sought consolidation in order to attain greater resources.

No longer was that the case by the 1970s. As middle-class white families favored suburbs in Wake County's Raleigh and Cary and suburban areas such as Parkwood, outside the Durham city limits, the Triangle cities looked to replicate the racial and class divide that increasingly polarized the metropolitan landscapes across the United States. In cities such as Detroit and Atlanta, fearful white parents—and some of their counterparts in the black middle class—saw urban neighborhoods as dangerous and city schools as unfit for their children. Historian Jack McElreath has shown that many families and schools in the Triangle did make a sincere effort to make integration work during the 1960s and 1970s. Some schools managed to avoid or at least minimize conflicts over student and teacher reassignments and school leadership decisions that plagued other communities. Yet the Triangle was hardly immune to the centrifugal forces of racial discrimination and economic inequality that were ripping cities and suburbs apart, exposing a rift between communities of privilege and disadvantage that politicians as much parents were, for the most, loath to address.

Raleigh and Durham in the 1970s tell a clear story of America's metropolitan possibilities—a tale of two cities. Both Durham city and county schools and Raleigh city and Wake County schools considered consolidation of their systems. School leaders believed that combining resources could at least arrest the growing race and class inequities across city and suburban lines. After all, consolidation of Mecklenburg County and Charlotte city schools in 1959 at least partly eased the path to desegregation in the years that followed.[74] In contrast, the Supreme Court's decision to block busing across county lines in *Milliken v. Bradley* (1974) ensured a radically segregated and unequal quilt of school systems across metro Detroit.[75]

Voters roundly rejected consolidation of both the Durham and Raleigh-Wake school systems in 1971 and 1972, respectively.[76] Some black Durhamites worried about losing control of their schools to white suburbanites, especially as they had fought hard for years to win political power in the city and did not mean to lose it as soon as they got it—not to mention concerns about their children being bused great distances into hostile suburban schools.[77] Meanwhile, white voters in the Wake and Durham County systems feared their children being bused into city schools or ceding access to their own affluent suburban schools. The divide seemed impassable. But city and county leaders in Wake attempted something audacious: in 1975, they went over the heads of voters and successfully sought a workaround from the state legislature that would allow them to merge schools anyway, without the consent of voters. Some suburbanites were outraged by the decision, especially in affluent communities such as Cary, where suspicion toward Wake's consolidated schools remained strong long after (see chapter 5).[78]

In the end, scholars of education viewed the new Wake County Schools as a striking success. Historian Gerald Grant even published a book in 2009 with the title *Hope and Despair in the American City: Why There Are No Bad Schools in Raleigh*.[79] Over the course of the 1980s and 1990s, consolidation permitted the county to spread resources and stabilize the class and race makeup of many schools—at least by the standards of urban public education in the United States. (Historian Matthew Lassiter has charted a parallel, modestly optimistic story in Charlotte's schools in his 2006 book *The Silent Majority*.)

Meanwhile, the gap between the city and county of Durham yawned ever wider in the years following the failure of consolidation. Affluent families—especially newcomers—chose not to move into neighborhoods within the urban system, viewing the city as increasingly dysfunctional and dangerous. Durham faced headwinds due to the waning tobacco industry, and many black parents in city schools could not afford to embark for prosperous suburbs. By the 1990s, the divide began to threaten city and suburb alike. A depopulating city school system saw student outcomes spiral downward, while the movement of families into suburban Durham and Wake Counties placed untenable pressures on their own systems such that they could barely keep up.

This is not a new story to those familiar with American urban history in the late twentieth century. In fact, the narrative of urban decline and suburban privilege is beyond cliché in almost every American city. But Raleigh and Durham offer a striking case study in the different paths of metropolitan growth that cities could take, especially as new industries and opportunities held the power to reshape the face of booming Sunbelt cities.

Research Triangle Park powered this change, sitting—paradoxically—at the very center of the Triangle itself but just at the edge of its cities and suburban communities. RTP's ability to draw scientists and engineers and their families, as well as laboratories, from across the nation and the world held the potential to transform schools and communities. One path led to increasing racial and class polarization across a dynamic but troubled urban landscape in Durham. Another led to a different, possible urban-suburban future—a still unequal but more integrated and less uneven one—in Wake County.

The Triangle might have pointed the way to markedly different fates for the postindustrial city in the 1970s, but the overall metro area itself was already becoming renowned as "the city of ideas." By the 1980s, Raleigh-Durham could boast of having the greatest concentration of PhDs in the country. And boast often it did. As Burroughs Wellcome, the National Humanities Center, and other institutions arrived in RTP, they added to the area's stock of PhDs and helped crystallize an image of the ideal space for intellectual labor to take place. If, by the 1980s, Americans came to believe a city could make nothing but ideas, it would look a lot like the Triangle.

Interlude

Sweet Gums, Traffic Jams, and Cilantro

Chemist Gertrude Elion expressed incredulity when the pharmaceutical firm Burroughs Wellcome first sent her packing to RTP in 1970. "We didn't see any sign of civilization," Elion recalled. "We wondered, 'What in the world are we getting into?'"[1] Indeed, as noted in a *New York Times* article, the verdant research park—"a landscape vivid with the brilliant hue of the sweet gum and deep green of the loblolly pine . . . [where] the hand of man is every where tastefully and somewhat sterilely evident"—was about as far from the gritty Bronx of Elion's youth as possible.[2]

When historian Peter Coclanis, then a postdoctoral fellow at Columbia University, was planning to visit UNC for a job talk over a decade later, a faculty member—a lifelong, inveterate New Yorker—joked about the prospect of moving to North Carolina: "You could spend a night in Chapel Hill," the professor said. "Maybe a weekend, but you could never live there." Coclanis, in fact, came to UNC to stay, becoming a distinguished professor of history and director of the Global Research Institute.[3]

Such doubts are not surprising, least of all coming from New Yorkers. "Northern scientists and intellectuals . . . are having trouble grasping the concept of 'brain drain to the South,'" as the *Times*'s Wayne King noted in 1977.[4]

Take the case of Tom Wenger. A Jewish kid from Long Island, Wenger grew up in a diverse community. "It had both Irish Catholics and Italian Catholics," he later joked. The public schoolers in his neighborhood lived in fear of the parochial school kids who worked out their pent-up anger by roaming the streets looking for boys like him to beat up. As Wenger moved up the chain of social mobility in postwar America, he learned more about the ugly realities of urban life. After medical school at Boston University, he continued his training at a Harlem hospital, which was engulfed by the chaos and poverty of New York in the early 1970s. "It was very like being on the front line of a war," he recalled, "only somebody else's body was at risk; not yours; your patient's was at risk and more than likely not going to make it."[5]

Coping with 100 emotionally draining hours a week of work in a massively underserved urban hospital was not easy on Wenger. So the budding doctor looked elsewhere to do his fellowship. Duke University was pioneering electrophysiology in the early 1970s, and the field appealed to him. But getting his wife on board with moving to the South was not easy either. The couple had never really heard of Durham, despite the fact that it was a much bigger city than Chapel Hill (albeit minuscule compared with New York). Ultimately his wife insisted on Durham because life in a tiny college town full of undergraduates—Chapel Hill—turned her off. "Frankly, we're in our mid-20s now," she said, "and the last thing I wanna do when I walk out of my house is to have undergraduates fucking under every bush." So Durham it was.[6]

The Wengers were part of a wave of outsiders who came to the Triangle beginning in the 1960s and accelerating in the 1970s and 1980s. They brought different sensibilities about issues such as culture, race, and religion to the Triangle, even if Raleigh, Durham, and Chapel Hill were widely reputed to be more progressive than the rest of the South. They established prosperous careers—Tom at Duke and, soon after, Burroughs Wellcome, and his wife with a successful dance company she founded.

Other affluent newcomers largely gravitated toward Raleigh, Chapel Hill, and the booming Wake County suburb of Cary, but the Wengers chose Durham. Still, their progressiveness had its limits. They were anxious about the quality of integrated schools, and realtors tended to steer these new, largely white families away from Durham City schools and toward suburban Durham County schools and neighboring Wake County. Although Wenger said he favored integration, he admitted, "It never even occurred to me to send them to public schools in Durham; I sent them to private schools."[7]

Segregation in schools may have persisted and reconstituted itself across the metropolitan landscape from the 1970s forward, but nevertheless, families like the Wengers found an appealing home with rewarding work amid the verdant laboratories of RTP and the rapidly growing suburbs of the greater Triangle. Affluent African American and Asian families joined them, albeit haltingly. For those with well-paid jobs in education, science, and tech and homes in affluent suburbs, the deal offered by the Triangle was satisfactory—even ideal, if they could accept the modest cultural offerings of the universities and local arts institutions.

By the 1980s, the Triangle had succeeded in diminishing the stigma of the South and winning a reputation as a place for innovative companies and people—with RTP at its center. Smita Patel moved first from India to New Jersey and then to North Carolina in 1981, after her husband, an engineer, accepted a job at Sperry Rand in Durham. The family moved into the suburb of Parkwood, next to RTP, and enjoyed the mild weather, short commutes, and friendliness of their neighbors, despite the dearth of local shopping and eating options. The Patels had to order groceries from a brother-in-law in New Jersey. "You were lucky to find cilantro around here, no?" Patel recalled.[8]

Engineer Chuck Till, who came to Raleigh from Atlanta in the 1980s to work at Northern Telecom in RTP, admitted wondering if coming to a metro area that numbered in the hundreds of thousands instead of millions would be a good choice. "There was the North Carolina Symphony," he said. "Probably not as good as the Atlanta Symphony, but at least there was one. There was an art museum. Probably not as good as the High Museum in Atlanta, but there was one. It was pretty good culture associated with Duke and UNC."[9]

As ever, the universities took a central role in allaying the anxieties of outsiders about what boll weevil–ridden pit stop they might be forced to accept if their employer moved to the park. Journalist Peter Range assured readers of the *New York Times* in the 1970s that Chapel Hill's more pious neighbors mostly "maintain[ed] a friendly respect for all of the hairy, book-toting atheists in their midst." It might not be the West Village or Harvard Square, but at least "the intellectual community has less arrogant scorn for its non-academic, more fundamentalist neighbors than any assemblage of eggheads east of the Iowa Writers Workshop."[10]

Tom Overman, a Chapel Hill native who returned to the village after working in advertising in New York and California, underlined this combination of provinciality and broad-mindedness. "The kind of people who come to this area have a big-city outlook even though this is a small, quintessential college town," he observed in 1983. "They are from all over the world. There is a cosmopolitan mix here." Overman admitted he missed the "amenities" of a big city, such as Thai restaurants, but he did not miss the traffic jams.[11]

The Triangle offered the city without the city—small but cosmopolitan, prosaic but stimulating—that is, the city of ideas.

4

"The Greatest Concentration of PhDs in the Country"

THE IDEA ECONOMY COMES OF AGE IN THE TRIANGLE

The 1983 sci-fi film *Brainstorm* offers a curious historical artifact of the Triangle's triumph as a postindustrial idyll. Shot in Raleigh and RTP, the film stars Christopher Walken as brilliant scientist Michael Brace, who works in the iconic, honeycomb-like building that Burroughs Wellcome built as its headquarters in 1971, based on a design by modernist architect Paul Rudolph. After work, Brace commutes by recumbent bike, riding through a leafy, green landscape of biotech companies to the eccentric Frank Lloyd Wright-esque home that he shares with his wife, Karen (Natalie Wood).

In classic 1980s movie fashion, the scientists soon learn that the military-industrial complex plans to use their inventions for nefarious purposes, but the film is less interesting for its plot than for its portrayal of RTP as a high-tech workplace. Brace and his coworkers are a quirky bunch, including a chain-smoking, straight-talking scientist memorably played by screen veteran Louise Fletcher. They cut up at work and wear casual, even shabby clothes; Fletcher's character is an older woman who seems to have eschewed marriage and kids. In short, they are the sort of unconventional, creative types who dream up great innovations in places like RTP.

Brainstorm's depiction of a green, serene space for tech workers represented a fulfillment of RTP's original vision: a Southern paradise of the smart.

By the early 1980s, that dream looked real enough. The Raleigh-Durham metro area's population grew by 23.4 percent between 1970 and 1980, and Governor Jim Hunt, a moderate Democrat who took office in 1977, committed the state to nurturing new industries with initiatives such as the North Carolina Biotechnology Center, founded in RTP in 1984.[1] The Triangle promised "graceful living," according to the Research Triangle Foundation, combining "the cultural academic atmosphere with small town living and cosmopolitan thinking."[2] North Carolina's cultural bonafides were proven by the fact that it boasted "the first state university . . . the first state-supported symphony . . . the first state museum of art . . . [and was] the first state to establish, with public funds, a school for the performing arts."[3] The park itself attracted seventeen new tenants in the 1970s, and another thirty-two the following decade as success built on success.[4]

If Chapel Hill was the "capital of the Southern mind," then the Triangle became increasingly renowned, by the 1980s, as a model of the economy of the future. RTP's fame spread around the world as companies such as Massachusetts's Data General (1977) and Japanese electronics manufacturer Sumitomo Electric (1983) came to the park.[5] An oft-repeated tale has it that a Japanese businessman, on hearing mention of North Carolina, responded, "Oh yes, we know that. It's in Research Triangle Park."[6] Indeed, RTP might not have swallowed up the entire state, but it increasingly subsumed the identities of Raleigh, Durham, Chapel Hill, and other nearby towns and cities in the popular imagination.

RTP's promoters stayed relentlessly on message. The brag that the Raleigh-Durham area possessed the highest percentage of PhDs in the country found its way into promotional materials, news reporting, casual conversation, and even historical scholarship. (Historian James Cobb briefly alighted on the Triangle's success in his seminal 1993 work *The Selling of the South*—noting, like so many others, the area's top rank in the nation as a home to PhDs.)[7] Governor Luther Hodges pledged back in 1955 that RTP would bring in "more PhDs than we've ever heard of here," and the statistics seemed to bear him out by the early 1980s.[8] As Hodges liked to say, the Triangle was "an idea that produced a reality"—and the reality was a city of ideas.

The architectural, economic, and social contours of this new postindustrial city can be found in the rapidly changing sprawl of a Sunbelt metropolitan landscape under Carolina blue skies. And the experiences of affluent workers and families who moved to live in the Triangle's suburbs and work in its equally verdant and spacious research park tell the story of an emergent class of professionals who would lead the way to the future—the folks who urbanist Richard Florida would characterize as the "creative class" decades later.

But before this class began to transform cities in the early twenty-first century, they lived and worked in Sunbelt suburbs. By looking at historic structures such as the Burroughs Wellcome building (1971; figure 4.1) and the National Humanities Center (1978), we can see how a new kind of space to work, married to a changing concept of work itself, was invented by architects, executives, and scholars in a profoundly rigorous and intentional way in the American South.[9]

Figure 4.1 The iconic Burroughs Wellcome, or Elion-Hitchings building, in 2016. *Source*: Photo by author.

A SPACESHIP LANDS IN THE SUNBELT

After IBM, one of RTP's biggest "gets" arrived in 1969. Burroughs Wellcome (BW), a major British pharmaceutical company, announced in August that it would leave suburban Tuckahoe, New York, citing "a lack of space for expansion," to build a $10 million facility in Research Triangle Park.[10] Like many manufacturing firms that had already left the Northeast for the South—as evidenced by the relocation of the American Association of Textile Chemists and Colorists from Massachusetts to North Carolina in 1964 to be closer to the new heartland of textile production—Burroughs Wellcome was one of many companies that sought lower costs for land and housing in the emerging Sunbelt.[11] (As noted in chapter 2, IBM also departed the New York City suburbs in the 1960s.) One executive said that land in the company's Westchester County home cost as much as 70 times more than in the Triangle.[12] With a ready supply of workers educated in biology and chemistry at area universities, and a more clement climate than New York, the Triangle well suited both BW managers and the workforce the firm hoped to employ. Executives were not attracted merely by cheaper land or labor, though; they favored RTP because it "promised to be an area of scientific and intellectual ferment," thanks to the nearby universities and the park's own strict emphasis on research work.[13]

The most striking thing about Burroughs Wellcome's move to RTP was undoubtedly its building, which was featured in countless stories about the park and the company to underline its radically futuristic veneer. The building, designed by celebrity architect Paul Rudolph, has been compared with everything from a honeycomb to a spaceship. It features "soaring inner spaces and a dramatic exterior . . . a symbol not only of the company's futuristic vision but also of the high-technology park," as local preservationists later put it. (The structure was later renamed the Elion-Hitchings building, after two Nobel Prize–winning scientists who worked at the pharmaceutical giant and did pioneering work on the early HIV drug AZT.)

The building became iconic precisely because it embodied the "science among the possums" aesthetic of Research Triangle Park: a symbol of the forward-looking, avant-garde, and knowledge-driven economy that had plopped down in the middle of the piney woods between

Figure 4.2 The juxtaposition of scientific research and architectural modernism within a verdant setting. *Source*: Photo by author.

Raleigh and Durham. From a distance, one can see the incongruity of the sharp lines and blocky spaces of the structure amid its bucolic surroundings. Yet Rudolph's design was meant to mirror the ridge of the building site, with chunks cascading down either side of its overarching A-frame structure like a pileup of tectonic plates. This choice gives the building its strikingly lapidary or "stacked" visual aesthetic. Large windows frame the forested rural area surrounding the building like a landscape painting, both highlighting its verdant environment and emphasizing the distinction between its high-tech, artificial internal environment and the natural world outside (figure 4.2).

The effect evokes nothing so much as modernism's melding of the natural and technological that geographer JB Jackson lampooned in his classic 1954 essay, "Living Outdoors with Mrs. Panther." It is a sardonic portrait of an affluent family that lives in a perfect, Mies Van Der Rohe–style glass and metal box in the countryside, which provides the illusion of an unmediated connection with nature.[14] In this way, Rudolph's design captured the aesthetic ambitions of high modernism—he was a student of Walter Gropius at Yale before earning his own global reputation as an architect—precisely at the moment when the movement was arguably passing its peak. Still, a structure such as the BW building was an undeniably prestigious project for both the company and the park. Indeed, the building itself was a testament to culture with a capital *C*. "The very fact that this building is standing here is a reflection of Burroughs Wellcome's interest in the arts," said vice-president Bill Sullivan in 1974.[15]

Pharmaceuticals stood out as a win-win in the postindustrial sweepstakes, considering that scientists could come up with wonderful new inventions in RTP and manual laborers could manufacture the pills in facilities elsewhere in the state. Indeed, the huge company's decision to relocate from New York's Westchester County was another milestone for the park. By 1979, the company employed 955 workers with a payroll of $17,800,000, and, as noted in the *Raleigh News & Observer*, 130 were PhDs, with 17 MDs—the most sought-after of knowledge workers.[16]

The facility not only brought white-collar jobs to RTP but it also generated twelve hundred jobs in Greenville, when the pharmaceutical company moved its manufacturing to the eastern North Carolina city, about a hundred miles from Raleigh. "I interviewed for my 1st job out of collage [sic] there in 1972," engineer D. Bruce Cohen recalled in 2016. "Everything was so different. . . . I remember being driven on two lane roads through pine trees until this futuristic building rose up to greet me for my interview."[17] As were many other visitors to RTP in the 1970s, Cohen was struck by the contrast between the Burroughs Wellcome structure and the narrow, seemingly rural roads leading to it. By the next day, the company was flying him out to Greenville to visit the manufacturing facilities there—less than a two-hour drive from RTP today, but a longer trip on the less-developed roads of the 1970s.

Greenville was not alone in greeting the spillover from RTP. Indeed, journalist Luther Carter noted that, because of the growth of RTP laboratories, "a number of new manufacturing plants more or less of the 'high-tech' variety have been established in the triangle area or just beyond it."[18] Burroughs Wellcome's presence in North Carolina, though, confirmed the fundamental division of labor that underlaid RTP: intellectual work in a pristine research park, and material production somewhere else in the state.

Even within the BW building one finds a complex map of postindustrial labor. Rudolph described his own aesthetic in terms of segmentation. Buildings, he said, needed "different kinds of space: the quiet, enclosed, isolated space; the hustling, bustling space, pungent with vitality; the paved, dignified, vast, sumptuous, even awe-inspiring space; the mysterious space; the transition space which defines, separates and yet joins juxtaposed spaces of contrasting character."[19] In fact, Rudolph's design might have captivated the eye and stirred a feeling of the future, but its angular lines and layered, geometrical surfaces never made a great deal of sense as a practical place to conduct business. Nobel Prize–winning chemist Gertrude Elion "complain[ed] as if from habit about Rudolph's large slanting beams, which jut into the lab spaces."[20] (Indeed, after its closure in 2011, the building was open to visitors for the occasional tour, but only if they signed a release and wore a hard hat in part to avoid bumping their heads on the sloping angles of doors and hallways.) In a bit of a holdover from the Space Age aesthetic of the 1950s and 1960s, the building looked as much like a form of futuristic transport as a workplace— "at once Escher-like with steps, angled walls, layered on more of the same," as chemist Sean Ekins observed after visiting the empty BW building in 2012.[21] Indeed, another employee recalled, "After years of being in and out of that building, I still had trouble finding what was where inside of it.[22]

The building was a striking relic of another era of corporate research. The pharmaceutical industry in the building's 1970s heyday was a "giant mass of people and knowledge," Ekins wrote, but it embodied an "upstairs/downstairs dynamic with the executives removed from the brains below. And then the partitioning by cave-like cubicles leaving only isolated whiteboards for sharing our ideas."[23] Architect Rudolph himself said that the building's A-frame design "allows the greatest volume to be housed on the lower floors and yet connected to the smaller mechanical system at the apex of the building. The diagonal movement of interior space opens up magnificent opportunities. Anticipation of growth and change is implicit in the concept."[24] It was a kind of cubist pyramid, with the largest space for working scientists at the bottom and a smaller clique of managers and machines at the pinnacle. Architecture critic Richard McKenna compared it with a cathedral.[25]

Many workers at BW appreciated both Rudolph's vision and the company's, holding fond memories of where they worked for decades. "I never found it claustrophobic during my 25 years," David H. Schroeder recalled years later. "The building was alive with interesting people."[26] Another scientist, Tom Wenger, remembered a small community where even top executives knew every janitor.[27] Still, cramped and segmented work spaces on the first floor contrasted with the gold fixtures of the deluxe executive bathroom and showers upstairs. The entire structure was oriented around brains and knowledge, but management was separate from the intellectual labor of the scientists who toiled below.

In a striking contrast, twenty-first-century theorists of the creative class tend to lump together a variety of workers—artists, designers, scientists, managers—in one group, even if that schema does not often accurately reflect the gradations of status and power in the workplace or wider economy. They are all "creative." Then again, perhaps the open or so-called smart office of the early twenty-first century mirrors the boundary-blurring social imaginary of the creative class, just as the Burroughs Wellcome building captured the way managers saw the "brains" in the 1970s. When Glaxo, the building's subsequent owner, left in 2011 for a renovated space elsewhere in RTP, that company dispensed with cubicles in favor of a layout with "no assigned personal work spaces."[28] Designers and managers presume that open, free-flowing spaces will prompt greater collaboration and creativity—a far cry from the myriad work warrens of 1970s corporate culture.[29] In any case, the building and the corporation that built it both reflected a division of labor that separated manufacturing from intellectual work such as research—as well as management from the brains below, as the film *Brainstorm* perhaps unintentionally implied in its "scientists versus corporate suits" narrative.

Yet, even if the BW building was a monument to an anticipated future of intellectual labor, the fruits of that knowledge work still ended up in a pill bottle. Indeed, IBM, Burroughs Wellcome, and other major tenants remained focused on making *something*—software, hardware, medicines, and so forth. RTP may have remained tied to a tangible, physical economy in the early days of its growth in the 1960s and 1970s—at times even requiring concessions to its no-production rule, as when IBM and Technitrol moved in—but the original ideal of purely intellectual work endured. Although the sciences and the humanities are sometimes viewed as mutually exclusive—even antithetical—camps today, they share the quality of being intellectual in nature. In the 1970s, the planners of RTP were eager to burnish the image of the park by adding an explicitly cultural component to its otherwise instrumental portfolio of computing, electronics, and pharmaceuticals. The arrival of the National Humanities Center in 1978 was, in many ways, the crowning moment of RTP's self-image as a place purely devoted to intellectual labor—the production not of something but of ideas in the most astringent sense.

INDUSTRIES WITHOUT INDUSTRY: AMBITION AND REALITY

Burroughs Wellcome and the National Humanities Center came to Research Triangle Park at a time when the political economy of the United States was shifting markedly toward the postindustrial. As the manufacturing heartland of the Northeast and Midwest suffered severe job losses and disinvestment in the 1970s, leaders in entertainment, software, and pharmaceuticals organized to press for policies on intellectual property and trade that protected the value of their products. The Copyright Act of 1976, for instance, dramatically expanded the power of copyright protection, and the Bayh-Dole Act of 1980 revolutionized higher education by permitting universities to commercialize and profit from their scientific discoveries. (The Association of University Technology Managers estimated in 2018 that more than two hundred drugs had originated in American university research labs since the law's passage.)[30] Crucially, Bayh-Dole accelerated the transformation of universities into entrepreneurial partners of private industry. From the 1980s onward, universities would not just provide employers with educated labor and scientific innovation; they would become businesses themselves.[31]

In short, business, government, and universities coordinated as never before to nurture the growth of a new knowledge economy. Even as capitalism besieged the ivory tower in the 1970s and 1980s, influence ran the other way as well. The university remained a model for knowledge production itself—just as it had for the designers who modeled RTP and other corporate parks after university campuses in the 1950s and 1960s.

"Academic ambience" continued to draw new companies and organizations to RTP, as journalist Luther J. Carter remarked in 1978.[32] The park gained seventeen employers in the 1970s, including a large Environmental Protection Agency (EPA) office, continuing the precedent established by the federal environmental health facility in the 1960s.[33] In fact, it was one of several organizations that distinguished both the park's strength in environmental and health sciences and its image as a pastoral space dedicated single-mindedly to intellectual work. Carter noted in 1978 that "there are now nearly 3000 Ph.D. scientists and engineers in the area and about 600 of them work in the park itself." Like many other observers, he was a bean-counter of PhDs. For example, he noted that the new Chemical Industry Institute of Toxicology (CIIT) employed "more than a score of Ph.D. staff scientists." CIIT chief Leon Golberg used the same ubiquitous language of concentration to describe his own institute's combination of scientific talent: "I don't think that there is anywhere else such a concentration of toxicologists," he said in 1978.[34]

Meanwhile, RTP took an important step to bolster its ties with the area's universities when it established the Triangle Universities Center for Advanced Studies (TUCASI) in 1975. Granting land to Duke, NC State, and UNC, planners intended to create a space where scholars and scientists could interact, pool resources, and work together—and, crucially, a place that was not explicitly devoted to corporate or government research but that included nonscientists, such as humanities professors.[35] As RTP's promotional materials put it, "Think of it like a park within the park!"[36]

Like RTI or the EPA, both CIIT and TUCASI were institutions dedicated to research rather than production in any direct sense. Engineers at IBM or chemists at Burroughs Wellcome might perform intellectual labor, producing ideas in the form of software or patents, but they did so as part of organizations made up of management, distribution, marketing, and production divisions—organized toward the end of *making something* in the real world.[37]

Being an information company with scientists on the payroll hardly meant that knowledge workers with the greatest credentials—those with PhDs—were anywhere near a majority of the workforce. As economist Candee Harris estimated in 1984, even in high-tech companies, 65 percent of the workforce was employed in production, 30 percent in administration and management, and a mere 5 percent directly in scientific or engineering work.[38] Charles Minshall, a scientist at Ohio's Battelle Memorial Institute, observed the year before that firms in computing, pharmaceuticals, and related fields "may have anywhere from 15 to 30 percent of their employment in the professional and technical category," while many research parks set a minimum threshold "8 to 12 percent" of such workers in their basic covenants.[39] In comparison, Burroughs Wellcome had nine hundred people working in the park, Carter noted, but only "about 100 of them are research scientists"—not counting the line workers in the Greenville plant or any of the company's other facilities.[40]

Even in a space restricted to the production of patents and scientific research, only one in nine employees was a scientist. Meanwhile, companies such as IBM and the telecommunications firm Nortel maintained large manufacturing workforces, belying the park's insistence on a strictly nonindustrial or even anti-industrial image. "This was the joke," engineer Chuck Till recalled. "Research Triangle Park but IBM had a manufacturing plant there. . . . Nortel had a manufacturing plant—it was probably the whole building—the whole complex was 700,000 square feet and manufacturing was probably 500,000 of the 700,000."[41] It was difficult to divorce the life of the mind from the business of the material world.

"INTANGIBLE ASSETS": THE HUMANITIES COME TO SCIENCE CITY

The idea of the city of ideas persisted nonetheless. It remained for another institution to come to RTP in the 1970s, further cementing the vision of a space devoted to high-level intellectual work, more so than even CIIT or RTI. Flanked by Duke University president Terry Sanford and UNC chancellor William Friday, banker Archie Davis broke ground on a site for the National Humanities Center (NHC) in April 1977.[42] Planning for the organization had begun in the early 1970s as scholars at the American Academy of Arts and Sciences, led by Columbia philosopher Charles Frankel and Harvard medievalist Morton Bloomfield, set out to establish a new center for humanistic scholarship in the United States.

Twenty-first-century readers might find the scholars' anxieties all too familiar, as even by the early 1970s, many worried that the humanities were losing ground and at risk of becoming irrelevant. Scientists in fields such as physics and computer science had proved their utility in the Cold War world of the 1950s, and social scientists had risen to prominence in diagnosing the social ills of the 1960s. But humanists feared shrinking into the shadows as American society moved into the 1970s.[43] As English professor Benjamin DeMott observed in 1975, the federal government had rushed to support scientific research through the National Science Foundation and National Institutes of Health in the postwar era, but the National Endowment for the Arts and the National Endowment for the Humanities were like afterthoughts—redheaded stepchildren of the Great Society, whose practical value to society (not to mention yearly funding) was tenuous at best. Hence, the need for a National Humanities Center. The institution would reconnect historians, philosophers, literary scholars, and the like to the pressing issues of the day.

As Frankel wrote in a 1977 mission statement, the NHC was "a response to the widely felt need within the academic world to revitalize the humanities, and to the growing recognition within the country at large that the humanities ought to make a larger contribution to public enlightenment and to the imaginative understanding of public issues." Frankel worried that humanists had lost the important role in public discourse that thinkers such as John Stuart Mill and William James had once enjoyed.[44] However, he insisted that "scholarship cannot and should not be shackled to problem solving. It must be free to follow crooked paths to unexpected conclusions."[45]

Indeed, the NHC was meant to be a site where scholars could follow their "crooked paths" unimpeded by any other material concerns. The nation, of course, already had centers devoted solely to scholarly work, such as Stanford's Center for Advanced Study in the Behavioral Sciences in California or the Institute for Advanced Study (IAS) at Princeton.

Since 1930, the IAS had provided free rein for intellectual giants such as Albert Einstein and quantum physicist Wolfgang Pauli to pursue their interests.[46] But such centers tended to focus on disciplines outside the humanities, such as math, science, and psychology.

The National Humanities Center would be just such a space for pure intellectual inquiry, bringing scholars in history, literature, and other disciplines to work for a time—typically an academic year—on a project. Here was an opportunity not just to bring a burnish of culture to a place that, in the end, remained a glorified business or industrial park but to refine the logic of RTP to its extreme. The NHC would be about the life of the mind, but without all that other *stuff*—distribution, marketing, production—and only a small staff of administration, library, and other support workers. Primarily professors from colleges and universities around the United States, the fellows were almost by definition PhDs, thus bolstering Governor Hodges's original ambition to bring in as many highly educated workers as possible. As fellows, the scholars' only job would be to sit and think, read, and write, freed from teaching obligations. It was an image of the information economy compressed into gemlike lucidity.

Indeed, the NHC did not produce anything in particular. Scientists at IBM or Burroughs Wellcome might spend their days engaged in intellectual work, but somewhere along the chain, something was made, a microchip or a pill, even if it might be manufactured elsewhere. NHC was important to RTP's image because it was strictly about the life of the mind, with few, if any, connections to a material economy—except, perhaps, in the books or journal articles that NHC Fellows might write after spending a semester or two in RTP.

A number of cities and states bid for the honor of housing the new center, and the committee ultimately settled on Research Triangle Park. Planners sought a "quiet atmosphere" and a hospitable setting for "young families," but not an "ivory tower." Columbia University had been an early contender, among eighteen others, but the Academy disdained New York "because of its high cost of living and troubled schools, its tight housing market for the middle class, and its atmosphere of crisis and conflict," journalist Michael Sterne reported in 1978.[47] (Key planner Charles Frankel taught at Columbia but lived in the Westchester hamlet of Bedford Hills.)[48]

RTP won in part because the NHC would not have to be tied too closely with one particular university, as it might have been at Columbia. It would benefit from the nearness of the Triangle's numerous colleges and universities without having any one as its "home" (like, say, IAS near Princeton). North Carolina also sweetened the deal by offering various perks, as state officials had done in luring IBM and federal research facilities in the 1960s. (As the American Academy of Arts and Sciences reported in 1977, "The business and academic communities of North Carolina have welcomed the Center enthusiastically, and have been very helpful as the Center has settled into its new home. This support has been material as well as moral, and has included the donation of a site for the Center's building and funds to finance its construction.") Local boosters raised $1.5 million for the center, RTP offered a $2.5 million building, and the Triangle universities promised $225,000 a year in support for the center's first half decade.[49]

The architecture of the center's bright, white, airy structure mirrored, in at least some ways, the futurism of Burroughs Wellcome's headquarters. It is a space designed for thought, for intellectual labor. Its modest offices have the feeling of monastic cloisters or grad student carrels, clearly modeled on the spatial layout of a university department. There is abundant light—itself a symbol of knowledge and enlightenment—and what President Robert Newman has described as a "seamless" (or perhaps seemingly seamless) interface with the pine forest surrounding it (figure 4.3).[50]

In this way, NHC continued the original assumption that underlaid RTP—that intellectual work is fostered by pastoral serenity, divorced from the truck and barter of the ordinary world. It is also a deeply American notion, reaching back to Thoreau's deep thoughts at Walden or possibly even the Jeffersonian ideal of the yeoman farmer, whose property ownership permitted space and an independent will unfettered by the impositions of others. As J. B. Jackson once noted, a green lawn has been a deep, if often implicit, aspiration of Europeans since they transplanted themselves to a new continent and began carving up a vast landscape into farms, cities, and, eventually, sprawling suburbs—much like RTP itself.[51]

Indeed, whereas today theorists such as Richard Florida and Charles Landry see innovation as emerging from the stimulation of people interacting in denser urban environments (the "creative city"), RTP was

Figure 4.3 The interior of the National Humanities Center. Ample windows fill the building with light and create a sense of unmediated contact with surrounding nature. *Source*: Photo by author.

premised on the idea of separating more conventional business and production activities from intellectual work in order to create a contemplative environment. That did not mean that the park (or NHC) lacked a theory of social interaction. After all, the park was all about bringing smart people together in one place, or a series of interconnected spaces, while providing access to the pleasures of cultural opportunities made possible by nearby colleges and universities—not within reach, exactly, but a half-hour's drive away

NHC itself was explicitly meant to bring scholars together in one space that was conducive to intellectual cross-pollination. Freed from teaching responsibilities, intellectuals could work in blissful isolation, but they also encountered one another at talks and seminars and, most important, in the open dining area that sits at the center's core. (As NHC's first director, Charles Frankel, put it early on, the center was meant "to encourage advanced studies in the humanities, to bring humanistic scholars together with scholars in other disciplines and with people in various fields of public life, and to enhance the usefulness and influence of the humanities in the American civic process.")[52] They might be separated from nearby computer scientists and chemists by broad lawns and security checkpoints, but within the NHC, bright minds would still mingle in a kind of ethereal, immaterial space. Creative thought and intellectual interchange would occur in a building where the outside was nearly unmediated by architecture (or at least appeared to be so).[53] "The walkways through the building were laid out to facilitate 'chance encounters' among scholars as they emerge for fresh air," noted an article in the *Christian Science Monitor* in 1982. "They are seen as a leavening influence in RTP's technical environment. . . . The day of my visit I was reminded of nothing so much as a very nice college dorm just before the semester begins and everyone gets swamped with work."[54]

The center's supporters were, of course, not keen to present it as the intellectual equivalent of spring break. Frankel was quick to caution that the NHC would "not exist to contribute to the leisure of the theoried class"—an apt and felicitous phrase, but in fact the center was the most idyllic spot in a place that was designed to be a postindustrial utopia.[55] It might not have been a space for leisure, but RTP as a whole demanded rethinking what kind of place and conditions favored a new kind of labor—one that held features in common for the chemist and the philosopher alike.

That landscape offered a curious compromise between distance and proximity, separation and interaction. RTP was an agglomeration of intellectual resources, with each cluster parceled out in a sprawling space; like the park, the center united brains in one place with a stated aim of spurring discussion and collaboration across disciplines. Meanwhile, it housed those brains in a luminous structure in a suburban landscape—and stored them in the little cloistered cubbyholes of the fellows' offices, which radiated out from the central meeting and dining space. (It was "a mixture of public and private spaces," as Frankel's successor, Director William H. Bennett, put it.)[56]

Like RTP in general, the NHC was framed as a place where highly educated workers could spend their time in reflection and contemplation, dreaming up ideas that would not be dreamed anywhere else. Its focus was solely on the intellect: even if the park included a fair amount of real material production of goods, RTP's image elided any real manufacturing in pursuit of an ideal that valorized the mind and immaterial creativity, as a space for privileged workers to ply their minds in a way distinct from the manual toil of manufacturing or low-level service workers. The National Humanities Center crystallized this idea in its most potent form: a clean, serene white space for scholarly work, far separated from the grubby world of work, and a complement to the similar work spaces of scientists and engineers in the park's computing, pharmaceutical, and chemical research facilities.

The arrival of the center was yet another coup for RTP's local planners and boosters, who had scored one success after another in attracting major corporate tenants, professional and industry organizations, and government agencies since 1965. It contributed to the Triangle's image as a city of ideas, a home to so-called idea industries, even if the handful of NHC fellows made for a relatively small and fleeting contribution to the local economy. Indeed, journalist Carter marveled at the acumen with which Frankel and his colleagues promoted the idea for the NHC in the mid-1970s and persuaded North Carolina leaders to put so much on the line to secure the deal. The scholars, after all, "had nothing much to offer but an idea." That capacious and slippery word—idea—comes up again and again.

The NHC itself was never terribly significant as a jobs engine, but it was as a potent symbol of the aesthetic and sociological ambitions that drove RTP from the beginning. Compared with the thousands of well-paying jobs generated by the likes of IBM and Burroughs Wellcome, NHC was a drop in the bucket; it essentially repatriated the professorial salaries of a few dozen "workers" to the Triangle area for nine months at a time. "This all adds up to handsome treatment for an activity which, while it may be good in itself, has no direct bearing on the problem the founders of the triangle park meant to address—that of expanding job opportunities in high-technology industry," Carter conceded. "But the center is an interesting new ingredient in a mix that does include better jobs."[57] (For a frame of reference, in 1978, IBM had roughly thirty-five hundred workers in RTP and twenty-five hundred in the greater Triangle; the NHC planned to bring in twenty-six fellows in 1978, eventually reaching fifty per year by 1980.[58])

The NHC might have had little direct economic impact, but it was one of a series of institutions in RTP that was funded in whole or in part by government and dedicated solely to research. Just a few feet away on TW Alexander Drive sits the North Carolina Biotechnology Center, which was the first such government-funded center of its kind when it was established by an ambitious Governor Hunt in 1984. The center has since played a significant role in promoting the biotechnology industry and helping to commercialize academic research in North Carolina (despite employing a staff that numbered only sixty-two in 2018).[59] The Biotech Center relied on funding from the North Carolina General Assembly, building on the scientific and medical resources of the universities and the park's demonstrated strength in attracting pharmaceutical and environmental health activities in the 1960s and 1970s. The number of biotech firms in North Carolina increased from six before the center's inception to eighty in 1998 and one hundred seventy-five in 2005, when the industry posted $4 billion in sales.[60] The center, in short, made good on Hunt's original plan to apply modest funds strategically to diversify the workforce in RTP, the greater Triangle, and the state as a whole. The governor also steered the founding of the Microelectronics Center of North Carolina, although its overall economic impact remains less clear.[61]

The biotechnology and microelectronics centers might have been more practical and consequential than NHC, but they shared with that organization a fundamental orientation toward research and research alone—the work of scientists, scholars, librarians—all while enjoying partial or complete support from government. The institutions that were built in the late 1970s and early 1980s bolstered RTP's reputation not only as a somewhat fancier version of an industrial park but as a place dedicated to ideas, which in itself was the biggest idea of all. Indeed, when NHC opened in 1978, Carter noted that RTP began "20 years ago as little more than a promoter's slogan. . . . But just as life sometimes follows art, it also sometimes follows promotion and PR, particularly if underlying the promoters' dreams there are a few sound ideas."[62] Life would continue to follow art in RTP, as the media fawned and the park's reputation spread around the world.

THE RESEARCH TRIANGLE AS A MODEL FOR POLICY MAKERS

In many ways, RTP mirrored the universities and the suburbs built to serve RTP workers, such as Parkwood in Durham or North Ridge in Raleigh. Education was the original idea industry, of course. Universities existed centuries before Gutenberg put ink and movable tiles to paper or water turned a wheel in a textile mill, and the physical landscape of the park had been deliberately designed by planners and tenants to evoke a campus atmosphere of open space, leafy trees, sun and shade. Indeed, as Tom White, president of the Greater Durham Chamber of Commerce, put it, universities were the model for the new idea economy itself: "The corporate campuses emulate the tranquil setting of our local college campuses. High-level intellectual inquiry requires peace and solitude in order to be creative and productive."[63]

What the Triangle offered, wrote Pulitzer Prize–winning Tennessee journalist Wendell Rawls Jr. in 1983, was "the good life." The area married the benefits of proximity to culture and—crucially—intelligent neighbors with the serenity and easy living of the suburban Sunbelt. After all, the three-county area of Raleigh, Durham, and Chapel Hill boasted more PhDs per capita than any metropolitan area in the country.[64] New Haven, Connecticut, and Boston, Massachusetts placed a poor eighth and eleventh place, respectively, and massive New York came in at number forty. "There soon will be 28 pure research facilities here," the reporter added, employing the familiar theme of purity to describe RTP's burgeoning economy.[65]

In fact, the Triangle was only one part of a broader discussion of the new economy amid the grinding economic transformations of the 1970s and 1980s. As the so-called rust belt of the Upper Midwest and Northeast continued to shed manufacturing jobs—which were lost to automation and low-wage, nonunion labor in the South, the West, and overseas—high-tech industries seemed to promise a cleaner, happier future. Ideas and educational institutions were central to this discourse. "In today's high-technology industries, proximity to raw materials or water transportation is not as important as it was for the auto industry," journalist Alexander Taylor noted in *Time* in 1982. "The entrepreneurial spirit now seems to flourish best near universities. There companies just getting started can find research help for their projects."[66] This was the new kind of metropolitan economy that sociologist Manuel Castells would later influentially dub "the informational city."[67]

Like Silicon Valley in California and Route 128—homeland of Michael Dukakis's "Massachusetts Miracle" of tech-led development—North Carolina stood out as a model of the new economy. Even as light manufacturing spread through the state's rural areas and small towns (belying the national narrative of deindustrialization), the Research Triangle of Raleigh-Durham and the booming financial capital of Charlotte represented the twin poles of a new white-collar, well-paid professional economy. As usual, an implicit narrative of modernization permeated news coverage, as journalists could not resist the "possums and laboratories" trope of high-tech progress side by side with the persistence of the state's rural, backward past. "Piedmont farming communities within the Triangle found themselves abruptly cheek-by-jowl with enclaves of Ph.D.'s and aerospace engineers," as Meredith College historian Thomas C. Parramore put it in a 1983 popular history funded by the National Endowment for the

Humanities. "The twentieth century seemed almost to have been bypassed in a headlong plunge from the nineteenth century into the twenty-first."[68] The Triangle, in other words, meant a shortcut from the "dark, satanic mill" of the nineteenth century—which North Carolina came late to, anyway—to the *Jetsons* world of a high-tech service economy, skipping the pesky middle stages of development.

The area's growth was borne out in demographic figures as well as the Triangle's resilience during the economic shocks of recession in the 1970s and early 1980s. Raleigh's population increased over 30 percent from 1960 to 1970, and the city drew more manufacturing jobs even as it remained less manufacturing-intensive than the state as a whole.[69] The metropolitan area's population expanded 26 percent between 1970 and 1980, whereas the national population increased only 10.5 percent during the decade. Clearly, the Raleigh metro area was scooping up a disproportionate part of the nation's shifting population.[70]

The local economy also demonstrated remarkable resilience. In 1975, for instance, the state posted an unemployment rate of over 10 percent, more than the nation as a whole, but the rate never rose above 5 percent for Raleigh residents. Later, when a painful recession hit the nation during the first year of President Ronald Reagan's term, Raleigh continued to enjoy a dramatically lower unemployment rate than the state; Wake and Durham counties enjoyed employment rates of 4.6 and 4.7 percent, respectively in 1982, almost half that of the state's rate of 9 percent.[71] Part of this resilience can be attributed to Raleigh's role as a center of education and government services, two industries in which employment tends to be less vulnerable to swings in the overall economy. But the Triangle's relative prosperity attested to its success in attracting dynamic firms that paid better wages than most in the state.[72]

Boosters have never been known for their reluctance to self-congratulate, and North Carolina's were no different. State officials trumpeted the Triangle's success in attracting good jobs and its evident demographic and economic good health as a sign of virtue and foresight. An RTP pamphlet stressed the "5,500 acres of gently rolling land" of the park, which boasted thirty-five research facilities by 1981. It emphasized the "university culture" of the Triangle, with the iconic steeples of Duke, UNC, and NC State featured at each corner of an "area rich in cultural and recreational opportunities as well as an intellectual and social climate which is fresh, hospitable and resourceful. It is a setting which breeds success."[73]

The promise of that university culture—with its connotation of education, enlightenment, and sophistication—was central to RTP's ongoing image management. "America's urban landscape is quickly shifting," cited a 1982 item in the *Christian Science Monitor*. The giants of the old economy, such as Detroit or New York, were being "eclipsed" by smaller burgs that combined the cultural benefits of the big city with a relaxed and affordable quality of life.[74] Culture was "just part of the good life," as the state's secretary of cultural resources, Sara Hodgkins, told the paper. "We don't consider music and art luxuries. In order to be a whole person, you need to experience these things." Boosters believed that arts could be as powerful an attractor as tax incentives or industrial revenue bonds, and Charles Reinhart, director of the American Dance Festival, commented, "When we first came to Durham, there was an immediate realization that the festival would be an economic help to the area. But then people became curious about us—'What is it?' " Local planners realized the potential utility of arts institutions for promoting development, and workers who relocated from places such as New York and Boston said they took advantage of such cultural opportunities, perhaps more often than they did back home.[75]

Around the same time, high-tech companies were looking for just such places to expand, away from the confines of Silicon Valley or Route 128. "Many states, in search of industries that are clean, fast-growing and pay good wages and fringe benefits to skilled workers, would like to attract such companies," Alexander Taylor reported in a 1982 *Time* article. "North Carolina is spending more than $24 million to build a microelectronics center near Durham in what is called the Research Triangle."[76] Microelectronics, a major priority of Governor Jim Hunt during his first term (1977–81), was an appealing target because it promised the potential of both high-brow intellectual work in RTP and manufacturing jobs elsewhere in the state. But the emphasis throughout was on ideas—"idea industries," as stated in the *Christian Science Monitor* article—clean, abstract, not *industrial* (figure 4.4). And there is no industry less industrial than the life of the mind: research, education, scholarship, and so forth.

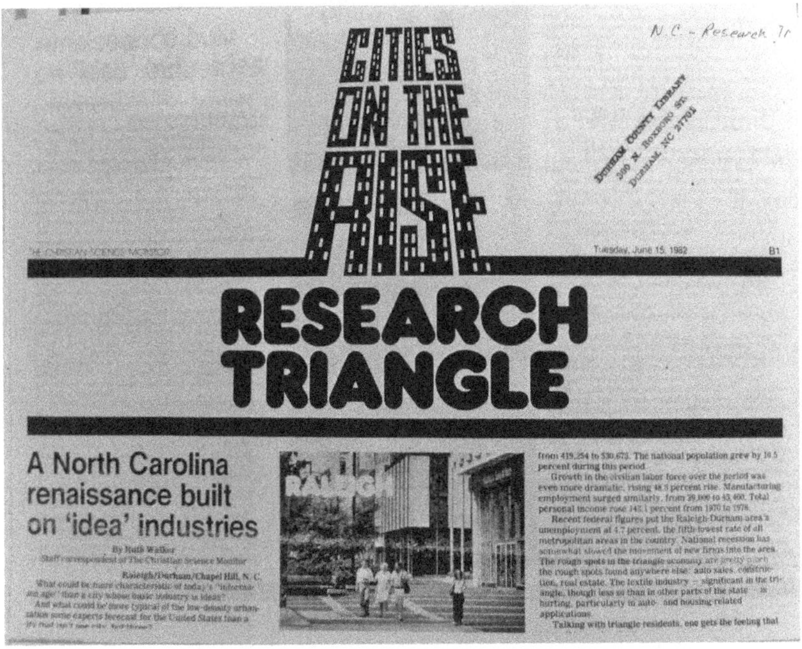

Figure 4.4 Glowing 1982 press coverage of the Research Triangle, "a city whose basic industry is ideas." *Source*: *Christian Science Monitor*.

RTP's progress was documented in a landmark study of research parks by UNC planning professors Michael Luger and Harvey Goldstein, who coauthored *Technology in the Garden* in 1991. They found that RTP drew "innovative people" thanks to the reputation of both the universities and the park, while "helping to create a special type of sociocultural milieu."[77] They also noted that university officials said that the existence of the park made it easier to recruit faculty. As always, the theme of recruiting people—innovative, talented, educated, creative—was central to the RTP project.

The Triangle was one of the "cities on the rise," according to the *Christian Science Monitor* in 1982. The paper had published a series on "vigorous and livable" cities, which "afford room to grow without being overwhelmed by big-city woes." The Triangle appeared to hold the key to combining economic growth, a good quality of life, and—most important—high technology. "What could be more characteristic of today's 'information age' than a city whose basic industry is ideas?" reporter Ruth Walker enthused.[78]

In her haste, Walker treated two intriguing assumptions as fact: that the various municipalities of the Triangle did, in fact, make up a single city, and that "ideas" were actually an industry. In many ways she was right, of course. The Triangle, less dense than even sprawling Sunbelt metropolises such as Los Angeles and Dallas-Fort Worth, is like those cities in being what geographers describe as "polycentric." The prosperous cities of America's postwar South and West often did not radiate from a traditional downtown or central business district, but rather embraced multiple urban cores. In this respect, the Triangle is the ne plus ultra of Sunbelt cities: it incorporates at least four major municipalities with their own downtowns and distinctive identities (Raleigh, Durham, Chapel Hill, and Cary) into a shared metropolitan landscape with a relatively empty space (RTP) at its core.[79] Metaphorically, the park is more like the spoke of a wheel than the pit of a peach.

Walker's idea of an idea industry is more curious, however. Park managers insisted on an anti-industrial image for RTP, despite the fact that IBM, Sumitomo, and other companies carried out manufacturing activities within its borders—an idea that planners resisted prior to the arrival of IBM in 1965. RTP's image remained much as portrayed in the film *Brainstorm*: quiet and bucolic (the word "pastoral" often came up in news coverage), populated by supersmart scientists and engineers and possibly the occasional scheming corporate executive—but almost never a blue-collar worker, whether in manufacturing or service roles.[80] (As I showed in chapter 2, the zoning rules of RTP took care to keep manual labor such as loading and unloading trucks invisible from the property line.) In addition, the research of Luger and Goldstein, among others, showed that RTP had spawned relatively little start-up activity compared with centers of innovation such as Boston and Silicon Valley. There were notable exceptions, such as SAS Institute (founded in Raleigh in 1976) and Quintiles (started in Durham in 1982), but overall, the park depended mostly on investment by well-established outside firms—a trend that continued into the early twenty-first century.[81]

The reality on the ground might have been more complex and mixed than the park's image of high-tech pastoralism suggests, but the image was what people saw—businesspeople at home and abroad, workers and visitors, and the casual reader of the *Times* or *Christian Science Monitor*. The promoters of RTP imagined a space for work that was distinctly *not* industrial, where people worked with their minds instead of their hands and made ideas—the formula for a new AIDS drug, for instance, or patents and copyrights or the design of a new piece of software. Diverse businesses, whether in computers, pharmaceuticals, or biotechnology, increasingly fell under the ambit of "ideas" and "information," which was taken for granted by journalists as part of one capacious information economy.

Research Triangle Park rapidly dwarfed its sisters, such as New Jersey's Princeton Forrestal Center or California's Stanford Research Park, becoming a commonly cited model for successful high-tech development in the 1980s and 1990s. The park "is now the largest research center of its kind in the world, operated by a nonprofit foundation on behalf of the area's three major universities," said Thomas C. Hayes in the *New York Times* in 1987, declaring that RTP was "North Carolina's high-tech payoff." Companies such as Burroughs Wellcome came not only for the area's universities but for its "easy mix of countrified and urban ways."[82]

When researcher Charles Minshall looked into the qualities that made a few research parks work while several imitators failed, he identified many of the features that defined RTP. "Very few industry, service, and office activity prospects are interested in raw land, or in building," Minshall wrote in a 1983 report for Battelle Memorial Institute. "Prospective tenants are much more quality conscious than ever before. High technology production, services, and research and development activities are being attracted to 'campus settings.' Attractive and high quality sites and buildings are very important—and factors like simple costs and basic bare buildings are not competitive."[83] (Minshall cited the "highly regarded" RTP as one of the chief examples in his study, along with Stanford Research Park and the high-tech cluster of Massachusetts's Route 128.[84]) The "campus feel" that tech companies sought extended to the rapidly growing metropolitan Triangle. As Raleigh newspaperman Ferrel Guillory put it in 1989, "More than any other, the word campus defines the three-city region known as the Research Triangle."[85]

Even by the early twenty-first century, no one would mistake Raleigh for a vast cosmopolitan metropolis—and far less so in the late 1980s and 1990s. But planners had designed a “technoburb” that appealed to high-tech firms, mostly from the outside, and the educated professionals they hoped to employ. The area benefited from relatively low costs for land and labor relative to the Northeast, the presence of an unusually robust higher education system, and energetic support from state government for new and emerging industries. Above all, perhaps, it benefited from expert branding and skillful outreach. This Sunbelt offshoot of high technology emerged at precisely the moment when Americans were becoming more broadly aware of large-scale shifts in employment and the structure of the economy, trends that had been developing since the 1950s but had not coalesced into a coherent narrative until the new economy or idea economy entered common parlance in the late 1970s and 1980s.

Grabbing footloose capital and educated workers who were nearly as mobile became an obsession for local, state, and national development officials by the early 1980s. The United Kingdom sought to recruit just such resources to science parks in places such as Cambridge and Edinburgh in 1983, placing ads in U.S. newspapers that touted the quintessential features of the ideal tech work environment:

> Association with a nearby university, technical center, or research institute; open, park-like surroundings on the outskirts of established communities; tax breaks; subsidized training programs; programs to recruit only high-technology or research-oriented enterprises; room for expansion, and organized park-wide seminars or other opportunities for exchanging resources and ideas.[86]

Universities? Check. Pastoral landscape? Check. A research-only environment, set apart from an urban center but providing at least some opportunity for interaction and intellectual stimulation. Check, check, and check. The sales pitch sounds familiar, because it is. British towns and cities realized they needed to draw new investment in technology to produce jobs and growth. “The idea,” they said, “has been traced to the success in the United States of North Carolina’s Research Triangle and, before that, of the property development projects sponsored by Stanford University that housed the pioneering Silicon Valley companies."[87]

Like the Japanese businessman who thought North Carolina was in the Research Triangle, anxious urban leaders and economic planners around the world had heard of the idea that transformed Raleigh, Durham, Chapel Hill and more. What the Triangle seemed to lack was a spillover of innovation and entrepreneurship beyond the bounds of corporate branch plants or even RTP itself. In the pioneering software firm SAS, it got just that.

5

Cary, SAS, and the Search for the Good Life

It was the early twenty-first century, and cartoonist Pick Cantrell was thinking of returning to his Tar Heel roots after a long sojourn working for newspapers in New York. His wife, Cam, a cinematographer, insisted that the Triangle was the place to be:

> We'll look in Raleigh-Durham-Chapel Hill. We can start a new life. Near family and friends. And it's beautiful down there. The Research Triangle is one of the most livable places in the country. Nice environment, less crime, slower pace, better quality of life than up here. Cost of living's a hell of a lot better, too. Good schools. Restaurants. Lots of culture with the universities close by. More Ph.D.s per capita than anywhere in the country. I've always loved that area.[1]

Pick was clearly a stand-in for author Doug Marlette, the man behind the long-running Southern comic strip *Kudzu*, who returned to his native Hillsborough, not far from Chapel Hill, toward the end of his life. Marlette's 2002 novel *The Bridge* might have been a deeply personal roman à clef, but its story invoked all the same quality-of-life and cultural considerations that drew many real-life Northerners—and not a few departed Southerners—to the Triangle in the late twentieth century.

No place embodied this vision of the good life more than Cary, a small town between Raleigh and RTP whose population grew a staggering 8,323 percent between 1950 and 2007. By the turn of the century, the town—a city, really, the seventh largest in North Carolina—boasted incomes and education levels dramatically higher than most U.S. cities and a reputation as one of the safest communities in the nation. (The median household income in 2016 was $100,167, nearly double the national figure the same year.)[2] It was part of Wake County Schools, even though its residents resisted, more than most others in Wake, the merger of city and county schools in the 1970s.[3] The county school system might have been considered among the best in the country, but those not content with it could choose from a number of private schools, including the Cary Academy, which was established by local tech billionaire Jim Goodnight in 1996.[4]

Cary seemed to fulfill the promise of the postindustrial economy that RTP planners aspired to build in the late 1950s, abounding with higher wages, more educated citizens, and better economic opportunities. Many residents worked in RTP; employers such as Oxford University Press (OUP) and American Airlines brought jobs to the community, and Goodnight's SAS Institute flourished in the software business.[5] The town's property market seldom dipped, even during recessions, and local officials continually worried about supplying enough water, roads, and schools for its ever-burgeoning population. The community's ranch homes, split-levels, and McMansions were decked out in tastefully neutral colors, and its commercial areas lacked loud, obvious signage, thanks to zealous policing of the local built environment.[6]

In short, Cary was what the late landscape writer J. B. Jackson called "the almost perfect town."[7] It mirrored RTP in its rigorous zoning and general lack of traditional manufacturing. Indeed, like the park, it was a space devoted single-mindedly to the interests and aspirations of the ascendant knowledge workers who flocked to Cary in extraordinary numbers, as employees of computing, pharmaceutical, and biotechnology firms largely disdained Durham—with its reputation for crime and segregated, dysfunctional schools—and opted for Wake County suburbs instead.

Like Durham County's Parkwood, it was a place designed with scientists, engineers, and their families in mind, but on a far bigger scale. And with the rise of the SAS Institute, perhaps the Triangle's most successful start-up, Cary gained not only an employer with a reputation for offering all the best perks an in-demand tech worker could hope to expect, but it also gained a whole new privatized science city unto itself, complete with day-care and health-care facilities and programs that offered employees privileged access to housing and schooling beyond its corporate campus. The press routinely praised SAS as among the best places to work and Cary as among the best places to live in the 1990s and early 2000s. Cary fulfilled the ultimate realization of Luther Hodges's "get more PhDs" strategy of the late 1950s, but the vision of the good life it promised was, in significant ways, confined to the knowledge workers who had the skills to work at SAS or the means to live in the increasingly prosperous town.

More than any other major city in the Triangle, Cary has RTP imprinted in its DNA. Durham had a long history as a manufacturing center, with a rich heritage of black cultural life and political leadership; and thanks to the presence of Duke University's medical school, it could have transitioned from the City of Tobacco to the City of Medicine with or without RTP. Raleigh likely would have grown and enjoyed a measured prosperity as the seat of state government even if the research park had never existed. But Cary was remade in the image of RTP—and Cary itself furnished the guidelines for a residential vision of the knowledge economy, as divorced as possible from the grubby realities of material production.

THE CARY EXPLOSION

Cary was almost made from whole cloth. In 1971, the town had only 7,640 residents, but the population tripled in the 1970s and doubled in both the 1980s and 1990s.[8] Early on, the community was known as Bradford's Ordinary, after an inn established there by William Bradford in the late eighteenth century. (The name perhaps foreshadowed its future reputation as an idyllic, if dull, town.) Relatively flat and dry, the area's topography favored the construction of the North Carolina Railroad, which, beginning in 1854, connected Goldsboro and Charlotte.

Though no station initially existed in the town, the train would stop there if hailed by passengers.[9] Officially incorporated in 1871, Cary got its name from Frank Page, a landowner who had purchased acreage around the rail line. An abstemious Methodist who abhorred drinking and dancing, Page admired Samuel F. Cary, an Ohio congressman and leader of the temperance movement. The town included prosperous free black families at the dawn of the Civil War and went on to include a black middle class that played a key role in the tumultuous transitions of desegregation and school integration in the mid-twentieth century.[10]

As with many small towns in the area, though, Cary spent most of the late nineteenth and early twentieth century on the periphery of larger settlements such as Raleigh, Durham, and Chapel Hill. Cary might have been an out-of-the-way village at midcentury, but it could claim a long history of commitment to education. It became the site of the first state-supported public high school in North Carolina when the Wake County Board of Education purchased the Cary Academy, a private school founded in 1870, following a push by the state's General Assembly to expand access to high school education in 1907. The townspeople have long cherished this distinction, as it symbolized an association of Cary with education that only grew stronger in the age of the Triangle's growth.[11] Indeed, one of the main lanes in Cary's historic downtown is Academy Street.

For most of the early twentieth century, the town served as a sleepy bedroom community for the nearby growing capital city. "In 1945 nearly everyone who lived in Cary, native or newcomer, worked in Raleigh," local historian Tom Byrd observed in 1994.[12] The town had few industries of its own—the Taylor Biscuit Company, founded in 1947, remained Cary's largest for decades—and locals clung to its predominantly residential character even as the community grew rapidly in the late twentieth century.[13] Byrd described the newcomers of the early postwar years as white middle-class families, many with steady, if modestly compensated, jobs in state government. That profile would change in the years after RTP, as private-sector workers with more bounteous salaries moved to the town. But their status as white and professional changed little, as in-migration dramatically reduced the African-American proportion of the population in a community that had been home to a relatively prosperous black middle class.[14]

Indeed, in many ways Cary recapitulated the story of RTP—the notion of a blank space where there was nothing and then there was something. Certainly, the town had a long history of its own, but its demographic and economic transformation since the 1960s was extraordinary. Cary's population doubled in both the 1950s and 1960s and then doubled again between 1970 and 1975, while the town's taxable property increased by 3400 percent from 1945 to 1971 (from $800,000 to $28,000,000).[15] By the early 1990s, more than 80 percent of the city had been built in the preceding two decades.[16]

Looking back from the twenty-first century, it is easy to think of the contemporary city as springing from the skull of Athena, fully formed as the affluent, professional paradise that is celebrated in the pages of *Money* magazine and *U.S. News and World Report*.[17] In retelling the story, one risks striking some notes harder and muffling others, resetting the tune of Cary's older history to the tempo of the town it became. Certainly, nostalgic local histories such as Byrd's 1994 *Around and About Cary* and Sherry Monahan's 2011 *Images of Cary* have rendered the town's historic black community virtually invisible. Reading back from the present, it is easy to assume that Cary was always white and affluent, with only its notable Asian-American population (8 percent in 2010) standing out as a major shift. In fact, the town was remade by tens of thousands of new families who came from other parts of North Carolina, the United States, and the world—but the Cary to be started in powerful ways from a template of the Cary that was.

Cary was one of a variety of options for newcomers, including new, middle-class suburbs in North Raleigh and Durham. Recall that Bill Bell had worked out of an IBM office in Raleigh's North Hills as the RTP facility was being built and first considered Parkwood as a housing option when he was recruited by the company in 1968 (see chapter 3). Unfavorable—and often racially tinged—comparisons between Cary and Durham have been common over the years. Veteran Durham journalist Jim Wise remembered Cary as "almost all white" in the 1960s, in contrast to the "eyeful of slums" on display in Durham. ("One visitor's impression was fixed when he passed a front yard complete with a mule.")[18]

Even before the founding of RTP, Cary was proving an attractive destination for young families in the 1950s. For example, architect and artist Jerry Miller came to Cary in 1957, having grown up in the small town of Sanford (today about a forty-minute drive from Cary) and studied architecture at NC State.[19] "I thought, why not move out to Cary," Miller recalled. "There was nobody out here, and it would be a quiet little community where one could move in to a little quiet village." Like many who came to work in the Triangle from around North Carolina, Miller was not exactly an outsider and certainly no Yankee—even if Cary eventually came to bear the humorous nickname of "Containment Area for Relocated Yankees." (Years later, Miller looked back and noted that his "people" down in Sanford, North Carolina, often asked how he could "stand to live with all these Yankees in Cary? I say, man, they're some of the best people around.")[20]

Miller was the quintessential joiner in the growing Cary. He built a career drafting designs for businesses such as Cameron Brown real estate and grocery chain Winn Dixie as well as numerous homes—including his own—in the proliferating suburbs of Cary, Durham, and Raleigh during the 1960s and 1970s. Miller became deeply involved with the worthies of local government, the Chamber of Commerce, the Jaycees, and the Rotary Club. He helped start the town's Lazy Daze Arts and Crafts Festival and contributed his careful line drawings of local scenes and buildings to *Around and About Cary*, which he and neighbor Tom Byrd first published in the early 1970s.[21] In a sense, Miller helped to envision Cary on two levels: first in designing the suburban ranch homes where many families raised their children, and then by committing its built environment to the memory of local history.[22]

Cary's fortunes flourished alongside both Miller's and RTP's. The decision by Chemstrand to relocate to RTP in 1960 was a major turning point for the research park, but the migration of two hundred and five families from Decatur, Alabama, was even more important for Cary. Town representatives were eager to woo the company and its workforce. Bob Coleson, the Chemstrand manager who oversaw the move, recalled one Cary booster "sketching the Research Triangle on a blackboard, drawing a vertical line through the middle of it, and saying, 'If you move east of this line, you can drive to and from work each day with the sun to your back.' "[23] The manager was sold. He liked the idea of a quiet town with only two police officers ("one for night and one for day") and its proximity to both work in RTP and shopping in Raleigh. The opportunity to avoid having to drive into a glaring sun twice a day did not hurt either—Cary was even favored by the motion of the planets.[24]

Those arteries of commerce and commuting made a big difference for the Triangle and for Cary in particular. In a preinterstate era, Raleigh, Durham, Chapel Hill, and Cary were connected only by mostly poor roads. As historian Tyler Gray Greene has shown, North Carolina's local roads remained ragged well into the 1950s despite spirited efforts from the 1920s to the 1940s to improve major highways. After 1956, the Federal Aid Highway Act dramatically expanded spending on infrastructure and increasingly linked rural and metropolitan areas of North Carolina, beginning with the construction of Interstate 40 in western North Carolina in the late 1950s. Then followed the highway's extension toward Raleigh and through the heart of RTP in the 1970s and 1980s, and the construction since the 1990s of the loop highways of I-440 and I-540 around greater Raleigh. Roadways such as I-40—choked though they were with commuters traveling among Raleigh, Durham, and Cary in the early twenty-first century—still drew communities closer that had been difficult to traverse by often unpaved and inadequate roads in the early days of RTP (figure 5.1).[25]

The arrival of IBM in 1965 set off an even bigger wave of migration. Newcomers stressed the quality of schools and the town's small size, as well as its convenient location between Raleigh to the east and RTP to the northwest. Like many others moving from IBM's facility in Endicott, New York, Lee and Becky Swanson were confirmed northerners, but they chose Cary so they could live in a community that was not occupied entirely by IBM workers. The white couple wanted to melt into the local community, and they felt rapidly embraced by the people of Cary—rather unlike the black Bell family's initial experience in Parkwood (see chapter 3). "They even had a big snow for us that first winter, and I thought that was real considerate," Becky recalled.[26]

For a Southern town of its time, Cary was unusually zealous about controlling and guiding growth. Perhaps its small size allowed citizens and

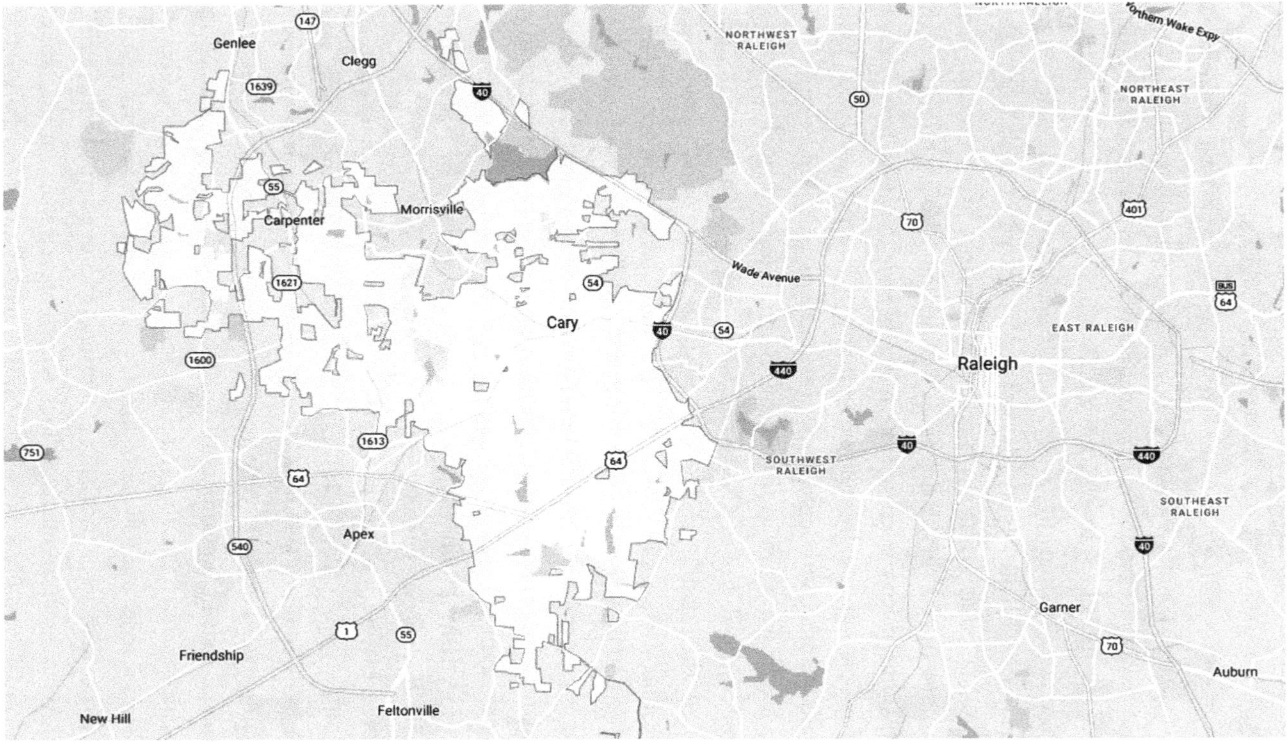

Figure 5.1 Map of greater Cary, North Carolina, ca. 2019. *Source*: Google Maps.

business and civic leaders to exert control over development right at the propitious moment when the city was about to take off in the early 1960s. The town set up a Planning and Zoning Board in 1949, which mandated building permits, street numbers on buildings, and zoning for particular uses.[27] A new zoning plan in 1963 expanded these regulations, segregating areas for traditional residences from mobile homes, and residential districts from business and industry. "Sometimes we made developers mad," zoning chief Frank M. Blackley (1957–63) boasted, "but we held their feet to the fire."[28] At one point, a man stood up during a hearing about the 1963 plan and claimed to be a private detective, threatening "to dig up dirt on each commissioner if they restricted the business zone," planner Jerry Turner said. The board eventually approved a modestly larger business zone than originally planned, although Turner insisted that veiled threats from the world's least discreet private investigator had nothing to do with it.[29]

Overall, the ability of Cary officials to steer development and bend it toward their vision of low-density, mostly residential growth was remarkable. Some locals scoffed at what they saw as intrusive, big-city style regulations, but younger families were glad that the rules forbade people coming to Cary to "build junk." In short, they wanted Cary to be a "planned, orderly town"; the 1963 plan projected an eventual population of fifty thousand.[30] Even that number appeared overly ambitious in the days before IBM. Surely the town would be swallowed by neighboring Raleigh before it ever got to that point, some thought.

During the years of the city's explosive growth, Cary maintained its serene, highly controlled image in other ways. In an expanding city that would soon come to accommodate more than one hundred and fifty thousand citizens in the twenty-first century, it was impossible to impose the kind of stylistic constraints that the Board of Design maintained in RTP, which dictated exacting standards for setbacks, footprints, and even architectural style. But it was not for lack of trying. Cary's careful zoning ensured that homes were not built in unusual styles or adorned with jarring colors. As architect and artist Miller, who designed many of the homes in Cary (including his own), said, Caryites would not abide the kind of loud colors that one found in other cities. "Cary is tough on construction," Miller said. "The zoning, and also the colors. Making sure that things have a color code, so you don't get all kind of red buildings and orange buildings. You can't do that here. . . . If you were to start a business here, you can't go out and get a big old neon sign. It's beige, neutral colors. . . . They control it to keep it from getting out of hand." Miller contrasted Cary with Durham, which he compared with Las Vegas. "Once things like that start happening, the town starts crumbling from the inside. . . . The quality of everything goes down. Over in Durham, you can go into some areas and you see all these different—they lost control over there. It looks tacky."[31]

It was a far cry from John Mellencamp's 1980s ode to American individualism and creativity—"Pink houses . . . ain't that America?"—but Cary managed to keep the aesthetic of a subdued, wholesome small American town that some homeowners craved through fastidious policing of the built environment. While Durham battled over ordinances regulating large signs and billboards, Cary largely avoided the louder or more unwelcome hallmarks of commercialism.[32] The convergence of demographic change and aesthetic choice is hard to miss: Durham became increasingly black up to the year 2000, and Cary's African-American population plummeted from 30 percent to about 8 percent by 2010, not so much because of displacement as due to the influx of white and Asian newcomers.

Indeed, Cary set itself apart in ways that went beyond the merely aesthetic—and which were potentially more consequential. Good schools had been central to the town's appeal for RTP since the park began to reshape the metropolitan landscape in the 1960s, and Cary was the site of the first school to integrate in Wake County.[33] In 1963, Gwendolyn Inez Matthews and five other young black women entered the doors of Cary Senior High School, enduring howls and taunts from white protesters.[34] (A black male student would not be granted entry until the following year.) "Gwen was strong," said her father, Alton Matthews Sr., who had lobbied for her to attend a formerly all-white school under the county's "freedom of choice" plan. "I felt she could take the smears and the insults, and I believed in the community too much to believe that anything would happen to her."[35] Still, a frightened Gwen did not want to return after one day at Cary High. Her parents urged fortitude and suggested that things would get better. In a sense, they were right. Within a week and a half, the protests died off; within a year, some white students began to speak to her;

and the young Matthews did well at the school—although she still sensed that teachers ignored her in class, assuming some kind of deficiency or lack of preparation on her part.[36]

Both Cary and Wake County fumbled through the unfolding path of desegregation in the 1960s, especially as new civil rights legislation and court rulings empowered the federal government to scrutinize local desegregation plans and push for more than token integration. To satisfy the demands of the Department of Health, Education, and Welfare (HEW), local authorities converted the previously black West Cary High into a mixed ninth-grade-only school; children in the higher grades attended a racially diverse Cary High, with "764 whites and 112 blacks for 12.8 percent integration" in 1967. That plan was soon challenged by white Cary parents, who called the West Cary move an illegal school merger. The case went to the North Carolina Supreme Court, but the parents did not prevail.[37] Ferd Davis, who would eventually become chair of the Wake Board of Education, tried to reason with them. "Essentially, 'Mr. Davis, please don't make me send my children to school with those Negroes,'" Davis recalled. "If they can't live with 10.9 percent integration in junior high school, then they can't live with anything."[38] But Davis also saw hope in the relatively peaceful and moderate transition to integrated schools in Cary and Wake County in general:

> It had been my observation that people in areas that were changing rapidly, like Cary, would accept something new more readily than people in an established area. I felt that if we could get some successful examples of integration in Cary, people in places like Wake Forest and Zebulon would see that the world was not coming to an end and would accept integration, too.[39]

Then came the question of merger, which bedeviled residents of both Wake and Durham. As Triangle residents wrestled with the dilemma of desegregation and potentially merging city and county schools during the 1970s, Cary citizens were among the most vociferous in opposing the possibility of combining the schools of Raleigh with those of suburban

Wake County. To be sure, opposition existed on a number of fronts—from affluent white suburbanites in Raleigh and Cary to African Americans in urban communities who feared losing control of their schools under a consolidated county system. Business and civic leaders feared that spiraling racial polarization would cripple city schools in Raleigh and damage the area's image, as the most privileged families moved to suburban Wake County and the city became increasingly marginalized.[40]

In fact, voters throughout Wake County rejected the merger in 1972, with Raleigh voters coming out against the plan along with suburbanites. But Caryites opposed the measure by a truly lopsided margin—5,098 against and only 866 for—citing concerns about a too-large bureaucracy and the loss of local control that communities enjoyed under the decentralized county system.[41] It was a curious irony, given that earlier in the twentieth century, rural and county school systems had looked with envy on wealthier, better-funded urban systems in North Carolina. As whites moved to the suburbs, the civil rights movement made historic gains, and African Americans increasingly moved to cities, the balance of power between suburbs and cities shifted, and consolidation with urban school systems suddenly looked less appetizing for white suburbanites. The situation tracked the same trajectory that occurred in Parkwood, as those in the affluent suburb seriously considered seeking annexation by the City of Durham to get better city services in the 1960s—but passionately rejected the idea by the 1990s, when a black-majority city successfully moved to absorb the community over virulent opposition.

In any case, local leaders pushed forward with a merger plan despite popular opposition, as the state legislature passed a bill in 1975 that allowed the school systems to merge with only the consent of the relevant local boards—in this case, Raleigh and Wake County. Thus Wake schools consolidated over the opposition of voters. The result was a county school system that boasted better performance and higher degrees of integration, more akin to Charlotte-Mecklenburg's consolidated system than the stark polarization that marked school systems in metro areas such as Durham and Atlanta.[42]

As Cary citizens fumed over the school merger, civic leaders eschewed industrial development. The town had few significant local businesses at the dawn of the RTP era. An entomologist at NC State had started Maxwell Insecticide in 1946; its small staff of ten developed agricultural chemicals into the 1960s, but the company later folded. At the same time, locals deplored the Cary Drum and Barrel Company, founded in 1950 to clean barrels shipped in from Philadelphia, because the firm let toxic chemicals run off into a ditch in town. Few grieved when the company eventually went out of business. Another firm, Harrisburg, PA-based AMP, made components for cars and planes on Cary's Madison Avenue from 1960 to 1987. But as a conventional manufacturing facility in the town, it was more the exception than the rule.[43]

Indeed, as light manufacturing spread throughout rural North Carolina in the 1970s and 1980s—and communities bid desperately for any new jobs and investment—the largely affluent and educated residents of Cary did not go chasing smokestacks. Like RTP, the booming town would be a nonindustrial, even anti-industrial space. "Most citizens were new," Byrd recalled, "and they had moved here because of Cary's residential qualities. One way to protect those qualities, they felt, was to keep out the noise, grime, and stench of industry." In fact, state development officials did not even bother to bring potential employers there because, according to Councilman Bob Hinshaw, "they'd been told we didn't want industry."[44]

However, town leaders realized that residents could be in a pinch by the late 1970s, as overdependence on housing as a source of revenue could lead to higher taxes. Although many new Caryites had come from Northern communities where property taxes were far higher, few were willing to give up the light tax burden they enjoyed in Cary.[45] The Chamber of Commerce soon took the lead, appointing Russell Buxton III, a former city manager of Rocky Mount in eastern North Carolina and the head of a local suburban developer, to lead a committee that would frame a new economic agenda for Cary. "The Chamber of Commerce is not going to go out and solicit a smoke-belching, noisy industry. . . . We are looking for clean industries that will provide jobs . . . that are highly capitalized, and are relatively low users of water and sewer services," Buxton promised residents in 1977.[46]

By the 1980s, Cary had managed to attract new employers by more actively recruiting businesses and relaxing some of its zoning regulations, including expanding access for industry beyond the town's old railroad corridor. Employers such as American Airlines' Reservation Center and Oxford University Press came to Cary, although they still hewed closely to the town's preference for "clean" industry. In the case of OUP, the world-renowned press had not decided to pull up stakes and move its entire operation to a suburb of Raleigh. Its core functions of editing, design, and management would remain in New York and London, but Cary would get a shipping and distribution center, recapitulating a pattern of outside firms retaining control and capital outside the South but outsourcing lower-skilled and ancillary activities to the region (see the discussion about IBM in chapter 2).[47] Still, OUP's distribution center might not have been a high-tech business requiring the skills of PhD scientists, but it was sufficiently clean and quiet to accommodate the Cary sensibility. The town also built its own "campus-like" settings for business, such as MacGregor Park and Regency Park, which included manufacturing, while allowing firms such as IBM to move workers from RTP to facilities in nearby Cary.[48]

In short, Cary was different from many small communities in the South, which would have been happy to get a pants factory, as Atlanta editor Ralph McGill put it in 1964.[49] Similar to the tightly controlled and antiseptic Research Triangle Park, where many residents worked, the town wished to re-create the bucolic and orderly aesthetic of the park in a residential setting. Nothing succeeds like success, as the saying goes, and Cary compounded success after success as it won a reputation for livability and quality of life. "While some investors groused about 'the high cost of doing business in Cary,'" given the town's exacting standards for zoning and aesthetics, Tom Byrd noted, "the petitions for annexation kept coming."[50]

Indeed, Cary's carefully crafted reputation might have been troubled by questions of desegregation and economic development in the 1970s, but its image was increasingly defined by the affluent workforce that resided there and the high-tech giant SAS Institute, which made its home in the town. SAS and Cary are hardly synonymous, but the firm became the town's foremost corporate tenant following humble beginnings in the 1970s. The company captured the reflection of both RTP and Cary in its own strange mirror: the knowledge economy as fortress, a mini-society unto itself.

SAS: QUALITY OF LIFE IN THE LIFE OF THE MIND

If Cary was among America's best places to live, SAS was indisputably among the best places to work. The company, which moved to Cary in 1980, was the quintessential university spin-off—a species that was relatively less common in the Triangle than, say, in Silicon Valley or Massachusetts's Route 128, where scientists and engineers founded major firms such as Hewlett-Packard and Biogen. SAS might have been the "Stepford software company," as *Forbes* put it in 1996—in other words, possibly too perfect. The company boasted a reputation for great perks, a relaxed work environment, and extreme employee loyalty. Founded by several graduate students from North Carolina State University in the 1970s, the company became the world's largest and most influential privately held software firm by the dawn of the twenty-first century. It provided statistical and data analytics tools prized by most major firms on the Forbes 500 and government agencies, including the Census Bureau and the Department of Agriculture. Devotees of SAS flocked to conventions and conferences in a manner akin to Deadheads following Jerry Garcia.[51]

Amazingly, SAS President and founder Jim Goodnight, a former NC State researcher, accomplished this feat without ever going public, wooing investors, or taking on debt, except for a mortgage to buy the first building in its fabled Cary campus in the early 1980s. Goodnight started the company with a handful of friends and collaborators from the Triangle's academic community, but he ended up exercising a strong and single-minded hold over the company he built after his original partners had cashed in or withdrawn their participation.[52]

In his early days, Goodnight worked for a time at General Electric as part of the space program in Florida. Having a security clearance was exciting, and the budding scientist dreamed of someday making $10,000 a year. However, he chafed at the restrictive culture of the company. "You could be questioned about being five minutes later arriving in the morning," Goodnight recalled. "I resented that, since I often came back at night to work. They didn't treat programming like a creative activity."[53] In his career, then, we see a glimmer of the yearnings that later gave rise to the flexible work culture of the creative class, who might be unencumbered by the constraints of traditional factory, office, or retail workers but who also put in time around the clock.

Goodnight had a faculty appointment at NC State, but that was essentially dependent on government funds, and his future was uncertain. The program that he and his coworkers had developed to analyze data for agricultural clients was growingly increasingly popular in the 1970s, sought after not only by agricultural firms but by pharmaceutical companies hoping it could help them make sense of massive amounts of data from clinical trials. "By 1976 we had 100 customers and the university didn't know what to do with us—they just weren't set up to run a commercial enterprise," Goodnight told the press in 1997. "So four of us left the university and founded SAS Institute."[54]

As demand rose for their product, Goodnight and his compatriots considered severing ties with the university and setting out on their own to provide services for businesses. The university agreed to turn over all copyrights in the work in exchange for a guarantee of continued updates and services—in part, perhaps, because it did not know what it was losing in the process. Goodnight and his partners already had a well-established group of clients, thanks to their pro bono work through the university, and SAS soon became one of the few highly successful start-up firms to achieve remarkable success with virtually no debt or venture capital. SAS was able to grow its business rapidly once it became a private firm, building on the crucial base that contacts at the universities provided but without the close scrutiny of academic administration.

Where SAS would live was another question. The pivotal moment in the company's history came when partner Jane Helwig, a documentation specialist, spotted a prime location for the firm to relocate. "I have found a really neat place," she told Goodnight and the partners. "It's got a lake behind it and everything." Goodnight concurred, agreeing that getting out of Raleigh and moving to a serene, semirural or suburban area would be good for the company. "We started building in, I guess, early '79 or late '78—one or the other, probably late '78," Goodnight recalled. "We actually moved in in January of 1980. Within about a year, we built this huge building and it would house over fifty people."[55]

Thus was the beginning of the story of SAS in Cary. The company took a novel tack in the 1980s, sponsoring child care for employees in part because Helwig wanted children and the company decided to accommodate her. ("The childcare was my idea," Goodnight said. "Jane Helwig had announced that she was going to have yet another baby. She seemed to love to have babies. She liked to cuddle them, or something like that.")[56] SAS also offered profit-sharing for employees, which Goodnight saw as a desirable alternative to paying them more and having their income taxed by the government. The executive knew that the question of benefits was a major consideration for academics, who were abandoning the comfort and security of academic employment to take a risk in the private sector. Reflecting years later, Goodnight explained that the company turned to profit sharing when it began to consider retirement plan options for employees. "We looked at the available options and decided to set up a profit sharing program. . . . I'd rather give it to the employees than give it to the government," Goodnight said, nodding to his own libertarian philosophy. "That's certainly been one of the guiding—in back of my mind—concepts. I don't want to make a huge profit so I can send it to Washington."[57]

As it grew in Cary, SAS became a creative company par excellence, employing an unusually high percentage of scientists as part of its workforce. Even the highest-tech firm typically employed a greater share of managers, clerical workers, and support staff than scientists and engineers, but in 1992, roughly half of SAS's employees were researchers.[58] Not only did the company make a product that was fundamentally intellectual property—a software package, immaterial except for the box and user manuals that came with it—but the product itself was entirely about manipulating information: crunching numbers, processing data, "drilling down" patterns and trends.[59] Even among tech firms, SAS dedicated a remarkable amount of resources to research and development: 31 percent of revenue in 1995, amounting to $174 million.[60]

As with RTP, the purely private space of SAS's campus was modeled on the university landscape from which Goodnight and his partners hailed. A 1983 job ad touted its "attractive, 100-acre lakeside campus in Cary, North Carolina—adjacent to the prestigious Research Triangle Park"

Figure 5.2 SAS employees frolic with frisbees in a 1996 profile of the company. *Source*: Will and Deni McIntyre.

that "provides a people-oriented atmosphere, conducive to personal productivity and inventiveness."[61] Reporters were obliging in describing the company's rapidly growing Cary headquarters as "campus-like."[62] In a 1996 *Forbes* article, Randall Lane mused that "With its leafy grounds and erudite name, it's easy to mistake SAS headquarters for a university campus." Next to the profile of the company, readers saw a photo of shirtless white men playing sports on the lawn outside company headquarters, barely distinguishable from college boys frolicking on the quad (figure 5.2).[63] As one newspaper put it in a 1989 about places to get "the best first jobs," SAS gave the impression more of "a well-funded research foundation than a commercial software house." The profile noted that the company's headquarters were "nestled among . . . lakes and trails" and "commonly referred to as 'the campus.'"[64]

Since the founding of RTP in the 1950s and the postwar transition from urban research laboratories to the suburban research campus (which historian Louise Mozingo beautifully charted in her book *Pastoral Capitalism*), business leaders increasingly viewed a work environment that resembled a college campus as the ideal way to foster innovation and coax the best work out of knowledge workers.[65] It is not surprising, then, that an institution devoted to the production and dissemination of knowledge—the college or, more particularly, the research university—would serve as the model for new economy landscapes in the private sector, including RTP, SAS, and, later, Google.

But the pastoral landscape itself was not enough to encourage quality intellectual labor, as SAS was among a number of firms to go beyond pursuing a particular architectural aesthetic to "pamper" (in *Forbes*'s term) the knowledge worker in a variety of new ways. A *Wall Street Journal* piece depicted SAS as "the workplace as clubhouse," saying the company "encourages innovation through an egalitarian culture, flexible schedules, few meetings, interdisciplinary project teams and generous perks intended to eliminate hassles. The perks include a private office for anyone assigned to a desk and an on-site health-care center, preschool, gym and hair salon."[66] In this regard, SAS Institute was almost a tiny city unto itself, with all the amenities—short of housing, which Goodnight and company later invested in off campus—that a town might offer.

Indeed, SAS was part of a movement among managers during the 1990s and early 2000s to rethink the workplace for highly educated, creative workers. Such considerations evidently did not matter at a chicken-processing plant or Wal-Mart, where supposedly low-skilled, interchangeable hands could do manual labor or routine interaction with customers without the coddling of generous corporate attention. The high end of the labor market was different. In 2004, a business columnist in the Philippines, Karen V. de Asis, urged companies to put "people first," "create an employee-first culture," "respect talent and expertise; and encourage employee success" in order to have a "fun and spirited" brand. SAS, de Asis said, was a fine example. After all, "it was featured as a Best Place to Work For in the Oprah Winfrey show."[67] The *New York Times* described SAS as "something of a workers' paradise," unlike other errant tech companies that overworked their people and stifled creativity. Everyone from the CEO down, allegedly, worked "just 35 hours a week," as "the company switchboard shuts down at 5 P.M., and the main gate is shut an hour later."[68] SAS could boast in 1999 that *Fortune* magazine ranked it number three on its annual list of best places to work. "There are some mighty good reasons for that, such as our amazing assortment of benefits, family-friendly business philosophy and an environment that encourages creativity and a balanced lifestyle," a job ad touted. "(We also happen to be one of America's largest and most successful software companies.)"[69]

Goodnight believed that such policies materially benefited the company in the long run. For one thing, the company could have saved as much $70 million each year by not having to spend time and energy hiring and training new workers to replace those who left.[70] Similar to the welfare capitalism of the 1920s—which offered employees recreational and other benefits in lieu of the siren song of unionization—Goodnight argued that proworker policies were simply "very good business sense." "The idea [is] that if we did not retain as many employees as we do, that we would have to have loss of productivity, loss of function, while a person is out or after a person has left," he said in 1999. "We would have to spend money training people, hiring people. Then that person, once they're on board, you're paying them for the first six months, and you're not getting any value out of them."[71] Giving employees free food, medical care, and flexible hours also was a form of compensation that Uncle Sam could not take a bite out of, as Goodnight readily admitted.[72] Above all, working at SAS meant accepting what *Forbes* called "The Goodnight tradeoff": "subpar wages for family-friendly perks and working conditions. With less than 4 percent employee turnover, few are complaining."[73]

Then again, generous benefits might have been more about managing the worker and getting the most out of him or her than fighting attrition. "I like happy people," Goodnight told the *Wall Street Journal* in 1998.[74] Smart people do more smart stuff when they are happy, as the theory goes. Knowledge workers could "concentrate on the work they're doing," he told reporters, if they did not have to worry about child care, lunch, or medical problems—or the consequences of leaving the office to take care of a sick child.[75]

A pioneer in the burgeoning field of "employee engagement"—which sought to build trust, camaraderie, and a feeling of belonging among white-collar employees—the company sponsored clubs and other worker activities, such as Toastmasters.[76] (Clubs got as much as $3,000 a year to fund their activities.) John Shafeei, an Iranian-born software developer, said he stayed at the company for over a decade because he "improved his speaking skills with the Toastmasters club, saved time by going to the company's on-site medical clinic and built up his leadership skills with an immigrant club he helped form." "It's helped me to create that great connection with other employees," Shafeei told the *Wall Street Journal* in 2008. "We're not competitors, but friends."[77]

Management guru Peter Drucker influentially made the same point in the late 1990s. Companies needed to satisfy not only shareholders but also

> the owners of the human capital that gives the organization its wealth-producing power, that is, satisfying the knowledge workers. For increasingly the ability of organizations—and not only of businesses—to survive will come to depend on their "comparative advantage" in making the knowledge worker productive. And the ability to attract and hold the best of the knowledge workers is the first and most fundamental precondition.[78]

But workplace conditions were about more than keeping people happy in a generic sense. Goodnight routinely stressed that SAS's policies were intended to create an environment that stimulated creativity. "Passion is contagious," he told the nonprofit Academy of Achievement in 1997. "Our employees as [sic] just as fervent about finding ways to help our customers as I am . . . just as committed."[79]

Art and technology went hand in hand when it came to spreading passion. As part of a series titled "Workspaces," the *Wall Street Journal*'s Nancy Holt marveled at not just the exotic rock collection that lined Goodnight's office but also the extent to which the company mobilized art and color to stimulate employees. "The software giant, which specializes in statistical analysis, even retains two artists in residence," Holt noted. "A company-financed trip to southern France inspired the three village scenes in his office. Colors are coordinated with a hand-painted clock. It's a setting designed to motivate employees, with perks such as an on-site health-care center, Montessori preschool, gym and hair salon."[80] *60 Minutes* reported on SAS for an adoring 2002 segment called "The Royal Treatment." Presenter Morley Safer noted how different the company was from others, where corrupt executives at, say, WorldCom or Enron "treated their publicly held companies as private piggy banks" while laying off workers and cutting benefits. SAS, Safer said, treated employees "like royalty." "If there is a heaven on Earth on the job," the veteran reporter said, "it is here: a design for living and working the good life."[81] (One wonders what it was like for Safer working at *60 Minutes*.)

Corporations increasingly dwelled on themes of creativity and innovation in managing their white-collar, high-tech workers, and learning how to foster these values became par for the course in the 1990s and early 2000s. Urban theorist Richard Florida captured the corporate imagination in 2002 with his *Rise of the Creative Class*, which lumped everyone from the bohemian barista in an electro-funk band to the advertising executive in a single group known as the "creative class"; the management philosophy of Goodnight and SAS in many ways anticipated Florida's preoccupation with creativity. Florida noted at the time that "managers typically tap only a small portion of workers' creative capabilities." To succeed, firms would need to "look more like an artist colony or inventor's laboratory than the office of today."[82] With its artists and art, SAS resembled the "artist colony" or "inventor's laboratory" or university campus that Florida might have imagined as the native home of the creative class. Hence, SAS's lavish fringe benefits and congenial work culture were necessary for capitalists like Goodnight to get the most out of their creative, high-tech knowledge workers.

But the SAS dream arguably came at a cost. "Depending on who you talk to, the world's largest closely held software company is either a workplace utopia or a bastion of smothering paternalism," journalist Timothy Schellhardt reported in 1998. Goodnight lived on the grounds of SAS's two-hundred-acre compound, residing in "a 7,500-square-foot colonial"—rather like a plantation or mill owner, where he could keep a close eye on his enterprise.[83] Indeed, local journalist Christina Dyrness saw the parallel all too clearly. "With a self-contained campus, little turnover and steady profits, SAS Institute is a high-tech, modern version of the old textile mill," she wrote. "Many have chafed at the idea, but there's no denying that James Goodnight, SAS founder, chairman and two-thirds owner, has made an indelible impression on Cary and the Triangle."[84] But as *Forbes* pointed out, "If SAS resembles a giant plantation, the serfs are certainly not complaining."[85]

Perhaps the word *slave* stuck too much in the craw of the *Forbes* journalist who wrote the mostly adoring piece, or maybe describing software engineers who made over $100,000 a year as "slaves" was simply too much. It would be better to call them high-tech serfs. In fact, in the twenty-first century, when tech giants such as Google and Facebook embarked on ambitious plans to create corporate-owned housing for their workers in the housing-crunched Bay Area, the SAS model looked prescient. As social critic Matt Christman put it in 2018, "The company town is back, baby!"[86]

In any case, the impression of old-school paternalism was inescapable to many journalists. They saw it not only in Goodnight's benevolent rule and tight control of the company and workplace but also in the magnate's growing influence outside the gates of his knowledge workers' paradise. He was, in fact, the city's largest landowner by 1998, and not just because of the SAS campus. Goodnight and his partners had gotten into developing residential and commercial real estate. "If employees buy a home in one of his subdivisions, they get 10 percent discounts on the land," Timothy Schellhardt reported in the *Wall Street Journal*. "They also get discounts on memberships at the country club he owns. And they are eligible for cheap fares on Midway Airlines, the region's principal carrier, in which he purchased a controlling interest last year." They even received benefits on tuition for the private school, Cary Academy, that Goodnight built a short walk down Research Road from SAS. (Despite the executive's greatest efforts, though, the *Journal* noted in 1998 that his son "refuses to attend the academy.)"[87]

Even these efforts contributed to the legend of SAS. Goodnight spent $15 million to start Cary Academy. The policy might seem "freakish," the company's vice-president for human resources conceded in 1999, but other companies had begun to study their methods.[88] As firms in the tech sector began to think about employee engagement and ways to combat burnout, Goodnight's generous version of corporate paternalism looked like a model worth examining. SAS certainly did not seem to resemble the "white collar sweatshops" that forced many white-collar tech "microserfs" into unceasing toil in the 1990s.[89]

If SAS did not quite reach the heights of new economy zaniness that came to define the famously quirky work environment of companies such as Google, it did bring a certain attitude of relaxed nerdiness to the office. "We certainly have some real individuals," Human Resources Director David Russo told reporters in 1992, pointing to the company's loose rules for work attire.[90] As the *60 Minutes* episode mused, an employee named Mark in t-shirt, khaki shorts, and sandals "adheres strictly to the SAS dress code—which is no code."[91] Mark also enjoyed a "flexible work schedule" that allowed him to work alongside his Elvis Costello LPs and complete only a 35-hour work week.[92] It might have been "pampering" to Morley Safer, but Goodnight responded quizzically: "What's wrong with treating your people good," after all?

Then again, he and his partners were able to follow their unique approach to management by keeping the company private and not having to answer to shareholders. Journalist Emery Dalesio noted that despite the fact that SAS flirted with an IPO in the early 2000s, the leaders vowed not to change the company's workplace culture. After all, the headquarters featured "a foam statuette of the patron saint of SAS programmers, Yoda from 'Star Wars.'"[93] The company, then, borrowed not just the spatial aesthetic of the college campus but also a bit of the autonomous and less regimented work culture of those original knowledge workers: academics. Here one also thinks of the idiosyncratic, vaguely bohemian scientists from the 1983 movie *Brainstorm*, which was filmed in RTP (see chapter 4).

The relaxed, family-friendly ethos of SAS seemed an outlier in more ways than one. It was not clear that this easygoing work culture prevailed outside the Cary headquarters. For instance, a *New York Times* profile of an SAS employee in New York, Michael Forhez, mentioned that he worked eleven-hour days—so much that he could not afford the time to cart a picnic basket around Manhattan all day for a romantic outing with his girlfriend in Bryant Park. Forhez was a business developer at SAS and wanted to meet a young woman at the HBO Summer Film Festival. However, he "had not really considered the logistics of an urban picnic." "Only later did he realize he would need to buy and fill a basket, keep its contents cool and lug it to and from his Upper West Side apartment," despite starting early and working late to make the grade at SAS.[94]

Forhez's story might be anecdotal at best, but it implies that the incomparable benefits enjoyed by people at the company's Cary headquarters were not necessarily shared by its raft of employees around the globe. As with any major American corporation, it might tell a story about its employees and their quality of life at home while outsourcing production or services to workers in another part of the world—even if the center was small-town, suburban Cary and the benighted fringe was New York City.

Whatever Goodnight's impact on Cary as an entrepreneur, business leader, and would-be paternalist, his influence is indisputable. Even as resolute a critic as local activist, teacher, and author Ella Arrington Williams-Vinson had nothing but good things to say about Goodnight in her 2001 local history, *Both Sides of the Tracks II*. "Cary is proud to recognize Jim Goodnight as its most famous citizen," Williams-Vinson wrote. "SAS is considered by many a place for every worker's dream. Thanks to Jim Goodnight for his unselfish concern for humankind, for education, technology, and for job opportunities for many. Jim Goodnight has put Cary on the world map."[95] For his part, artist Jerry Miller also heaped praise on SAS. "That guy Jim Goodnight has done more for Cary than anyone else. He started a business, he's got thousands of people in Cary working for him. The area he's built is gorgeous. That is a *plus* for Cary. There's nothing wrong with it. And one time everybody got all upset with [former mayor] Koka Booth because he worked for SAS, they said he would let SAS do whatever they want. I don't care if he did or not. Whatever they did was good! Whatever they did for Cary was a plus, . . . Everything he's got is self-contained, I tell you that now. They have their own doctors, nurses, daycare centers, schools."[96]

In short, thanks to Cary's city fathers and the ambition of Jim Goodnight, the almost perfect town came full circle. RTP created the template for a high-tech economy and brought thousands of affluent, educated, mostly (if not entirely) white families to a new suburban enclave of upper-middle-class privilege. SAS reproduced the image of an all-white, serene, green, postindustrial landscape that the research park and Cary had already approximated. Here was the best place to work, the best place to live, the safest city in America, the greatest concentration of PhDs—all the superlatives that proved the postindustrial or high-tech economy was a success, the wave of the future, crashing right into the heart of North Carolina with the softest sound.

THE GOOD, BORING LIFE

For some, SAS and Cary epitomized the good life in a new, knowledge-intensive postindustrial capitalism. As in highly educated suburban communities around cities such as Boston, Philadelphia, Denver, and San Francisco, a new class of knowledge workers began to assert their primacy in the political economy of the contemporary United States. Scholars such as Lily Geismer and Rachel Guberman have shown how a socially liberal, affluent class of voters in metropolitan suburbs helped give rise to a new constituency within the Democratic Party of the late twentieth century. These were the "suburban liberals" (in Geismer's term) who eschewed racism and embraced a mildly meritocratic and technocratic view of politics, albeit without a strong vision of redistributive social justice.[97]

Those suburban liberals were the voters of Cary, as well as Parkwood and other white-collar enclaves of the Triangle—not necessarily conservative, but also not particularly liberal. The once-solidly Democratic Cary of old gave way to a more competitive two-party system as thousands moved to the city from the 1960s to the early 2000s. Cary voters split their tickets to support Republicans such as George H. W. Bush and Jesse Helms at the national level but Democrats at the state and local level, consistently voting with the national majority in presidential elections; the town registered majorities for Presidents Bill Clinton, George W. Bush, and Barack Obama.[98] The knowledge workers of Cary, SAS, and RTP were, in many ways, the harbingers of politics to come.

In terms of economic development, SAS represented an ironic sort of cul de sac. As one of the Triangle's biggest firms, it represented the area's innovative culture at its best: leveraging academic talent to create a genuinely new company that produced a palpably irresistible product. Alongside Quintiles—which became one of the world's largest contract research companies on the outskirts of RTP, after being founded by UNC biostatistics professor Dennis Gillings in 1982—and open-source software company Red Hat, SAS stood out more as the exception than as the rule.[99] After all, RTP had been dominated by large corporate employers recruited from outside, despite the ambition of Romeo Guest, Luther Hodges, and others to "hatch" indigenous industries rather than depend on outside investment.[100]

But just as some academics were reluctant to abandon the security of tenure at a university, SAS employees were conspicuously absent in terms of spawning the new firms that social scientists study as evidence of innovation and start-up culture. Maryann Feldman and Nichola Lowe determined in 2015 that SAS, despite being a spin-off itself, "has not resulted in many next generation start-ups."[101] The company's remarkably low level of turnover was the clearest symptom of "the problem," such as it was. By providing a desirable and flexible work environment, SAS retained talent and investment in hiring and training at the larger cost of dampening the creativity of employees who might innovate after they are laid off or leave of their own accord.[102]

Any tally of the plaudits for Cary and SAS is necessarily partial and incomplete. In 1985, *Working Mothers* magazine praised SAS early on for its work conditions; and *60 Minutes* lauded the company in the wake of the dotcom bust and revelations of corporate chicanery at Enron and Worldcom in the early twenty-first century. Cary ranked number five on *Money* magazine's best places to live in 2006; *Forbes* called it, along with Raleigh, the country's second biggest "brain magnet" in 2011. For his part, Jerry Miller insisted that Cary is "the greatest town in the world."[103]

The town's pristine lawns, the tasteful and restrained aesthetic of homes and businesses, the verdant lanes of shopping centers and suburbs—it all added up to an ideal place for an educated, affluent professional to raise a family. But there is another lens to consider. One man's suburban paradise is another's antiseptic nowhere. "Cary, NC is boring," one online commenter warned a Floridian considering relocating there in 2006. "Really boring."[104]

Ben Drasin, a computer programmer who lived in Cary during the 1990s, echoed this assessment. "Boring! All housing and strip malls," Drasin, a native Californian, said of his new home:

> I made a few friends at the Triangle Vegetarian Society but other than that it was all work and no play. My co-workers . . . were pretty much all very committed Christians who got married and had kids in their early 20s so we had little in common outside of work.

Compared with California, he found the available cultural, culinary, and recreational opportunities severely wanting.[105]

Durham might have had "grit," as reporter Jim Wise put it, but picturesque Cary was sanded smooth. The agricultural scientist Sarah Taber mirrored Drasin's observation about the placid, insular nature of the area's culture. "It's challenging to get to know people in the Triangle as they seem pretty happy with their existing social circle, even in tech," Taber said in 2018. "Whereas in Charlotte it's a lot easier to get introductions. . . . I jokingly tell people I like Charlotte better because at least they're greedy enough to learn your name."[106]

If RTP was, as geographers David Havlick and Scott Kirsch aptly put it, a "production utopia,"[107] then Cary was its residential equivalent: clean, highly ordered, largely devoid of signs of old-school industry. *Utopia*, though, comes from the Greek meaning "no place." Coining the term in 1516, Sir Thomas More might have intended it to signify a place that does not—indeed, could not—exist. But in Cary, the term works on two levels—both as a place that is too good to be true, and as a place that lacks a sense of place.

Geographer Edward Relph wrote movingly about this concept in his 1976 classic, *Place and Placelessness*.[108] Although it is debatable whether any place can be truly "placeless," Cary was very much part of a larger place—the Research Triangle—whose evolution paralleled and mirrored the town's own development from the 1960s on. And that place, as deliberately contrived and designed as were Cary's tony subdivisions, in many ways fulfilled RTP's original mission of attracting jobs, educated workers, and prestige by the early twenty-first century. In the age of gentrification, the

Triangle would continue to win favorable press coverage, especially as its universities, cultural institutions, and tech companies spawned a hip local scene in the 1990s and 2000s. Journalists and academics might have held up Durham or Raleigh as a model of the new creative class city—an Austin or Portland by way of Mayberry—but Cary was hardly anyone's idea of a hip destination, even if it housed many creative workers and their families.[109] The new metropolitan landscape of the knowledge economy, even in its moment of success, continued to struggle with problems such as segregation, sprawl, and inequality, as the experience of the Triangle in the early twenty-first century makes clear.

Interlude

The Islamic School in Parkwood

The Triangle Bridge Club. A falafel place called Mediterranean Grill and Grocery. A convenience store and the Al-Huda Academy. To their left, baseball fields and to their right, the modest office of the Parkwood Homeowners Association. A church stands across the narrow bend of Revere Road, and the Parkwood Elementary School is a few steps away. The model community designed for the scientists and engineers is not the same place it was when, in the 1960s, it was an award-winning all-white suburb.

Nazeeh Z. Abdul-Hakeem helped bring a *masjid* and Islamic academy to Parkwood's small and declining shopping center in the early 2010s. Abdul-Hakeem, a native of Goldsboro in eastern North Carolina, had studied geography at Durham's North Carolina Central University and, later, urban planning at UNC-Chapel Hill, before converting to Islam in 1979.[1] He enjoyed a fruitful career as a planner with the City of Durham in the years that followed, but he also played a central role in transforming what began as a small prayer group at Duke University into a robust Muslim community in Durham, centered on the *masjid* Jamaat Ibad Ar-Rahman. The community had grown and flourished among African Americans in greater Durham, as well as the many newcomers from Africa, Asia, and elsewhere who practiced Islam and had relocated to work in the Triangle.[2]

Yet growth brought challenges for Abdul-Hakeem's community, changes that captured in miniature the broader demographic shifts of the metropolitan Triangle since the 1970s. Muslims from different ethnic and national backgrounds took on a greater presence within the Jamaat community, creating tensions with an older base of support that was predominantly African American. Meanwhile, moving into Parkwood presented its own potential for conflict; Jamaat's leaders sought to develop a second location there (the original *masjid* being in Durham's Hillside Park), and the neighborhood had its own complicated history with racial prejudice. Parkwood was already home to a number of Muslim residents, largely of Pakistani origin, but some locals feared that Jamaat's purchase of the shopping center would end the ability of the Christian church across the street to use its lot for parking or as a beginning and ending point for the neighborhood's annual Christmas parade. Muslim leaders provided assurances that such activities would not be prohibited in the future, though anxieties persisted on both sides.[3]

Parkwood's journey paralleled the rise of a new multiethnic suburbia throughout the United States in the late twentieth and early twenty-first centuries, as the collapse of formal segregation and a steady of influx of new Americans reshaped not only cities but, increasingly, their suburbs as well. But the Triangle's progress toward racial integration—including neighborhood desegregation, city-county school consolidation, and the rise of a new generation of black elected leaders since the 1960s—could not always mask the continuing antipathy between its cities and suburbs or the desire among some to police boundaries of identity and privilege.

The trajectory of Parkwood was uniquely symbolic, given the neighborhood's history with the City of Durham. When Durham sought to annex the community in the 1990s, residents waged a vociferous and determined campaign of opposition. Becoming part of the city meant higher taxes and poorer services, they argued, and the motives of Durham's leaders were questionable. ("This is just another ploy for the city to raise their tax base to get a better bond rating," resident and developer Sol Ellis and his wife Helen wrote in 1997, "so they can make low interest loans to developers for downtown projects that keep on raising the tax rate for it's [sic] citizens."[4]) Parkwoodians, perhaps unsurprisingly, wished to enjoy the benefits of suburban life between Durham and RTP without paying city taxes—much as the park itself wished to remain a shiny citadel beyond the grasp of city voters and tax collectors.

But a deeper animus abided as well. Amid American flags and garbage cans adorned with a skull and crossbones, middle-class white residents expressed their disdain for the majority-black city, with a child holding up a sign reading, "Is This What We Are to You?" They even posed for a picture holding up letters that spelled out "Durham City Symbol" behind the overturned trash cans—an arresting assertion of both suburban privilege and racial and class identity.[5]

Ultimately, efforts to block annexation failed in 1997, and the community became part of Durham.[6] In the early twenty-first century, the formerly all-white Parkwood was increasingly diverse; by 2015, the community around Al Huda Academy remained nearly two-thirds white, but black, Latinx, and Asian residents accounted for 25.26 percent, 9.25 percent, and 4.27 percent of the population, respectively. The neighborhood had been 81.25 percent white as recently as 1990. Notably, the white population of Parkwood declined by over 19 percent between 1990 and 2000, whereas the number of black residents increased by nearly 70 percent—a change that might reflect white opposition to annexation by the City of Durham or the merger of city and county school systems in the 1990s.[7]

The story of Durham and the greater metropolitan Triangle parallels communities across the United States that have become more broadly diverse since the passage of the Immigration Act of 1965. That act lifted racist restrictions on migration from abroad and led, at least in part, to the influx of workers from Asia, Africa, and Latin America into the tech industry. Scholars such as Mike Davis and Wendy Cheng have documented this transformation in books such as *Magical Urbanism* and *The Changs Next Door to the Diazes*, in studies that center largely on the West Coast. Similarly, anthropologist Stanley Thangaraj has explored the increasing diversity of Arab and Asian communities in the suburbs of metropolitan Atlanta in his study, *Desi Hoop Dreams*.[8]

However, North Carolina's part of this story of cultural, demographic, and economic change has rarely been told. Notably, anthropologist Hannah Gill and sociologist Sarah Mayorga-Gallo have begun to narrate the story of the massive demographic shifts that have reshaped North Carolina in the late twentieth and early twenty-first centuries, focusing largely on the profound in-migration of Latinx people since the 1980s in both rural and urban quarters of the state. Such change has prompted fresh encounters and sometimes uncomfortable adjustments in the urban neighborhoods of Durham as much as smaller, agricultural towns like nearby Siler City in Chatham County, which saw its population grow by 75 percent between 1990 and 2016.[9]

The arrival of Asian, Latinx, and other immigrants to North Carolina was particularly pronounced in the Triangle, although it remained part of a larger story: the transformation of a biracial apartheid state into a multiethnic polity starting in the 1960s, not long after the founding of RTP. "In 1970, the racial and ethnic composition of the Triangle could be described as either black or white," planning scholar William Rohe noted. "At that time 71 percent of the Triangle's population was white, 28 percent was black, and all other racial and ethnic groups made up slightly more than 1 percent of the area's population." Employment opportunities in RTP began to change this demographic, by small steps, in the 1960s and 1970s, but the Triangle's multiculturalism flourished from the 1980s forward. Its Latinx population grew by 561 percent in the 1990s, compared with a simultaneous 159 percent in the area's Asian population. Although the region boasted a lower proportion of Asian residents than the nation as a whole—4.3 percent in Raleigh versus 5.1 percent nationwide—it had developed a more ethnically diverse community than the state as a whole. Morrisville, a small community near RTP, saw a 1,036.9 percent increase between 2000 and 2010, when Asians made up least 27 percent of the town's population.[10]

The Islamic school in Parkwood's shopping center is a small detail in the overall mosaic of the Triangle's transformation since the 1950s, but it is a telling one. It was a bellwether of the promising cultural efflorescence of the region as well as the potential for contention between people and communities with different priorities and interests across the metropolitan landscape. Boosters had enticed corporate investment and skilled workers to the Triangle by playing up a reputation for tolerance and moderation that was more aspirational than factual in the 1960s, and it seemed sufficient to satisfy executives at IBM or Burroughs Wellcome. But the metro area faced new challenges by the dawn of the twenty-first century, when the dual prospects of high-tech growth and gentrification once again shuffled the deck of race and class, opportunity and inclusion, as a new kind of city and a new kind of suburbia grew among the kudzu and loblolly pine of the Triangle.

6

"We Think a Lot"

THE TRIANGLE IN THE AGE OF GENTRIFICATION

On the outskirts of Durham, a sign on Durham-Chapel Hill Boulevard directed drivers to the nearby Research Triangle Park. Some wag had scrawled "We think a lot" on the sign in spray-paint, right below the name of the famed institution (figure 6.1).

The sign was eventually replaced. But the dig seemed to be a nod to the alternative metal band Faith No More, whose 1985 hit "We Care a Lot" irreverently skewered the pieties of 1980s politics by sneering at "disasters, fires, floods, and killer bees, about the NASA shuttle falling in the seas, about starvation and the food that LIVE AID bought."[1] Whoever defaced the RTP sign had a sense of humor, apparently poking fun at the intellectual arrogance of the people who developed new software, pharmaceuticals, and medical treatments in the tree-lined corporate park.

Not far from this sign, in 2001, Durham's soon-to-be mayor, Bill Bell, walked through a landscape of boarded-up buildings and vacant lots on the city's West End shortly before taking office. Bell commented on the poverty, underdevelopment, and violence that afflicted this community—a two-year-old girl had died in a drive-by shooting not long before—and pledged his support for "large-scale neighborhood revitalization" in Durham.[2]

Figure 6.1 Graffiti on a sign guiding motorists to RTP in 2013. *Source*: Photo by author.

Bell got his wish. The former IBM engineer-turned-politician became mayor in 2001 and oversaw an extraordinary remaking of downtown Durham and its surrounding neighborhoods. Following Bell's inauguration, "$1.7 billion in public and private investments have flooded the 0.8-square-mile area in the form of tech start-ups, world-class restaurants, and trendy hotels," journalist Sarah Willets reported in 2017. "Downtown will add thirteen hundred new housing units in the next few years—ten times the number of units that existed in 1995."[3]

At last, it seemed the city of Durham was reaping the benefits of high-tech postindustrial prosperity that the campaign for the Research Triangle had been promising since the late 1950s. Food trucks, cafes, condos—the Bull City had arrived at the "creative" destination that local elites set out for it more than forty years earlier, long before anyone had ever heard of a food truck. The *New York Times* raved in 2011 about the area's "design collectives and rehabbed downtowns," where one hundred fifty thousand college students attended school and a former vegan could be found roasting hogs (presumably organic). The Triangle was North Carolina's "Axis of Cool," the newspaper of record declared—akin to Los Angeles's famous hipster enclave of Silver Lake, only "with a few more 'yes ma'ams' "—reiterating the familiar journalistic trope of liberal modernity sidling up to Southern traditionalism.[4]

Indeed, the Triangle of the twenty-first century is a quintessential case of answers that raise new questions, solutions that birth new problems. In the early 2000s, the city of Durham seemingly escaped the pattern of deindustrialization, disinvestment, and white flight that had dogged it since the 1960s. There were biotech start-ups and the beautifully refurbished and thoroughly gentrified space of the American Tobacco Campus in downtown. There were breweries and bakeries where, as recently as the late 1990s, few Triangle residents either dared or cared to go. Yet Durham in the era of the knowledge economy also revealed the lacuna of this brave new world—shortcomings that threatened the promise of a high-tech future that would benefit all.

Nearby, Research Triangle Park also found itself facing the perils of success. In the 1950s, the idea of a high-tech hub in the woods between a few small Southern cities in a state still plagued with poverty and Jim Crow might have sounded implausible, at best, to many reasonable ears. The state did not have the benefits of advanced industry, venture capital, world-class universities, or proximity to a major metropolitan area, things that had helped make greater Boston a hearth of the new knowledge economy in the late twentieth century.[5] Raleigh, Durham, and Chapel Hill boasted some respected colleges and universities—they were not working with nothing—but outsiders, especially from the metropolitan North, were understandably skeptical in the 1950s and 1960s.

Yet the park succeeded in its quest to lure big employers such as IBM and Burroughs Wellcome and, later, the likes of Glaxo and Sumitomo—this in a high-tech update of the time-honored tradition of so-called smokestack hunting. While Alabama, Tennessee, and South Carolina tilted toward a strategy of winning heavy-industry jobs in auto manufacturing, North Carolina worked assiduously on two tracks: manufacturing jobs for its towns and rural areas, and a concerted focus on high-end services such as finance in Charlotte, tech in the Triangle, and real estate everywhere.[6]

At the end of the twentieth century, RTP could claim “137 organizations with over 41,600 employees, including 104 research companies with over 40,000 research employees” within its sixty-nine hundred acres.[7] Notably, the years after 2000 saw a steady uptick in start-ups outside the limits of the park, thanks in part to tech accelerators such as RTP’s AgTech and the efforts of Durham’s Center for Entrepreneurial Development, a nonprofit founded in 1984 to connect potential innovators with investors.[8] The Triangle metro area had finally succeeded in developing the culture of enterprise and innovation that had largely eluded it in the park’s first forty years, although local venture capital funding remained a shortcoming; in 2014 it still came predominantly from outside the state.[9]

In the new postindustrial world, progress was as Janus-faced as ever. In the age of the hipster, the Triangle had evolved the kind of creative local culture that boosters had somewhat implausibly promised investors in the early 1960s. In the throes of the so-called back-to-the-city movement, Durham and Raleigh filled with young professionals whose parents likely would have eschewed downtowns just a decade or two earlier. Yet each of these successes contained the seed of its own failure: downtown renewal endangered the living standards of long-time residents, who could not afford rising rents and property values, ironic in a metro area long reputed for its affordable cost of living. And hip new start-ups did not necessarily want to locate in the stuffy, sprawling, suburban-corporate landscape of RTP. Instead, they favored greater density and street-level interaction—the very qualities that park planners sought to hammer out of existence in their designs and zoning regulations of the late 1950s and early 1960s.

The plan had worked, but it created a new kind of metropolitan economy that no longer fit the dream of midcentury technosuburbia. How local residents and policy makers tackled these challenges speaks to the fundamental paradoxes facing cities, even—or especially—prosperous ones in the twenty-first century.

BILL BELL AND THE NEW DURHAM

The promise of the creative city proffered a devil’s bargain: growth for the benefit of the highly educated and affluent, and hardship for the poor, working class, and lower-middle-class people who had long resided in Durham.

It was a story of gentrification so hackneyed and predictable as to rival the stuff of romance novel plots—at least for anyone who has followed the life of American cities in the late twentieth and early twenty-first centuries.

The Triangle's struggle was, in a way, more emblematic than most: nothing here was an accident. The region set out in the late 1950s specifically to recruit well-educated, affluent workers to remake the local landscape, as well as the large corporations that would employ them. The Triangle was an expressly articulated effort to bring more privileged and educated people into these communities—a kind of gentrification by design that transcended neighborhood- or even city-level debates about the future of development. It was gentrification on a sustained, decades-long, and regional scale, well before the term *gentrification* itself was coined.

Indeed, in the early twenty-first century, the Research Triangle seemed to have achieved its original 1950s-era objectives. Corporate laboratories, government agencies, and foundations came to Research Triangle Park and increasingly sprouted up in the surrounding metropolitan area of Raleigh, Durham, Chapel Hill, and Cary. Educated workers from around the country and the world migrated there to work and raise families. The metro economy remained resilient, with consistently low unemployment and stable growth even during the recessions of the 1980s, 1990s, and early 2000s. (The Triangle weathered the Great Recession of 2008 better than most American metropolitan areas, though the rest of the state, hit by punishing job losses, told a somewhat different story.) Raleigh, Durham, and Cary won plaudits in national media as among the "best places to live" and "most creative" or "brainiest" cities in the country.[10]

Indeed, Governor Luther Hodges's goal to "bring in more Ph.D's than we've ever heard of here" came true.[11] His gnomic saying in 1962 that RTP was "an idea that produced a reality" seemed apt in the 2000s. It was almost as if North Carolina's leaders in academia, business, and politics had made the idea a reality by sheer force of will.

Presiding over all this was Bill Bell, the IBM engineer who came to Durham in 1968 and received a frosty reception when he sought to buy a home in the new RTP suburb of Parkwood. Bell subsequently pursued a career in local politics as a county commissioner in the 1970s, and he helped steer the controversial merger of the Durham City and County school systems from 1988 to 1992—a goal delayed long after the City of Raleigh and Wake County merged their own systems over local opposition in the 1970s.[12] Around the same time, Parkwood was annexed by the City of Durham in the face of vociferous protests and determined legal challenges. By 2001, Bell was mayor of Durham—as well as Parkwood, the community that at first kind of, sort of rejected him.

In a sense, Bell was the philosopher-king of Durham in the creative age. An IBM engineer, a black man, and an upwardly mobile striver who came to the area during a time of tumultuous social change, he was the quintessential politician for Durham during the time of its rapid revitalization—or gentrification—in the 2000s and 2010s. He proved to be a unifying leader, widely regarded as a capable steward of the city during a time of rapid cultural, demographic, economic, and technological change. (As one prominent Caryite indelicately put it in 2015, "He's kept everybody down. He's kept them quiet. If you don't, they'll—it'll all go crazy over there"[13]). Bell oversaw the remaking of downtown Durham, which brought significant new investment in dining and retail and new housing to the city center (figure 6.2).

Figure 6.2 The new downtown Durham in 2010. *Source*: Photo by author.

For Bell, as for the founders of RTP, the outcome looked like pure "gravy" in the early twenty-first century: jobs, growth, rising wages and housing prices. For Bell in particular, his tenure must have felt like a vindication. In the long and troubled story of Durham, ever since he arrived in 1968, the city had managed to chart a course toward revitalization and at least a degree of racial compromise between the long-deadlocked foes of inner-city and suburban Durham. Indeed, the Triangle looked to many observers like the model of a new creative economy. It might not have been as famous or innovative as Silicon Valley or as politically liberal as Massachusetts's Route 128, but it provided a vision of high-tech suburban prosperity that rivaled any similar metro area in the United States—an economy driven by universities, technology, and an educated middle and upper-middle class. And with a lower cost of living than its peers and Southern charm to spare, the Triangle appeared to be the apotheosis of the new creative economy in its comfiest, most middle-of-the-road iteration.

GENTRIFICATION BY DESIGN

Indeed, the Triangle in the early twenty-first century basked in good press—as it had become used to for several decades—but few locales earned greater praise than Durham. The former tobacco town, long viewed as hardscrabble, dangerous, and dysfunctional by nearby suburbanites, had remade itself as the City of Medicine—harking back to Representative Nick Galifianakis and Senator B. Everett Jordan's risible 1967 claim that North Carolina would be great for doing lung cancer research considering it already knew so much about tobacco.[14] Duke University was by far the city's largest employer; biotech start-ups appeared in and around downtown by the 2010s; and the old tobacco warehouses had been remade as dining, shopping, and office spaces in the American Tobacco District beginning in the late 1990s.[15]

By the early 2000s, *gentrification* had gone from an activist buzzword to a fixation of American culture at large. The less privileged and their allies and advocates decried its effect, while gentrifiers—sometimes referred to euphemistically as "urban pioneers"—increasingly used the term in a neutral or even positive way; for instance, "the neighborhood is slowly gentrifying."[16]

Typically, gentrification refers to the occupation of a poor or working-class neighborhood by more affluent people who change the cultural profile of a neighborhood—dollar stores replaced by cafés, bodegas by beer bars or bakeries—and drive up property values, making home prices, rents, and taxes unaffordable for the original residents. At times, critics speak of the gentrification of an entire city—say, Washington, D.C., or San Francisco in the early twenty-first century—as demographic change and displacement occur on a larger scale.[17]

Yet the Research Triangle represents the gentrification of a multi-county metropolitan area, even the willing of it into existence, a feat of branding that dwarfs the enterprising developers who coined names such as "TriBeCa" and "SoBro" (yes, the South Bronx). The founders of RTP intentionally and openly sought to import educated people with higher incomes to transform Raleigh-Durham and the larger economy that surrounded it.[18]

Of course, they could not have called their plan "gentrification"; the word did not exist yet. It first appeared in the *New York Times* in 1972 in a piece about Londoners who feared the practice of real estate sellers' taking a deposit from a buyer before promptly increasing the sale price. ("What mugging is to a dinner-party conversation in New York," the paper reported, "gazumping is in London.")[19] The word originated in a classic bidding frenzy, as middle- and upper-class Londoners attempted to buy up homes in traditionally working-class areas of the city. The trend can be viewed as an early harbinger of things to come, first in major metropolises such as London and New York—the first *New York Times* reference to gentrification in a U.S. context followed in 1974—and later in other cities throughout the rust belt and Sunbelt where a combination of deindustrialization, suburbanization, and white flight emptied formerly dense urban communities.[20]

The South had few big, populous cities prior to the heyday of cars and cul-de-sacs after World War II, but metropoles such as Atlanta continued to witness dramatic shifts of population that moved tax revenue to the suburbs and concentrated poverty closer to downtown in the 1970s and 1980s. Sunbelt cities might have lagged behind New York or London, but they nevertheless saw their own gentrification occur in the late twentieth century—a sort of reverse current of the youngish and educated back into neighborhoods where property values had cratered and schools were viewed as off-limits to anyone fortunate enough to escape them. Consider Atlanta's Inman Park since the 1980s, or Charlotte's North Davidson arts district in the 1990s and 2000s.[21]

The rise of gentrification brought the same ills pretty much everywhere it happened: higher property values improved the local tax base but also increased the tax burden for homeowners and rent for tenants of modest means, eventually outpricing those who had lived in the community the longest. This displacement has received scorn from social critics, long-time residents, and even the original gentrifiers who sometimes cannot afford to stay in their chosen neighborhood. For other newer, more affluent residents, the appeal of urban life—a "back to the city" movement that the *New York Times* recognized as early as 1974—has often prompted an uneasy acceptance of the inequities that the process is known to cause.

When looking at North Carolina, though, it is perhaps more helpful to think of gentrification not on a neighborhood or even city level but on a regional one. In this sense, North Carolina was itself a poor neighborhood in search of jobs, investment, and tax revenue in the 1950s, when Research Triangle Park was founded. Local elites clearly understood that high-tech development was a vehicle to bring more affluent people and better jobs to the state. Long before the terms *gentrification* and *creative class* were in common circulation, North Carolina leaders explicitly set out to gentrify Raleigh, Durham, and Chapel Hill by appealing to an educated, professional workforce.

They succeeded. By most measures, Triangle residents earned higher levels of wages and education by 2000, particularly in the core counties of Durham, Orange, and Wake. Broadly speaking, the numbers speak for themselves. In seven counties of the greater Triangle, population grew dramatically from 1950 to 1990—rising from 419,523 to 889,331, or an increase of nearly 112 percent. By 2010, that number had climbed to 1,634,847 in Chatham, Durham, Franklin, Johnston, Orange, Person, and Wake Counties. A typical male in Chatham County in 1950 had completed 7.4 years of school, with a woman achieving 8.1. By 1990, 70 percent of local residents had at least a high school degree. The same figures were 8.6 for men and 8.9 for women in Durham County in 1950, whereas nearly 80 percent had completed high school or greater in 1990. In more affluent Wake County, men and women had completed 9.2 and 9.9 years of school in 1950, respectively, whereas 85.4 percent had a high school degree or greater in 1990.[22]

Trends in the early twenty-first century showed an even sharper rise, as university populations and high-tech growth left Durham, Orange, and Wake with a striking proportion of residents holding a bachelor's degree or greater. The U.S. Census Bureau estimated that about 46.9 percent of Durham residents had a bachelor's degree or higher between 2012 and 2016, compared with 29 percent for the state as a whole, 50.1 percent in Wake, and 57.7 percent in Orange.[23] Incomes followed the same upward trajectory. Wake's median income in 1950 was $2,011, surpassed only by Durham's $2,264. By 2010, positions had reversed, with Wake enjoying a median of $63,770 and Durham $49,894.[24]

These metro areas were the drivers of growth in one of the most rapidly growing states in the United States. North Carolina had "become a magnet for young, well-educated workers who are flocking to cities like Charlotte and Raleigh for jobs in banking, tech and research," as NPR's Reema Khrais noted in the run-up to the 2016 presidential election. In fact, Wake and Mecklenburg Counties (the latter being the home of Charlotte, the Carolinas' largest city) accounted for roughly half of the entire state's growth in the early to mid-2010s.[25]

Yet with growth and revival inevitably came their cousins, gentrification and displacement. If the cost of living in Durham remained well below that of New York or Los Angeles, it still grew at a rapid clip in the early twenty-first century in a way felt by the most vulnerable Durhamites—especially those of the black working class, who had been abandoned in the city during the age of white flight. Despite the prodigious growth of the city center in the 2000s, inequality increased: the poverty rate rose from 2000 to 2015, 15 percent to 19.2 percent. "From 2000–2001, median rents in Durham went up by 22 percent and median home values by 42 percent," Sarah Willets reported in 2017, when trends had only accelerated. "The result has been an affordable housing crisis."[26] In a bitter irony, the forces of abandonment and immiseration that characterized many American cities during the age of the urban crisis of the 1970s and 1980s reversed in ways that disadvantaged those who remained.[27]

The facts are depressingly familiar and not particularly unusual. Economic growth, investment, and in-migration of the more privileged and better-off citizens disrupted the lives of the less-well-off in Raleigh and Durham. The mechanisms are neither obscure nor difficult to understand. People with more money and education come to an older inner suburb or center-city neighborhood. They appreciate the historic built environment or the urban vibe and they buy houses, retooling them and driving up both home values and property taxes. Both renters and homeowners feel the effects in different ways. "We're building for the whiter, richer new people that are moving to town," Durham Councilwoman Jillian Johnson, a critic of the unequal impact of development, observed in 2017. "We're not building grocery stores and pharmacies and banks in east Durham, and that's what we need to be building."[28]

As Tyran Hill, a policy officer at the North Carolina Housing Coalition, pointed out in 2017, development was leaving many low-income and even middle-class families behind. "The more desired locations and areas of Raleigh have a lot more building revitalization going on," Hill said, "and it makes it a lot more difficult to acquire those lands at a price point in which the fair amount of subsidy and investment that is required would offset those additional land costs that would make it affordable for low income wage workers." Even as advocates like Hill worked to make affordable housing possible, the escalating prices of in-town real estate made their job doubly difficult. A firefighter in Raleigh had to commute an hour into the city he served because the only housing he could afford was on the urban periphery.[29]

Meanwhile, some affluent residents of the Triangle were not keen on building new, affordable housing, as a controversy over Habitat for Humanity's plan to build new units in Cary in 2017 showed, evoking intense local opposition.[30] Hill, a member of Habitat for Humanity of

Wake County's Affordable Housing Policy Committee, commented on the thorny politics of privilege and inclusion:

> The biggest difficulty when it comes to educating people who have NIMBY [Not in My Backyard] tendencies is that in revitalization and in creating these new units, the fabric of your neighborhood is going to have to change. People don't want to accept that for whatever reason; they want to maintain that while still benefiting from the financial investments, which is an unrealistic mentality to carry. A lot of people believe that it's going to bring down their property values, and it's going to bring crime, and it's going to increase traffic. . . . The money line that kept getting used in the council meeting I was in in Cary was, "I'm for Habitat, I love Habitat and building Habitat homes, but I don't think Habitat belongs here, we should find another place and I will help you build those homes."[31]

The citizens of Cary were, as ever, fixated on maintaining the architectural and demographic character of their community. Meanwhile, Orange and Durham Counties have made similar efforts to increase the stock of affordable housing through modest increases in property taxes that would fund new housing, but such measures have not kept up with the need for both rental and owner-occupied dwellings in the metro Triangle.[32]

The historic communities surrounding downtown Durham have felt this impact more acutely than elsewhere in the Triangle, as the pristine college town of Chapel Hill and the sleepy capital city of Raleigh had experienced white flight less acutely. Older bungalows in central Durham became increasingly desirable to young professionals, much as the lofts of Sharon Zukin's late 1970s Manhattan or similar housing stock had become in Charlotte or Atlanta in the 2000s. The iconic African American community of Hayti had been bulldozed to make way for the Durham Freeway in the 1960s in a quintessential case of urban renewal gone wrong and partly in an effort to ferry travelers to and from Research Triangle Park. Decades later, those black families who remained faced a new threat of rising costs and neighborhood change.[33]

Unsurprisingly, in an era of growing economic inequality that reaches back to the 1970s, economic development in the Triangle has been highly uneven.[34] Better jobs, higher wages, and higher levels of education in general have almost indisputably benefited the Triangle and North Carolina as a whole, with multiplier effects for families and communities throughout the state. Yet scholars and policy experts have pointed out that Raleigh and Durham boast some of the greatest economic inequality and lowest social mobility among American metropolitan areas. The gap between the best and worst off has grown within the Triangle, and within the state as a whole, as economic growth has proceeded apace for most of the last fifty years. In fact, residents of the major metropolitan areas of Charlotte, Fayetteville, Greensboro, and Raleigh experience lower economic mobility—the chance that someone born into a lower socioeconomic stratum will move to a higher one—than their peers in 90 percent of other cities.[35] Meanwhile, parts of poor and rural North Carolina have infant mortality rates that rival those of much less developed countries; the rate for African American women in eastern North Carolina was 16.6 deaths per thousand births in 2013, versus 5.4 for white women and 5.96 for the nation as a whole across ethnic groups.[36]

High-tech growth resulted in a distinctly Tar Heel paradox. As columnist Sandy Grady remarked in 1990,

> The image of North Carolina as "progressive" is a genteel hoax. Sure, it has a couple of great universities, some good writers, the gleaming towers of Charlotte, the brains of the Research Triangle. But there's a dark underside: low wages, high infant mortality, subpar schools, low SAT scores. The state's caught between the Bible Belt and the Sun Belt. Between 1865 and 1990.[37]

Grady's candor was welcome. Few have repeated it, but historian Peter Coclanis acknowledged the shocking disparities in development and opportunity that stretched over the Triangle and its hinterland. Traveling through rural eastern North Carolina and South Carolina in 2005, the UNC professor saw the roadside littered with check-cashing places, pawnshops, and dollar stores that, to one degree or another, prey on the working poor.

This chronically depressed part of the country was just an hour or two from suburban prosperity and corporate laboratories. "I mean, really, do places like Chapel Hill or Cary—which is to say, an affluent university town and a self-contained sleep storage unit for RTP, respectively—seem to be suffering from globalization?" Coclanis asked. "Talk about Abundant Life! Globalization? Sure, I got faith! All God's tenured professors got faith!"[38] The awesome effects of "brain power" were little felt only a few miles from downtown Raleigh. "You can drive 75 miles outside the Triangle and wonder, 'Where in the hell is this? It doesn't look like—doesn't taste, doesn't sound, doesn't act anything like where the airport was,'" as former Nortel engineer Chuck Till reflected in 2016.[39]

The relentlessly positive coverage of North Carolina in local and national media disguised the dark underside of high-tech postindustrial growth. Both within the metro Triangle and the state of North Carolina, large divisions between the fortunate and the least fortunate have persisted well into the twenty-first century—in spite of high-tech success.

Both the metro Triangle and North Carolina as a whole continue to suffer from wide inequality and persistent poverty despite promising economic growth over decades. Historian Bryant Simon has shown how grinding disadvantages have affected those in rural and small-town North Carolina in his book *The Hamlet Fire*, about a 1991 accident that killed twenty-five people in a low-wage chicken-processing plant less than two hours from Raleigh.[40] Even the metropolitan economy of North Carolina's Piedmont—the cities of Charlotte, Greensboro, Raleigh, and Durham, where growth has been concentrated in recent decades—has shown signs of falling short in terms of innovation and entrepreneurship.[41] The fact remains that economic growth and technological innovation, while good at raising tax revenues and wages for some, still have not, by themselves, eroded the enduring structure of racial and economic inequality that has defined North Carolina, and the South as a whole, for generations.

Why is it so difficult for a poor child in Durham or Wake or any North Carolina county to climb the ladder to the glittering and sophisticated prosperity so seemingly within reach in nearby RTP? The answers should be no more surprising than the questions. For most of the twentieth century, the political culture of North Carolina celebrated education, science, and progress in general—as well as a stubborn commitment to probusiness conservatism. The history of the Research Triangle is deeply entwined with what historian William Chafe called North Carolina's "progressive mystique." The state's image as more enlightened and moderate than other members of the former Confederacy belied a bedrock of conservatism committed to the maintenance of low wages and little regulation, as state leaders deflected demands for racial or economic justice in the pursuit of investment from outside capital.[42]

This savvy combination has been key to the success—such as it is—of RTP, the Triangle, and the state. As the late sociologist and state legislator Paul Luebke argued, North Carolina's leaders have always been split between "traditionalists" and "modernizers." The former have been more conservative, typically tied to low-tech, labor-intensive industries such as furniture and textiles—and, hence, resolutely antiunion. The latter were nominally more progressive, those with interests in finance, real estate, and, indeed, high technology who might not have been as committed to an antique social order as their more conservative peers but still did not favor the interests of organized labor.[43]

The founders and captains of RTP—Archie Davis, George Watts Hill, and George Simpson—fell, for the most part, into the modernizer camp. As Doug Edgeton, president and CEO of the North Carolina Biotechnology Center, emphasized in 2015, "[North Carolina is] a smart state, a business-friendly low-cost state, with a wide and deep life science infrastructure."[44] Behind those words was the whole story: brains plus "low-cost" had long been the Triangle's formula, and the state's. Elites could attract jobs and grow the economy, but they showed relatively little interest in taking on the woeful conditions of many workers or the ingrained structural poverty across the state in a serious way.[45]

The Triangle also has come up short on more prosaic measures that do not have to do with life and death so much as growth and investment. RTP has drawn major employers and in-migrants from outside the state, but besides a few major firms such as SAS (founded in 1976) or Quintiles (1982), it has not historically generated a great deal of local innovation, at least in the late twentieth century. This deficit began to diminish in the 2000s as more start-ups emerged in Raleigh and Durham with the help of the Council for Entrepreneurial Development (CED), which was founded in 1984 and aimed to support innovation and channel investment to start-up firms.[46] But unlike Boston and San Francisco, the Triangle has spun off relatively few major companies or new technologies. AZT might have been developed as an HIV drug there, AstroTurf and Ctrl+Alt+Delete might have come from the minds employed at RTP, but they did not generate the kind of entrepreneurial activity that builds dense local networks of partnership and collaboration and keeps profits within the local economy.[47]

Scholars have advanced a few reasons for the laggard aspect of the Triangle. One is a lack of venture capital. Compared with Boston, San Francisco, and New York, a limited amount of investment was available in a chronically poor state like North Carolina to promote local entrepreneurs who had an idea and a vision. The Triangle simply did not produce the likes of Hewlett-Packard (1939), Apple (1976), or Google (1998) in the San Francisco Bay Area or Biogen (1978) in greater Boston. "You need a lot of filthy-rich people who are willing to gamble, knowing that nine out of the ten things that they invest in are gonna be bombs but one out of ten they're gonna get a great return," Chuck Till observed, comparing his experience with that of friends and peers in California. "I still don't think you got a lot of that in North Carolina." Moreover, as geographer William Graves argued, Southern bankers traditionally have had a conservative and risk-averse approach to investing in chancy new enterprises, unlike their counterparts in the Northeast or West Coast.[48] "RTP clearly is in but not of the South," geographer Susan Walcott concluded in 2001, "a global node station whose affluence assists the state coffers but exists more as an island than an example of Carolina dynamism." Like Graves, she credited "a paucity of local financiers" with inhibiting the "difficult transition" to a truly dynamic local economy.[49] Hence, what finance capital existed in Raleigh, Durham, Charlotte, or Winston-Salem was not necessarily forthcoming.

In fact, RTP represents, if nothing else, the greatest success of venture capital in North Carolina's history. That was evidenced when Archie Davis and George Watts Hill managed to scare up enough money from bankers, industrialists, and other businesspeople across the state in 1959 to buy out the original investor, New York textile magnate Karl Robbins, and put RTP on a sound financial footing as a nonprofit. Those donors were the original angel investors.[50]

Finally, the relative job security offered by the Triangle might, by itself, have inhibited potential entrepreneurship. Jim Goodnight was a researcher at NC State when he conceived of launching SAS Institute, but he did not enjoy the privilege of tenure, of a more or less guaranteed lifetime job; he and his compatriots were willing to set off and try something new. Professors at UNC or Duke could have started their own businesses to commercialize new technologies, but leaving behind a stable salary and benefits was a disincentive. Meanwhile, RTP had focused on recruiting huge corporate employers that also guaranteed generous benefits, such as IBM. And SAS ironically became a symptom of the problem itself: the lavish rewards of working there and solicitous attitude of managers toward work-life balance meant that loyal workers were unlikely to disembark for possibly greener, but still riskier shores. "[SAS is] a very comfortable place for a lot of people, and they don't really have—they don't have the energy, effort, or impetus to go leave," as the CED's Jay Bigelow put it. "It's not cutthroat."[51] The Triangle's historical reliance on a handful of big corporations might have smothered the potential for start-up innovation.

For all these reasons, the Triangle has not managed to hatch new industries—as Romeo Guest dreamed of in the earliest days of the Triangle in 1954—in the same way as Boston, Austin, or the Bay Area.[52]

CREATIVITY: ITS PROMISES AND PARADOXES

The Triangle might have lagged in terms of start-up growth or social mobility, but it could cherish a singular innovation: an influential strategy of mobilizing the cultural capital of universities, local lifestyle amenities, and a sense of place as drivers of high-wage growth. RTP focused on attracting educated labor and knowledge-based production as early as the 1950s, yet it found its pop sociological apotheosis in Richard Florida's creative class in the twenty-first century. Of course, many scholars had already written about the importance of arts and cultural institutions to cities, beginning with Sharon Zukin's pioneering 1982 study of gentrification in *Loft Living*, and further elaborated in Charles Landry's 2000 *The Creative City*.[53] But Florida was a man who met his moment in 2002, when his book *The Rise of the Creative Class: And How It's Transforming Work, Leisure, Community and Everyday Life* captured the zeitgeist of an American economy just emerging from its hangover from the high-tech boom of the 1990s.

Florida proposed that a new class was coming to the fore—indeed, one that already had taken what Marxists might call the hegemonic position in a changing society.[54] Old distinctions between the poor, working class, middle class, and elite were being superseded by a new group: the broad swath of workers who used their intellect and creativity primarily on the job, from the barista in a band to the computer programmer to the visionary CEO. United in the fact that their work required more thinking than rote repetition, they were the vanguard of a new economy and a new class paradigm.

Florida's message was, in many ways, a sugar high too great to resist. Cities that had lost investment, jobs, and population in the late twentieth-century wave of deindustrialization and financialization of the U.S. economy, like his beloved Pittsburgh, could look to the author's prescriptions for a ray of hope.[55] Focus on cultivating a tolerant, interesting local environment, with coffee shops, art galleries, and gay pride parades, Florida argued; then a city could lure the educated workers who would refill depleted urban tax coffers, drive up property values, and make old downtowns thrive again. Anxious local leaders across the United States took up the message, and Florida was suddenly a consultant whose services could help Green Bay, Wisconsin, or Memphis, Tennessee, become more "creative."[56] If his message was perhaps too easy—slap a pride sticker on your lonely burg and the techies will come a-calling—it also was not entirely wrong. Many American cities did, in fact, see a major revival in the early twenty-first century, a trend that, arguably, Florida intuited sooner than many others.[57]

Durham is a perfect example. It was a postindustrial city, in the sense that its tobacco-processing industry had declined rapidly so that by 1987, American Tobacco had left downtown and basically vanished by the time

Liggett & Myers departed the city in 2000. Meanwhile, its downtown had languished as white flight led the whiter and more affluent citizens to suburban Durham or Wake County.[58] In the years after 2000, though, the change in Durham was striking: coffee shops, whiskey bars, music venues, breweries, new apartments, and all the accoutrements of urban revival found in basically every other gentrifying city in the United States. In moves rich with symbolism, both Brightleaf Square in 1981 and the American Tobacco Campus in 2004—"the largest historic preservation in the history of North Carolina," according to planning scholar William M. Rohe—reoccupied old warehouses with new retail and dining spaces, much as textile mills and other factories had been repurposed in cities like New York and Gastonia.[59]

Durham was creative; it had strong universities, educated workers, and arts institutions; and the people and businesses came. In fact, the pioneers of RTP—most of which was in Durham County but remained insulated from annexation by the city because state legislators passed a 1985 law forbidding it—had anticipated all this change with a kind of breathtaking foresight.[60] Forty-five years before *The Rise of the Creative Class*, men such as Romeo Guest and George Simpson argued that North Carolina needed to leverage its cultural and intellectual resources to lure both educated workers and more technologically advanced companies to the state. Museums, theater, art, and, above all, universities were the keys to attracting brains, which the Triangle's early boosters saw as the key to development. They were Florida long before Florida.

Where has this prescient economic development strategy left the Triangle, and North Carolina as a whole? One problem with writing about the Triangle is that almost no one is willing to say anything bad about it. The relentlessly cheerful booster spirit of Romeo Guest, George Simpson, Luther Hodges, George Watts Hill, and Archie Davis has soaked into the metropolitan fabric of the Triangle in many regards. Activists make noise about the lack of affordable housing, the problems of traffic and sprawl, and the yawning gap of racial and overall economic inequality in the metro Triangle. But in general the region in the twenty-first century mirrors the loving national media coverage it has managed to attract and cultivate since the 1990s: a robust recipe of smart and creative people, economic growth, easy living, and political moderation.

In fact, Florida found the Triangle wanting in terms of creativity in his 2002 book. "The Research Triangle lacks the 'hip' urban lifestyle found in places like San Francisco, Seattle, New York and Chicago," he wrote, citing a researcher at the University of North Carolina who rued that the only fun local activity was to "visit the hog farms."[61] Its boring suburbia and sprawl rendered it less delectable than San Francisco's Mission District or other paradigmatic cases of the hip new capitalism. The urbanist reassessed his views in later years, however, naming Durham–Chapel Hill as the second "brainiest" metro in America in a 2010 *Daily Beast* report.[62]

At the same time, rival urbanist Joel Kotkin consistently made a different case: that the prosperous, if sometimes dull, suburbs of cities such as Raleigh, as well as Dallas and Salt Lake City, represented the vanguard of twenty-first-century urbanism.[63] As metastasizing housing prices in so-called global cities such as New York and Los Angeles drove out all but a small elite, Kotkin insisted that the main action of American life would happen in sprawling and increasingly diverse suburbs in the twenty-first century.[64] "In the coming decades the 'luxury city' may be a place with a significant increase in high-end dwellings but not many more people," Kotkin argued in 2010, noting that a $50,000 income bought more than twice as much house in Atlanta as in New York. "Over the past few decades even educated workers, particularly when they enter their thirties, have tended in increasing numbers to leave more expensive cities for less expensive cities like Phoenix, Dallas, Atlanta, and Raleigh-Durham."[65]

In fact, the Triangle of the twenty-first century sat in something of a middle spot between Florida and Kotkin's competing visions of creative cities and family-friendly suburbs. "From its biscuits to its boutiques," as one *New York Times* profile said in 2009, "the Triangle occupies a happy place between slow-paced Southern charm and urban cool."[66] Its radically dispersed population—among the lowest-density metro areas in the United States—might have meant traffic, but it also led to relatively lower housing prices than other major cities and the possibility of having a comfortable,

Figure 6.3 A vision of RTP's future. *Source*: Research Triangle Foundation.

serene suburban life as a tech worker in Raleigh, Durham, Chapel Hill, Cary, or their more distant surrounding counties.[67]

In the end, *New York Times* pundit David Brooks might have had the better part of the argument. The Triangle was the land of his "bobos"—bourgeois bohemians—who enjoyed both high levels of education and professional attainment as well as a taste for the arts and culture. Brooks introduced the term in his 2000 *Bobos in Paradise: The New Upper Class and How It Got There*, a book that was at least as insightful as *Rise of the Creative Class*. With a jaundiced but none-too-secretly loving eye, Brooks looked at the hard-working strivers who pursued higher education and won a place in corporate America and the professions.[68] They were the "knowledge workers" about whom management theorist Peter Drucker and sociologist Daniel Bell talked in the 1960s and 1970s, the symbolic analysts who economist Robert Reich wrote about in his 1992 *The Work of Nations*, and the creative class that Florida popularized in 2002.[69] Whatever name you choose—knowledge worker, creative, bobo—the Triangle was a place tailor-made for them.

RTP: A *JETSONS* SUCCESS IN A HIPSTER ERA

No part of the Triangle represents its paradoxical combination of success and failure more than Research Triangle Park itself. RTP bagged the big corporate tenants like IBM and Glaxo, enforced its rigid, austere sense of corporate aesthetic conformity, and eluded political control by the neighboring city of Durham. It had its own zip code and post office: a letter could be sent to Research Triangle Park, NC.

As a consciously contrived place, it seemed to have realized its goal of a perfect, antiseptic space for research, innovation, and contemplative thought. RTP represented midcentury modernism at both its finest and most pedestrian. As the writers of *VICE* magazine remarked in 2005, "Sorry, dude, but the future is slick and modernist. If you really want to get futury go back to the late 50s."[70] That is RTP at its core.

Yet the park faces serious challenges in the new century. It remains dependent on large corporate tenants, which could lay off large numbers of employees—as IBM did during the Great Recession in 2010—or, worse, leave entirely.[71] In this sense, RTP falls into a longer Southern history of efforts by states and localities to recruit employers from outside the region for the basic reasons of jobs and investment rather than fostering local entrepreneurship.

More relevant, though, is the legacy of the park's rigorously corporate-suburban aesthetic. What appealed to executives, scientists, engineers, and planners in the 1960s is not necessarily the cutting edge of development or tech in the twenty-first century. The Jane Jacobs–inspired vogue for density, interaction, and walkability embodied by the movement for "new urbanism" runs counter to the regimented, clean, separated look of RTP.[72] When the park began to evolve, corporate leaders wanted to have their workers cordoned off in discrete fiefdoms, with little more than a few pine trees lining the road, a company logo at the entrance, and a secured gate for entry to their suburban campuses. Interacting and intermingling were not encouraged, so much so that for much of RTP's history, there were barely any coffee shops, bars, or restaurants within easy reach of the park and its employees.

In the twenty-first century, RTP's leaders recognized this quandary. The zoning rules and property covenants that governed the park strongly inhibited the development of any housing or retail within its space, but RTP President Bob Geolas wanted to change that. "It's kind of an old model," Geolas admitted in 2016.

> In the 1960s, it was the future model. People wanting to escape the chaos of the urban cities, they were completely enamored of the new, American, suburban lifestyle. Mom, dad, and the two kids, in a ranch house in the suburbs. . . . When you say to someone we need to rethink the park, you need to bring amenities into the park—there are no amenities in the park—there is no residential, no retail. . . . We're seven thousand acres, half the size of the island of Manhattan, and you can't buy a cup of Starbucks coffee.[73]

If what young professionals wanted in the twenty-first century was the urban life and sense of community of downtown Durham, then RTP would try to give it to them.

Planners aimed to reformat the park for a way of living and working that departs sharply from the big corporate campuses of the 1960s (figure 6.3). The first step was the Frontier, a project launched in 2015 that rehabilitated several older office buildings as a space for start-ups and coworking. Gone were the single employers that occupied a low-density footprint on a lush, suburban lawn; instead, entrepreneurs and inventors could interact in fluid, shared, open spaces, and new firms could perfect their technologies in a low-cost setting before raising the capital to take a product to market and move into larger environs. Inside, bulletin boards enticed workers to running clubs and movie nights, and people from multiple firms milled around the same coffee machine. Outside, a Cuban food truck offered its treats in the parking lot. There were kickboxing classes and happy hours with free beer on Thursdays. Such changes reflected a conscious intention to model space after an idea of what a funky, Floridian environment of innovation in New York or San Francisco might look like. RTP's leaders want to remake at least part of the park around the virtues of interaction and collaboration, in contrast to the model of older research and development firms that wished to keep workers separated in order to protect intellectual property and other corporate secrets.[74]

Just as important, a new Park Center aims to give RTP a promenade it never had, a core and a sense of place. "A trip through RTP always feels Orwellian," journalist Lisa Sorg noted in 2015, nodding to "large, somber buildings veiled by noble stands of pine trees" and "blocky, corporate mausoleums."[75] But the Frontier and the Park Center are meant to diminish, at least, a feeling of chilly absence that many visitors to the park have reported over the years. Planners envision a Park Center with dining and retail, grocery stores, housing, and hotels, all in a walkable space not far from where I-40 cuts through the heart of RTP. In a historical irony, the park's founders considered building a "science city" with its own on-site housing and amenities in the late 1950s before quickly shelving the idea. In the twenty-first century, RTP aims to remake itself in just such a way, "to offer the kinds of 'experiences,' " as Geolas put it, that contemporary tech workers allegedly crave.[76]

It remains to be seen whether the ambitious redesign of RTP can transform its place within the sprawling metropolitan landscape of the Triangle, as start-ups pop up in downtown Durham and Raleigh and residents are vexed ever more by the woes of traffic. In an ideal world, the Park Center would become a desirable destination in its own right, a central node within a denser and better-connected Triangle. In 2020 there are hopes—which have been routinely dashed since the 1980s—that significant mass transit such as light rail could interconnect the municipalities of Chapel Hill, Raleigh, and Durham with RTP, although the political logistics of working out a plan with multiple cities, counties, the state, and the federal government have long impeded progress. The issues of traffic, sprawl, unaffordable housing, and economic inequality continue to pose serious challenges to the Triangle's future as a prosperous and equitable place for all its residents.[77]

In the end, RTP has the curious distinction of being an almost axiomatically successful effort to create a somewhere from whole cloth, at branding a place—"the Triangle," a term that did not exist prior to 1954, has come to define the entire metro area—but it resulted in an absence at its core. Countless visitors to the region have driven through RTP and wondered how they missed seeing it, because the stands of pines and endless driveways to corporate office parks do not strike them as a place in any meaningful sense.[78]

In the twenty-first century, park officials hope to manufacture a new identity within RTP's suburban lanes of sterile corporate campuses, in much the way that its original boosters invented the idea of the Research Triangle from basically nothing in the 1950s. Whether or not the effort succeeds is difficult to predict, but the trends of contemporary urbanism and tech investment run toward density, agglomeration, and walkability instead of sprawl and sterility. At the same time, though, Kotkin and Brooks are correct to recognize that the suburban life remains appealing to many of the people who will work in the software and biotech firms of the Triangle, much as it did for their precursors in the 1970s or 1980s. In that sense, the Triangle struck a critical balance between urban and suburban—at least for a privileged group of knowledge workers, now known as the creative class. Or, as RTP's Kristie VanAuken put it in 2018: "The value proposition here is right in the sweet spot."[79]

THE BRAIN, THE BUS, AND THE TRAILER

Can RTP and the Triangle as a whole overcome the shortcomings of the region's original 1950s vision? Can high-tech development not only produce better jobs, higher wages, and worthwhile innovations but also result in a broad-based prosperity that includes as many people as possible across a constellation of diverse communities?

The answer lies in the nature of what some scholars have called "cognitive capitalism," an economy driven by immaterial labor and the production of similarly abstract goods: affect and information.[80] Since at least the 1960s, many thinkers have pondered what a future economy and a future city might look like, especially if automation and other new technologies were to supplant older, manual labor jobs and result in a new kind of political economy. As manufacturing diminished as a proportion of employment in the United States, industries such as education, entertainment, and software accounted for an increasing number of workers in the late twentieth century.[81] Whether they are called "knowledge workers," a "new class," "symbolic analysts," or the "creative class," there is clearly a segment of the workforce that is more educated and lives and works in a manner that is different from that of the past. And since the 1950s, American cities and suburbs have pursued those workers for both their cultural cachet and the potential tax revenue they might generate.

In this book I have argued that the rise of this cognitive capitalism has been too little recognized by scholars and policy makers. Or, if it has been acknowledged, observers have treated its emergence too often as something natural or inevitable—the logical outcome of economic and technological developments of postindustrial capitalism in the late twentieth century. Rather, RTP illustrates that this new political economy was part of a concerted *cultural project*, one that explicitly valued certain types of labor and industries—and, by extension, certain kinds of people—as more important than others.

The Triangle is perhaps the most representative and unique example of a deliberate attempt to create a landscape expressly intended for education, research, and innovation—in short, "brains," the Triangle itself being a "brain magnet." The late-twentieth-century effort to retool the national economy toward postindustrial ends was hardly unique to North Carolina. Since the 1970s, the quest for the knowledge economy has swept America, from Cambridge to Raleigh, to Salt Lake City, to Seattle.[82] Austin in particular mirrors the Triangle model, with the centrality of the University of Texas to its postindustrial boom in the late twentieth century; the city's preference for light, nonpolluting industries; and its persistent pattern of racial and class inequality, as geographer Eliot M. Tretter has argued.[83] In the Research Triangle, as in Austin, universities were the magic totem for creating a metropolitan economy based on creativity, intellect, and knowledge—the key forces in a political economy that not only valorized knowledge production but lent privilege to its makers as a core component of the blueprint for the future.

This vision of a new economy emerged, unlikely as it may seem, among a handful of academics, bankers, and politicians in the Jim Crow North Carolina of the 1950s. If, as political scientist V. O. Key said in the 1940s, the North Carolina of that era was run for the benefit of a "progressive plutocracy," we might say its post-1960s political economy was organized around a progressive bobo-ocracy, exemplified by nothing so perfectly as the Research Triangle, and perhaps the banker suburbs of Charlotte.[84]

Questions of equity and social justice remain unremittingly present amid the twenty-first-century celebration of creativity and urban revival in Raleigh and Durham. And although the Triangle's problems stem, significantly, from the South's own historical legacy of economic and racial injustice, it is hardly an outlier. In the early years of the twenty-first century, a robust discussion broke out about inequality across the tech world, particularly Silicon Valley. Critics increasingly pointed out that racial and gender imbalances pervade employment in the most cutting-edge firms, with women, African Americans, and Latinos highly underrepresented. Meanwhile, the glaring economic divide between the best-educated and most affluent knowledge workers and everyone else became impossible to ignore as gentrification unfolded in cities from the 1970s onward. Sharp and sharpening inequities, in short, could be found both within the high-tech industry itself and across the broader metropolitan landscape.[85]

This widening gap was as impossible to ignore in the 2010s as it had been in prior decades, as Google buses roamed the streets of San Francisco and Mountain View, ferrying employees to and fro. Frustrated locals even took to blocking roads and throwing rocks at the buses in 2013 and again in 2018; they were fed up with skyrocketing housing prices and the privatized transit system enjoyed by their tech betters. "Warning: Two Tiered System," protesters declared, while another sign put a sharper point on the message: "Die techie scum. No one wants you here."[86] In 2016, the Bay Area boasted the third highest level of income inequality of any metropolitan area in the nation—with San Francisco, formerly a working-class port city and stronghold of cultural and political radicalism, becoming iconic as the acme of tech success.[87] Inequality, it could be said, is more a feature of the knowledge economy than a bug.

We live in an age of smart phones, smart cars, even smart refrigerators. "Smart" has become the alpha and the omega, just like creativity and innovation—roseate words that almost no one can possibly be against. Who could oppose creativity? The imperative to generate jobs for symbolic analysts undoubtedly opened the door to the good life for some, as North Carolina has done since the 1950s. But whether cognitive capitalism can deliver more than membership in an exclusive club for certain favored groups and communities remains to be seen. The knowledge economy continues to be an elitist formula for development and growth—one that occludes many in pursuit of the interests of the most educated and credentialed among us.

A stone's throw from RTP, an abandoned mobile home once sat. Perhaps it still does. When I trespassed inside in 2010, its floors were littered with empty prescription bottles and other various and sundry traces of a disordered life. This thing, once a home, was in the shadow of a beautiful laboratory building that belonged to a multinational corporation. It was a nettlesome reminder not only of the past but of the present. For all its successes, the boons of technology and investment and growth, the Research Triangle could not solve the riddle of achieving economic growth while ameliorating social inequity, perhaps because it was not designed to do so in the first place. North Carolina in the early twenty-first century never managed to achieve a sufficient escape velocity to leave the burden of its past behind. But if you think of it, what place ever has?

Epilogue

THE FIGURE OF THE KNOWLEDGE WORKER

It's a creative community. With plenty of educated men and women.

—State-sponsored ad for the Research Triangle, 1965

Progress goes where there's brains and water.

—Durham banker John S. Stewart, 1967

The genius of the place was the making of the place.

—Raymond Williams, 1973

Ever since Sir Thomas More proposed the idea of utopia in 1516—Greek for "no place"—humans have imagined what an ideal society would look like.[1] Subsequent dreamers from the Puritans, to the utopian communities of the nineteenth century such as Brook Farm or New Harmony, to the hippie communes of the 1970s attempted to make real, on soil and stone, schematics for a perfectly realized social order. Communist revolutionaries remade society again in the Soviet Union and China in the twentieth century. Meanwhile, nations built entire new cities out of ambition and necessity across the globe, in Magnitogorsk and Los Alamos, Brasilia and Islamabad, as historians such as Stephen Kotkin and Kate Brown have shown in their chronicles of such artificial places.[2] The hope for a perfect city or society was rather like the poet Adrienne Rich's idea of "the dream of a common language" in the 1970s—an idealistic goal worth yearning for, but one that remained problematic and, possibly, impossibly elusive.[3]

Some visitors and critics have seen Research Triangle Park as a no place in its own right, albeit not in the way that Thomas More intended—a bland, almost unnoticeable nothing in the pine forests of Durham County.[4] RTP, of course, has never been a utopian project on the scale of a new national capital or a socialist revolution. It was, however, a highly ambitious, coordinated, and long-term project to re-create a region in a new image, beginning in the impoverished North Carolina of the 1950s and leading to the much-lauded Triangle of the early twenty-first century. The tightly regulated architecture, landscaping, and zoning of the research park bore the fingerprints of idealistic and obsessive enterprises of the past. And its original goal of importing PhDs to remake the local economy was social engineering at its gentlest and most genteel. RTP also happened to invent a whole new approach to economic development that placed art, creativity, and cultural capital at its center, an approach that became ubiquitous in the United States by the end of the twentieth century.

Chief among the aims of this book has been to illustrate how Americans have thought about knowledge and work—how the former was made and where the latter happened. These themes were especially salient in the late twentieth century, as the relative decline of manufacturing as a proportion of employment (deindustrialization) and the rise of postindustrial jobs in services reshaped the way Americans thought about and experienced their working lives. Simultaneously, the ethos of the information economy drove leaders, whether in Congress or the local city council, to promote policies that favored intellectual property rights, high-tech development, and industries such as entertainment and finance. (The late Judith Stein and other historians, including myself, have traced this process with a critical eye, from the 1960s forward.[5]) Knowledge was the coin of the realm, and brains were how you got more of it.

Hence, looking at a place expressly designed for the creation of knowledge provides a way to trace how an idea was conceived in the 1950s and 1960s and brought to realization by the end of the century. The idea? That intellectual labor was the wave of the future, and public policy should favor both high-tech industries and the educated workers they employed. RTP and the Research Triangle as a whole offer an early and crucial example of a development strategy based specifically on leveraging intellectual and cultural resources—such as universities and the arts—to present an attractive image of a place to live for an emerging class of scientific and technical workers. Indeed, the aim was not merely to create an image of a place but to invent an entire place itself, from RTP to its neighboring suburbs and cities.

Such an approach became increasingly common after World War II. Orange County, California, filled with Lockheed-Martin engineers and their families, who were hungry for the largesse of the Department of Defense and the hard-core conservatism of affluent Los Angeles suburbs, as Lisa McGirr and other historians have shown. Margaret Pugh O'Mara examined the rise of intellectual and high-tech enclaves from Silicon Valley to Philadelphia in her essential book *Cities of Knowledge*. More recently, Rachel Guberman argued that "quality of life"—a stubbornly amorphous term—had come to dominate urban and suburban politics for the middle class in Denver and Colorado as a whole since the 1960s, and Lily Geismer followed the political ambitions and ideology of the affluent denizens of the outskirts of brainy Boston.[6] By the 1990s, policy recommendations for urban revitalization that centered on arts, culture, and the tastes of an educated elite abounded, until Richard Florida synthesized and popularized this approach with his expansive concept of the creative class in 2002. RTP was arguably the birthplace of what economist Ann Markusen has termed "creative placemaking."[7]

All this is to say that the idea of attracting educated, well-paid residents to a city or suburb is hardly a breakthrough of Archimidean proportions. Communities across the United States have long lusted after the tax base and spending power of the middle and upper classes. The Triangle was only one of the places where this solicitous pursuit of the educated took place in the late-twentieth-century United States. But it was perhaps the most intentional effort—contrived from thin air, a plan consciously articulated and persistently pursued beginning in the 1950s. Crucially, its founders emphasized creativity and culture in ways—inchoate at first, perhaps—that spread far from the Triangle and ultimately congealed into a specific way of thinking about class and the economy that continued to influence public policy in the twenty-first century. RTP offers us a vision of the future as it was understood at midcentury. It is a blueprint of an economy dedicated to intellectual labor and the production of knowledge, of what a world made for brains would look like.

If RTP was the blueprint, then the creative Triangle of today is the building. In this book I intended to look at both, to see how, as Governor Luther Hodges put it, an idea becomes a reality, an ambition becomes a real, felt thing of glass and steel, Astroturf and asphalt. Indeed, this book has used the concepts of space and place to trace how ideas about both knowledge work and knowledge workers were inscribed in the landscape, from the original zoning rules and design aesthetic of RTP to the laboratories and offices where its denizens came to work at places such as IBM and Burroughs Wellcome. From the green, suburban setting to the clean, angular lines of the buildings' exteriors, to the layout and organization of the offices within, these spaces reflected evolving ideas of where the workers of the future would work and how best they would do so. (Historian of science William Rankin aptly described such spaces as reflecting the "epistemology of the suburbs"—a design approach common to corporate research laboratories after World War II.[8]) The National Humanities Center carried this vision further, crystallizing, in the late 1970s, a model of a space devoted purely to contemplation, reading, and writing. It was full of books and open spaces where the creative worker—in this case, the scholar—could do his or her work with flexibility and freedom.

And what better represents the ethos of a knowledge-based economy than academia? In a literal sense, the college or university provided the model of the new idea economy. These institutions were, after all, devoted almost exclusively to the production and dissemination of knowledge; their only output was credentials and diplomas, in addition to books, articles, and perhaps patents. Richard Florida and others have repeatedly stressed the centrality of universities to economic development and urban prosperity, citing how cities with major research institutions such as Austin and San Francisco have enjoyed the greatest advances in quality of life and job growth in the late twentieth and early twenty-first centuries.[9]

RTP illustrates how this model of a new economy was based significantly on universities—the original brain magnets—as planners both public and private strove to re-create the intellectual environment of the campus in a new, postindustrial, suburban format for work. This was where smart people did smart things: studying (the university), living (the suburb), and thinking, researching, and writing (the park)—an entire life cycle for the maturation of the middle-class egghead. It is not surprising that scholars and journalists have been entranced by this vision of the future, which resembles their own lives of knowledge work. In many ways, including the scientists and executives, the professors and consultants who promoted the concept, the creative economy was an ode to themselves.

The world around RTP mirrored in home life and recreation the ambitions of this class. Developers founded Parkwood in the 1960s next to RTP as an idyllic ranch-house-age suburb, with a homeowners association to police the landscape—rather as the Board of Design did within the park—and, for much of the 1960s and 1970s, an all-white population. Both the suburb and the research center were grounded squarely in veneration of the ideal of the park, similar to the leafy, dispersed ideal of the college campus. The tremendous subsequent growth of nearby Cary only expanded on this model of highly educated suburbanites and easy living on a more ambitious and affluent scale. Its famed SAS Institute brought "the good life" to the workplace starting in the late 1970s, becoming not only the largest privately held software company in the world by 2009 but also a celebrated case study of how benevolent, flexible management can foster the creativity and loyalty of privileged knowledge workers.[10]

Each of these locales—from RTP to Cary to gentrifying Durham—have witnessed the ideal of the knowledge economy realized in real space, piece by piece, ever closer to a future defined by the creativity and intellectual work of a certain class of workers. People's mental conception of the ideal future tells us much about not only where the culture is going but also what it is. What is the best kind of job? A creative one is better than an uncreative one; a knowledge job is better than digging ditches. In Florida's clever but reductive dichotomy, jobs that require brains fall on one side of a line—far distant from the low wages, marginal status, and rote, allegedly unthinking repetition of other jobs in factories, retail stores, and offices.[11]

Looking at this genealogy of the knowledge worker lets us consider a much bigger trajectory of history. Where we want to go or have wanted to go tells us a great deal about where we are or have been. Even in the earliest days of the United States, the founding fathers—children of the Enlightenment—privileged the power of knowledge in ways both prosaic and grandiose. From the Constitution's mandate for copyright and a postal service—an early and critical vector of the spread of information, as historian Paul Starr has shown—to Jefferson's lyrical image of knowledge as a candle that lights another without extinguishing itself, the founders believed in knowledge as a good in itself.[12] Most poetically, John Adams described this sense of a future made better by knowledge in a 1780 letter to his wife, Abigail:

> I must study Politicks and War that my sons may have liberty to study Mathematicks and Philosophy. My sons ought to study Mathematicks and Philosophy, Geography, natural History, Naval Architecture, navigation, Commerce and Agriculture, in order to give their Children a right to study Painting, Poetry, Musick, Architecture, Statuary, Tapestry and Porcelaine.[13]

One generation does the hard stuff so the next may do the less difficult tasks—and in turn, the succeeding generations can devote themselves to the airier things, art and the life of the mind. The concept of the knowledge economy is an echo of an enduring aspect of America's enlightenment legacy.

Indeed, this somewhat Whiggish sense of history and progress speaks to habits of mind long established in the United States. Knowledge is good. Creativity is good. Curiously, creativity has both a shorter and longer story of its own; for much of Western history, "to create" was a term reserved for God alone, for only God could make something out of nothing.[14] Use of the words *create* and *creativity* was relatively uncommon in the English language until the mid-twentieth century, when it picked up considerably, to the point that those terms in the twenty-first century are so common as to be banal. Indeed, creativity, innovation, and the ability to make something out of nothing have become the most totemic power in postindustrial America. This book argues that Americans increasingly valorized concepts such as creativity, education, information, and knowledge from the mid-twentieth century to the early twenty-first. That turn—as much cultural as it was economic or technological—had real implications for policy, whether regarding copyright law, trade policy, or local questions of development and gentrification.

In a society that prized education and intellectual and social capital above all, the brain workers mattered most. That figure might have been the scientist or engineer or, perhaps, professor in the 1960s; historian Jamie Cohen-Cole has discussed the importance of intellectuals' own self-conception of having "open minds" and how much that image mattered in the context of the Cold War struggle.[15] The category might have grown both wider and more shallow since the 1970s, as thinkers such as Daniel Bell and Herman Kahn imagined a "new class" that included not only scientists with horn-rimmed glasses and pocket protectors but also a greater variety of postindustrial workers. The ever-changing concept of the knowledge worker reached its apotheosis in Florida's creative class—but its message remained the same. Knowledge and culture were now the fuels of capitalism; those who possessed them, whether an artist, businessperson, or scientist, were important and needed to be catered to. Everyone else could go jump in a lake.

Of course, one lives not just by thought alone, any more than by bread. The economy of the twenty-first-century United States might have seen a shrinking portion of the workforce engaged in traditional manufacturing, but such activities still accounted for a large portion of output—8.8 percent of workers but 12.5 percent of GDP in 2013, for instance.[16] Meanwhile, the work of life continued on the backs of home health aides bathing the elderly and infirm; floor personnel in retail stores and "pickers" hunting toilet paper and tube socks in Amazon warehouses; and, indeed, factory workers sweating away everywhere from Gastonia to Guangzhou.[17] The life of the mind remains stubbornly embedded in the world of the body, even in the information age. One is left to think of the consultants and theorists and local development officials who espouse creativity as akin to a diametrically opposite image—the anonymous hordes of lurching, foot-dragging zombies of horror films, who also cry out for "Brains . . . brains . . ."

There is, of course, nothing wrong with brains, or creativity, or innovation. Science and technology have improved the lives of people all over the world since at least the dawn of the industrial revolution, if not since the invention of the umbrella two thousand years ago. Although anxieties about automation have persisted over centuries, few can argue that a drug that saves lives from HIV or the invention of Ctrl+Alt+Delete—both outgrowths of RTP—was a detriment to humanity.[18] We need the human ingenuity that Silicon Valley, the Research Triangle, and other high-tech locales have succeeded so well in providing.

Indeed, the city of ideas remains a fond dream, and understandably so—an aspiration keyed to a centuries-long desire for progress as much as the pragmatic objectives of economic development or our contemporary zest for new gizmos. Most (if not all) Americans would agree that a world with more art, education, and scientific progress would be a better one, and places that nurture innovation and creativity are valuable in their own right. Yet the gossamer visions of the new and the good, sweet to the eye, should not cloud our ability to see who and what our pictures of the good life show us—and what they risk obscuring.

The story of RTP shows us, at the very least, what a highly conscious strategy of economic development based on assets of culture, knowledge, and science can achieve—when it is executed in the most effective and sustained way, over the course of decades: greater investment and wages, a degree of spillover innovation, and a decent quality of life for some, but also persistent inequality and a picture of the future that has little place for those without the best starting position. Anyone who is concerned with the future of capitalism and the prospects of all people, from the top to the bottom of the socioeconomic hierarchy, has to reckon with this question. (In 2017, journalist Sam Kriss memorably described the emerging landscape of the tech economy as a "lanyard-based class system," referring to the color-coded name tags that are common at academic and business conferences.[19])

Who will we be? What will we do, day in and day out, at work? If the future is only a playground for the affluent and educated, an endless multiplication of the manicured lawns of SAS or the whiskey bars of downtown Durham, who gets in and who is left out? Surely everyone is creative in their everyday lives in ways big, medium, and small. If we favor an economy dedicated to the idea of ideas, we would benefit from a far more capacious notion of what creativity and innovation really mean. It is something worth thinking about.

Notes

PREFACE

1. Interview with Farooq Mazhar, Raleigh, North Carolina, August 7, 2018.
2. For examples of "stuff" or "things" discourse, see Robert Teitelman, "On the Nostalgia for Manufacturing," *Huffington Post*, October 20, 2010, https://www.huffpost.com/entry/on-the-nostalgia-for-manu_b_770400; Aditya Chakrabortty, "Why Doesn't Britain Make Things Any More," *Guardian*, November 16, 2011, https://www.theguardian.com/business/2011/nov/16/why-britain-doesnt-make-things-manufacturing; Neil Irwin, "Growth in Global Trade Is in Ideas, Not Stuff," *New York Times*, April 29, 2014, https://www.nytimes.com/2014/05/01/upshot/big-growth-in-global-trade-is-in-ideas-not-stuff.html; and Larry Wines, "Cyberian Economics 101," *LA Progressive*, February 8, 2015, https://www.laprogressive.com/information-based-economy/.
3. For a typically boosterish rundown of accolades, see "Raleigh Ranks Among Best Places," *City of Raleigh*, July 10, 2018, https://www.raleighnc.gov/home/content/PubAffairs/Articles/Accolades Raleigh.html.
4. Richard Florida, *The Rise of the Creative Class: And How It's Transforming Work, Leisure, Community, and Everyday Life* (New York: Basic Books, 2002).
5. Alex Sayf Cummings, "Of Sorcerers and Thought Leaders: Marketing the 'Information Revolution' in the 1960s," *The Sixties: A Journal of History, Politics, and Culture* 9 (2016): 1–25; Peter Drucker, *Landmarks of Tomorrow: A Report on the New "Post Modern" World* (New York: Harper & Row, 1959); Fritz Machlup, *The Production and Distribution of Knowledge in the United States* (Princeton, NJ: Princeton University Press, 1962); Daniel Bell, *The Coming of Post-Industrial Society: A Venture in Social Forecasting* (New York: Basic Books, 1973); Manuel Castells, *The Informational City: Information Technology, Economic Restructuring, and the Urban-Regional Process* (Oxford: Blackwell, 1989); and Margaret Pugh O'Mara, *Cities of Knowledge: Cold War Science and the Search for the Next Silicon Valley* (Princeton, NJ: Princeton University Press, 2004).

6. LaDale C. Winling, *Building the Ivory Tower: Universities and Metropolitan Development in the Twentieth Century* (Philadelphia: University of Pennsylvania Press, 2017); Lily Geismer, *Don't Blame Us: Suburban Liberals and the Transformation of the Democratic Party* (Princeton, NJ: Princeton University Press, 2014); and Andrew T. Simpson, "'We Will Gladly Join You in Partnership in Harrisburg or We Will See You in Court': The Growth of Large Not-for -Profits and Consequences of the 'Eds and Meds' Renaissance in the New Pittsburgh," *Journal of Urban History* 42 (2016): 306–22.
7. Stefano Lucarelli and Carlo Vercellone, "The Thesis of Cognitive Capitalism: New Research Perspectives. An Introduction," *Knowledge Cultures* 1 (2013): 15–27; see also Michael Hardt's and Antonio Negri's treatment of the "informatization of production" in *Empire* (Cambridge, MA: Harvard University Press, 2000), 280, and the role of immaterial labor as the hegemonic "tendency" within contemporary capitalism in *Multitude: War and Democracy in the Age of Empire* (New York: Penguin, 2004), 107.
8. Yann Moulier Boutang, *Cognitive Capitalism* (Cambridge: Polity Press, 2011), 50. The original French edition was published in 2007.
9. Boutang, *Cognitive Capitalism*, 55.
10. The company TaskRabbit is part of the "gig economy," founded in San Francisco in 2008 as RunMyErrand and later acquired by Swedish furniture giant IKEA in 2017. See Louis Hyman, *Temp: How American Work, American Business, and the American Dream Became Temporary* (New York: Viking, 2018), 9, 294; and Nick Statt, "HBO's Silicon Valley Takes a Direct Shot at the Tech Industry's Obsession with AI," *The Verge*, May 8, 2017, https://www.theverge.com/2017/5/8/15582040/hbo-silicon-valley-season-4-episode-3-intellectual-property-recap.
11. Richard J. Herrnstein and Charles Murray, *The Bell Curve: Intelligence and Class Structure in American Life* (New York: Free Press, 1994), 114–15; and David Brooks, *Bobos in Paradise: The New Upper Class and How They Got There* (New York: Simon & Schuster, 2000); Florida, *Rise of the Creative Class*.
12. Derek Hyra, "The Back-to-the-City Movement: Neighbourhood Redevelopment and Processes of Political and Cultural Displacement," *Urban Studies* 52 (2015): 1753–73. For the most influential twenty-first-century take on widening inequality and social stratification, see Thomas Piketty, *Capital in the Twenty-First Century* (Cambridge, MA: Harvard University Press, 2014).
13. On greater geographic mobility in America, see Bill Bishop, *The Big Sort: Why the Clustering of Like-Minded America Is Tearing Us Apart* (New York: Houghton Mifflin, 2008). On multiethnic cities, see Wei Li, "Anatomy of a New Ethnic Settlement: The Chinese Ethnoburb in Los Angeles," *Urban Studies* 35 (1998): 479–501; Mike Davis, *Magical Urbanism: Latinos Reinvent the U.S. City* (New York: Verso, 2000); Stanley Thangaraj, *Desi Hoop Dreams: Pickup Basketball and the Making of Asian American Masculinity* (New York: New York University Press, 2015); and Wendy Cheng, *The Changs Next Door to the Diazes: Remapping Race in Suburban California* (Minneapolis: University of Minnesota Press, 2013).

INTRODUCTION

1. Don Hoefler, "Silicon Valley U.S.A.," *Electronic News*, January 11, 1971; Margaret Pugh O'Mara, *Cities of Knowledge: Cold War Science and the Search for the Next Silicon Valley* (Princeton, NJ: Princeton University Press, 2004), 97–141.
2. The seminal works on Research Triangle Park include Albert N. Link, *A Generosity of Spirit: The Early History of the Research Triangle Park* (Research Triangle Park, NC: Research Triangle Foundation, 1995); Michael I. Luger and Harvey A. Goldstein, *Technology in the Garden: Research Parks*

and Regional Economic Development (Chapel Hill: University of North Carolina Press, 1991); and William M. Rohe, *The Research Triangle: From Tobacco Road to Global Prominence* (Philadelphia: University of Pennsylvania Press, 2011).

3. James C. Cobb, *The Selling of the South: The Southern Crusade for Industrial Development, 1936–1980* (Baton Rouge: Louisiana State University Press, 1982).
4. "North Carolina: An Economic Profile," *Monthly Review of the Federal Reserve Bank of Richmond*, November 1962, 2–4.
5. As numerous historians have shown, overly enthused boosters have made glittering claims about economic growth and capital investment in the South ever since Reconstruction. See, for example, Lawrence H. Larsen, *The Rise of the Urban South* (Lexington: University Press of Kentucky, 1985), 142–44.
6. "North Carolina: An Economic Profile," 2–3.
7. C. B. Deane, "Complex Factors Enter into State's Low Wage Pattern; Lack of Education Is Sharply to Fore," *Greensboro Daily News*, August 14, 1955, in Romeo Guest Papers (hereafter cited as RGP), Duke University, Durham, North Carolina, box 10, Newspaper Clippings, 1956, 2 of 2.
8. Richard Lloyd, "Urbanization and the Southern United States," *Annual Review of Sociology* 38 (2012): 485–86. For the classic view of the South as a colony, see W. J. Cash, *The Mind of the South* (New York: Knopf, 1941), vii. See also Keri Leigh Merritt, *Masterless Men: Poor Whites and Slavery in the Antebellum South* (Cambridge: Cambridge University Press, 2017); Lawrence Goodwyn, *The Populist Moment: A Short History of the Agrarian Revolt in America* (New York: Oxford University Press, 1978); and David L. Carlton and Peter A. Coclanis, *Confronting Southern Poverty in the Great Depression: The Report on Economic Conditions in the South and Related Documents* (Boston: Bedford Books of St. Martin's Press, 1996).
9. David Carlton, "The Revolution from Above: The National Market and the Beginnings of Industrialization in North Carolina," *Journal of American History* 77 (1990): 445–75.
10. Memo to Phyllis Branch, November 5, 1954, in Romeo Guest Papers, 1925–87 and undated (RGP), Think Up/Start Up Era, box 10, Advertising and Related Correspondence, 1954, 1.
11. Romeo H. Guest to Mrs. Julius Cone, December 22, 1954.
12. Stephen J. Appold, "Research Parks and the Location of Industrial Research Laboratories: An Analysis of the Effectiveness of a Policy Intervention," *Research Policy* 33 (2004): 225–43; Susan Walcott, "Growing Global: Learning Locations in the Life Sciences," *Growth and Change* 32, no. 4 (Fall 2001): 511–32.
13. "The universities, black areas, and the wine-and-cheese crowd in Charlotte all backed Obama, while [Hillary] Clinton ruled only the white rural counties," pundit Robert Novak commented on the 2008 Democratic primary in North Carolina. "This shows that she failed to reach beyond her standard base in North Carolina." Robert Novak and Timothy Carney, "Racial Divide Guarantees Obama Nomination," *Human Events*, May 7, 2008, https://humanevents.com/2008/05/07/enpr-racial-divide-guarantees-obama-nomination/. For a more historically informed perspective, see Kevin Kruse, *White Flight: Atlanta and the Making of Modern Conservatism* (Princeton, NJ: Princeton University Press, 2007); Matthew Lassiter, *The Silent Majority: Suburban Politics in the Sunbelt South* (Princeton, NJ: Princeton University Press, 2006); and Dan T. Carter, "North Carolina: A State of Shock," *Southern Spaces*, September 24, 2013, https://southernspaces.org/2013/north-carolina-state-shock.
14. David Havlick and Scott Kirsch, "A Production Utopia: RTP and the North Carolina Research Triangle," *Southeastern Geographer* 44, no. 2 (2004): 266–67.
15. "The Research Triangle," *Greensboro Daily News*, November 14, 1965, in RGP, Think Up/Start Up Era, box 10, Clippings, 1954–82.

16. Robert H. Kargon and Arthur P. Molella, *Invented Edens: Techno Cities of the Twentieth Century* (Cambridge, MA: MIT Press, 2008); Margaret Pugh O'Mara, *Cities of Knowledge: Cold War Science and the Search for the Next Silicon Valley* (Princeton, NJ: Princeton University Press, 2004); Lindsey A. Freeman, *Longing for the Bomb: Oak Ridge and Atomic Nostalgia* (Chapel Hill: University of North Carolina Press, 2015).
17. "Regional Planning in Research Triangle Area," *Durham Morning Herald*, September 30, 1957, in RGP, box 10, Newspaper Clippings, 1957, 1 of 2; Link, *Generosity of Spirit*, 73.
18. William J. Mallett, "Managing the Post-Industrial City: Business Improvement Districts in the United States," *Area* 26, no. 3 (1994): 276–87; Jason Hackworth, *The Neoliberal City: Governance, Ideology, and Development* (Ithaca, NY: Cornell University Press, 2007).
19. Arthur Johnsey, "Explanation Is Given of Research Triangle," *Greensboro Daily News*, October 18, 1957, n.p., RGP, Think Up/Start Up Era, box 10, Advertising and Related Correspondence, 1954.
20. David R. Goldfield, *Cotton Fields and Skyscrapers: Southern City and Region* (Baltimore, MD: Johns Hopkins University Press, 1989).
21. Blaine Brownell, *The Urban Ethos in the South, 1920–1930* (Baton Rouge: Louisiana State University Press, 1975), 47.
22. Steve Kichen, "The Biggest Privately Held Tech Companies," *Forbes*, November 14, 2006, https://www.forbes.com/2006/11/13/private-technology-companies-pf-ii-cx_sk_1113sf.html#2dfeac9c6a9d.
23. William T. Polk to Romeo Guest, December 5, 1954, in RGP, Think Up/Start Up Era, box 10, Letters (Copies), 1953–54.
24. Lassiter, *The Silent Majority*; Christina Greene, *Our Separate Ways: Women and the Black Freedom Movement in Durham, North Carolina* (Chapel Hill: University of North Carolina Press, 2005).
25. Fritz Machlup, *The Production and Distribution of Knowledge in the United States* (Princeton, NJ: Princeton University Press, 1962).
26. *The Port Huron Statement of the Students for a Democratic Society, 1962* (New York: Students for a Democratic Society, 1962), http://www.historyisaweapon.com/defcon1/porthuron.html.
27. Daniel Bell, *The Coming of Post-Industrial Society: A Venture in Social Forecasting* (New York: Basic Books, 1973); Alain Touraine, *Post-industrial Society: Tomorrow's Social History: Classes, Conflicts, and Culture in the Programmed Society* (New York: Random House, 1971); Robert Reich, *The Work of Nations: Preparing Ourselves for 21st-Century Capitalism* (New York: Alfred A. Knopf, 1991); Richard Florida, *The Rise of the Creative Class: And How It's Transforming Work, Leisure, Community, and Everyday Life* (New York: Basic Books, 2002).
28. O'Mara, *Cities of Knowledge*; Stephen J. Pitti, *The Devil in Silicon Valley: Northern California, Race, and Mexican Americans* (Princeton, NJ: Princeton University Press, 2003); Lily Geismer, *Don't Blame Us: Suburban Liberals and the Transformation of the Democratic Party* (Princeton, NJ: Princeton University Press, 2014); Willow Lung-Amam, *Trespassers? Asian Americans and the Battle for Suburbia* (Berkeley: University of California Press, 2017); Eliot M. Tretter, *Shadows of a Sunbelt City: The Environment, Racism, and the Knowledge Economy in Austin* (Athens: University of Georgia Press, 2016).
29. Alex Sayf Cummings, "Of Sorcerers and Thought Leaders: Marketing the Information Revolution in the 1960s," *The Sixties: A Journal of History, Politics, and Culture* 9 (2016): 1–25.
30. Bill Bishop, *The Big Sort: Why the Clustering of Like-Minded America Is Tearing Us Apart* (New York: Houghton Mifflin, 2008).
31. Jamie Peck, "Struggling with the Creative Class," *International Journal of Urban and Regional Research* 29 (December 2005): 746.

1. IMAGINING THE TRIANGLE: THE UNLIKELY ORIGINS OF THE CREATIVE CITY IN THE COLD WAR SOUTH

1. C. B. Deane, "Complex Factors Enter into State's Low Wage Pattern; Lack of Education Is Sharply to Fore," *Greensboro Daily News*, August 14, 1955, in RGP, box 10, Newspaper Clippings, 1956, 2 of 2.
2. Ann Markusen, Peter Hall, Scott Campbell, and Sabina Deitrick, *The Rise of the Gunbelt: The Military Remapping of Industrial America* (New York: Oxford University Press, 1991); and Bruce Schulman, *From Cotton Belt to Sunbelt: Federal Policy, Economic Development, and the Transformation of the South, 1938–1980* (Durham, NC: Duke University Press, 1994).
3. Kari Frederickson, *Cold War Dixie: Militarization and Modernization in the American South* (Athens: University of Georgia Press, 2013).
4. George L. Simpson, "The Research Triangle of North Carolina," February 5, 1957, in Research Triangle Foundation Papers (hereafter cited as RTF), North Carolina Collection, University of North Carolina at Chapel Hill, folder 4, Research Triangle Committee Inc., General, 1956–58, 6, 12–13.
5. For example, see "North Carolina—Research from the Mountains to the Sea," *Wall Street Journal*, November 9, 1959, 4; "Live a Full Life with Chemstrand Research Center," *Science* 131 (March 18, 1960): 885; Luther J. Carter, "Research Triangle Park Succeeds Beyond Its Promoters' Expectations," *Science* (New Series) 200, no. 4349 (June 30, 1978), 1469.
6. Richard Florida, *The Rise of the Creative Class: And How It's Transforming Work, Leisure, Community, and Everyday Life* (New York: Basic Books, 2002); and Charles Landry and Franco Bianchini, *The Creative City* (London: Demos, 1995).
7. James C. Cobb, *The Selling of the South: The Southern Crusade for Industrial Development, 1936–1980* (Baton Rouge: Louisiana State University Press, 1982).
8. Memo to Phyllis Branch, November 5, 1954, in RGP, box 10, Advertising and Related Correspondence, 1954, 2.
9. Memo to Phyllis Branch, 1.
10. Memo to Phyllis Branch.
11. Luther J. Carter, "Alabama Cotton Town Takes Off into the Space Age," *Science*, New Series, 55, no. 3767 (March 10, 1967): 1224–29; see also Monique Laney, *German Rocketeers in the Heart of Dixie: Making Sense of the Nazi Past During the Civil Rights Era* (New Haven, CT: Yale University Press, 2015).
12. Blaine Brownell, *The Urban Ethos in the South, 1920–1930* (Baton Rouge: Louisiana State University Press, 1975), xvi.
13. Phil Clarke to Morris Sabin, June 11, 1954, in RGP, box 10, Letters (Copies), 1953–54, 1.
14. Clarke to Sabin, 2.
15. Fred Linton to Romeo Guest, January 11, 1955, in RGP, box 10, Correspondence, 1955, January, 1–2.
16. Louis R. Wilson, *The Research Triangle of North Carolina: A Notable Achievement in University, Governmental, and Industrial Cooperative Development* (Chapel Hill, NC: Colonial Press, 1967), 3–5.
17. Linton to Guest, 1–2.
18. Wilson, *The Research Triangle of North Carolina*, 8.
19. "Southern Research Through the Years," *Southern Research*, https://southernresearch.org/about/timeline/; and Charles X. Larambee, *Many Missions: Research Triangle Institute's First 31 Years, 1959–1990* (Research Triangle Park, NC: Research Triangle Institute, 1991), 25.
20. William T. Polk to Romeo Guest, December 5, 1954, in RGP, box 10, Letters (Copies), 1953–54, 1.

21. Romeo H. Guest to Dr. W. M. Murray Jr., January 21, 1955, in RGP, box 10, Correspondence, 1955.
22. "Research Triangle Plan Adopted," *Greensboro Daily News*, November 8, 1955, in RGP, box 10, Research Triangle Correspondence, 1955.
23. Elizabeth Tandy Shermer provides a valuable account of Hodges's energetic efforts to recruit foreign capital by stressing the state's business-friendly—low-tax and antilabor—climate in "'The South's No. 1 Salesman: Luther Hodges and the Nuevo South's Transatlantic Century," in *Outside In: The Transnational Circuitry in US History*, ed. Andrew Preston and Doug Rossinow (New York: Oxford University Press, 2017), 204–29.
24. Luther H. Hodges, *Businessman in the Statehouse: Six Years as Governor of North Carolina* (Chapel Hill: University of North Carolina Press, 1962), 203.
25. "Hodges Cites Research Plan," *Raleigh News & Observer*, March 26, 1955, in RGP, box 10, Research Triangle Correspondence, 1955.
26. James C. Cobb, *Industrialization and Southern Society, 1877–1984* (Baton Rouge: Louisiana State University Press, 1982), 107.
27. "Estimate of Personnel for the Research Triangle Park," January 22, 1958, in RGP, box 11, Research Triangle, History, 1958–60, 1977–78, 2 of 2, 2.
28. Margaret Pugh O'Mara, *Cities of Knowledge: Cold War Science and the Search for the Next Silicon Valley* (Princeton, NJ: Princeton University Press, 2004), 97–141.
29. "New Plan Launched to Attract Industry for Durham Section," in RGP, box 10, Correspondence, 1955, January.
30. Romeo Guest to John K. Voehringer Jr., December 28, 1954, in RGP, Think Up/Start Up Era, box 10, Letters (Copies), 1953–54.
31. Romeo H. Guest to Senator Arthur Kirkman, January 6, 1955, in RGP, box 10, Correspondence, 1955.
32. Russell A. McCoy Jr. to John P. Swain, January 7, 1955, in RGP, box 10, Correspondence, 1955.
33. Frank P. Bennett to Romeo Guest, February 1, 1955, in RGP, box 10, Research Triangle Correspondence, 1955.
34. William A. Newell to Kenneth Kramer, June 3, 1955, in RGP, box 10, Research Triangle Correspondence, 1955, 2.
35. Walter W. Harper to Romeo Guest, August 2, 1954, in RGP, box 10, Letters (Copies), 1953–54.
36. Memorandum to R. H. Guest, February 10, 1955, in RGP, box 10, Correspondence, 1955, 1.
37. N. J. Demerath to L. Hodges, April 5, 1955, in RGP, box 10, Research Triangle Correspondence 1955, p. 2.
38. Albert N. Link, *A Generosity of Spirit: The Early History of the Research Triangle Park* (Research Triangle Park, NC: Research Triangle Foundation, 1995), 29.
39. Simpson, "The Research Triangle of North Carolina," 4, 10.
40. "Minutes of the Working Committee of the Research Triangle Development Council," July 21, 1955, in RTF Papers, 2–3; and "Minutes of the Meeting of the Development Committee," September 12, 1955, in RTF Papers, 2.
41. Simpson, "The Research Triangle of North Carolina," 5.
42. "Memorandum to Members of the Research Triangle Committee," December 4, 1956, in RGP, box 11, Governor Hodges's Archival Papers, 1955–57, 1.
43. William F. Little to George Simpson, February 20, 1957, in RGP, box 11, Governor Hodges's Archival Papers, 1955–57, 1.
44. Little to Simpson, 1.
45. Little to Simpson, 2.
46. George Simpson to Robert Hanes, February 26, 1957, in RGP, box 11, Governor Hodges's Archival Papers, 1955–57, 1.

47. Simpson to Hanes, 2.
48. Link, *Generosity of Spirit*, 52.
49. "Karl Robbins, 67, Textile Man, Dies," *New York Times*, March 14, 1960, 29.
50. Karl Robbins to Luther Hodges, May 14, 1957, in RGP, box 11, Governor Hodges's Archival Papers, 1955–57, 1.
51. "New Soviet City to Spur Siberia," *New York Times*, June 9, 1957, in RGP, Box 11, Governor Hodges's Archival Papers, 1955–57.
52. Karl Robbins to Luther Hodges, June 18, 1957, in RGP, box 11, Governor Hodges's Archival Papers, 1955–57.
53. "Research Park Development Begins," advertisement, *New York Times*, January 6, 1958, 75.
54. O. Mac White, "Secret Was Problem," in RGP, Box 10, Newspaper Clippings, 1957, 2 of 2.
55. Romeo Guest to Karl Robbins, July 25, 1957 in RGP, box 11, Governor Hodges's Archival Papers, 1955–57.
56. White, "Secret Was Problem."
57. H. K. Nason to D. S. Mims, January 30, 1957, in RGP, box 11, Governor Hodges's Archival Papers, 1955–57.
58. "Proposed Statement of Principles for the Research Institute of the Research Triangle," April 23, 1957, in RGP, box 11, Governor Hodges's Archival Papers, 1955–57.
59. George Simpson to Robert Hanes, March 25, 1957, in RGP, box 11, Governor Hodges's Archival Papers, 1955–57, 2.
60. George Simpson to F. L. Fish, June 20, 1957, in RGP, box 11, Governor Hodges's Archival Papers, 1955–57; and Robbins to Hodges, May 14, 1957.
61. Romeo Guest to Luther Hodges, September 11, 1957, in RGP, Box 11, Governor Hodges's Archival Papers, 1955–57.
62. George Simpson to Luther Hodges, May 22, 1957, in RGP, Box 11, Governor Hodges's Archival Papers, 1955–57, 1–2.
63. David Havlick and Scott Kirsch, "A Production Utopia: RTP and the North Carolina Research Triangle," *Southeastern Geographer* 44, no. 2 (2004): 263–73.
64. "Scientific City," in RGP, box 10, Newspaper Clippings, 1957, 2 of 2.
65. Wilson, *The Research Triangle of North Carolina*, 14.
66. Romeo Guest to Claude Q. Freeman, July 22, 1958, in RGP, box 11, Research Triangle, History, 1958–60, 1977–78, 2 of 2.
67. William M. Rohe, *The Research Triangle: From Tobacco Road to Global Prominence* (Philadelphia: University of Pennsylvania Press, 2011), 67–69.
68. George Simpson to Luther Hodges, November 6, 1956, in RGP, box 11, Governor Hodges's Archival Papers, 1955–57, 1.
69. Simpson to Hodges, November 6, 1956.
70. "Conditioned for Research . . ." pamphlet, in RGP, box 10, Duke University, Advertising and Related Correspondence, 1954, 3.
71. Romeo H. Guest to William E. Bunney, June 8, 1953, in RGP, box 10, Correspondence, 1951–53, 1.
72. "Research Park Development Begins."
73. "Research Triangle," advertisement, *New York Times*, November 17, 1957, AS9.
74. "Research Center Planned by IBM," *New York World-Telegram and Sun*, September 27, 1956, in RGP, Think Up/Start Up Era, box 10, Newspaper Clippings, 1957, 2 of 2.
75. Guest to Bunney, 1.
76. G. H. Law to G. L. Simpson, November 20, 1956, in RGP, box 11, Governor Hodges's Archival Papers, 1955–57, 1.

77. P. Aydalot and D. Keeble, *High Technology Industry and Innovative Environments: The European Experience* (London: Routledge, 1988); and Manuel Castells and Peter Hall, *Technopoles of the World: The Making of Twenty-First Century Industrial Complexes* (London: Routledge, 1994).
78. John Leland, "On a Hunt for Ways to Put Sex in the City," *New York Times*, December 11, 2003, F1–F9.
79. "Research Staffs Being Beset By Problem of Where to Live," *New York Times*, June 16, 1962, 47.
80. "Research Triangle."
81. "Research Triangle."
82. "Man and Mind Work Better Where Life Is Stimulating," advertisement, *New York Times*, November 17, 1957, AS2.
83. "RTI: An Independent Research Organization in a Stimulating University Environment," *Operations Research* 10, no. 4 (July–August 1962): xxvi.
84. D. G. Crosby, "The 'Research Triangle' of North Carolina," July 21, 1958, in RTF Papers, folder 4, Research Triangle Committee Inc., General, 1956–58, 1.
85. Wilson, *The Research Triangle of North Carolina*, 16.
86. "Real Estate Notes," *New York Times*, July 21, 1959, 46; and William M. Freeman, "New Commerce Chief Pledges Research Step-Up," *New York Times*, February 2, 1961, 46.
87. "North Carolina—Research from the Mountains to the Sea," *Wall Street Journal*, November 9, 1959, 4.
88. "Mechanical Research," advertisement, *New York Times*, September 23, 1962, 176; and "Live a Full Life with Chemstrand Research Center," *Science* 131 (March 18, 1960): 885.
89. "Senior Project Engineers," *New York Times*, February 21, 1960, F15.
90. "Big Research Center," 48.
91. Thomas O'Toole, "Computer to Aid Three Campuses," *New York Times*, February 15, 1966, 25.
92. "In Our Research Triangle Are Three of the Nation's Leading Universities and More than 450 Scientists," *Wall Street Journal*, September 16, 1966, 5.
93. "A Lot of Yesterday's Science Fiction Isn't Fiction Anymore," *Wall Street Journal*, November 24, 1965, 12.
94. "Carolina Shows How to Do It," *St. Petersburg (FL) Times*, January 8, 1965, 6A.
95. "Suncoast Research Triangle," *St. Petersburg (FL) Times*, January 10, 1965, 2D.
96. " 'Research Triangle' Important," *Bend Bulletin*, August 25, 1962, 4.
97. "Triangle," *Eugene Register-Guard*, October 23, 1962, 12A.
98. Ralph McGill, "Education, Economic Progress Inescapably Together," *Miami News*, May 31, 1964, 6A.
99. "University Complex Is Urged Upstate," *New York Times*, February 12, 1967, 71.
100. Blake Gumprecht, "The American College Town," *Geographical Review* 93 (January 2003): 51.
101. Gumprecht, "American College Town," 51; Havlick and Kirsch, "A Production Utopia," 273; and "North Carolina: Pacesetter of the Advancing South," *New York Times*, January 2, 1957, 63.
102. Simpson, "The Research Triangle of North Carolina," 7.

2. "NOT A SECOND RUHR": BUILDING A POSTINDUSTRIAL ECONOMY IN THE 1960s

1. William M. Freeman, "New Commerce Chief Pledges Research Step-Up," *New York Times*, February 2, 1961, 46.
2. David Havlick and Scott Kirsch, "A Production Utopia: RTP and the North Carolina Research Triangle," *Southeastern Geographer* 44, no. 2 (2004): 263–77.

3. "Development of the Research Triangle Site," 1957, in RTF Papers, folder 5, Research Triangle Committee, Inc.: Announcements, 1957, 1.
4. Louise A. Mozingo, *Pastoral Capitalism: A History of Suburban Corporate Landscapes* (Cambridge, MA: MIT Press, 2011), 161–66.
5. Joe Duke, " 'Research' Zone Planned," *Durham (NC) Sun*, August 3, 1959, in RTF Papers, folder 1189, Zoning: 1958–63, 3-A.
6. George A. Moore Jr., "The Research Triangle Park," November 9, 1960, in RTF Papers, folder 20, Archie Davis: General, 1960–62 and undated, 7.
7. Admittedly, Moore went on to say that some kind of material production, for prototypes and pilot plants, would have to be permitted in one way or another.
8. For the definitive account of RTI, see Charles X. Larambee, *Many Missions: Research Triangle Institute's First 31 Years, 1959–1990* (Research Triangle Park, NC: Research Triangle Institute, 1991).
9. Romeo H. Guest to Senator Arthur Kirkman, January 6, 1955, in RGP, box 10, Correspondence, 1955; "Proposed Statement of Principles for the Research Institute of the Research Triangle," April 23, 1957, in RGP, box 11, Governor Hodges's Archival Papers, 1955–57, 1.
10. George L. Simpson, "The Research Triangle of North Carolina," February 5, 1957, in RTF Papers, folder 4, Research Triangle Committee Inc.: General, 1956–58, 2, 9.
11. "Astra Patents New Radiation Process for Making Pneumatic Tires," ca. June 19, 1960, in RTF Papers, folder 291, General, 1961: Astra Reprints, 1961, n.p.; and "Research Triangle Soon to Add Another Member," *Greensboro Record*, December 1, 1960, F6, in RGP, Think Up/Start Up Era, box 10, Newspaper Clippings, 1957, 2 of 2.
12. Robert F. Campbell, "Modern Science Leads Industrial Development," *New York Times*, November 17, 1957, AS3.
13. "Research Triangle Soon to Add Another Member."
14. James B. Shea Jr. to Members of the Council, February 2, 1961, in RTF Papers, folder 289, General, 1961: American Association of Textile Chemists and Colorists, 1961, 1.
15. Mark Clark, *Dyeing for a Living: A History of the American Association of Textile Chemists and Colorists: 1921–1996* (Research Triangle Park, NC: American Association of Textile Chemists and Colorists, 2001), 130.
16. Clark, *Dyeing for a Living*, 110.
17. Clark, *Dyeing for a Living*, 140.
18. G. P. Paine to James B. Shea Jr., June 23, 1961, in RTF Papers, folder 289, General, 1961: American Association of Textile Chemists and Colorists, 1961, 1.
19. G. H. D., "AATCC Makes a Wrong Move," *Textile Industries*, September 1961, in RTF Papers, folder 289, General, 1961: American Association of Textile Chemists and Colorists, 1961, n.p.
20. Clark, *Dyeing for a Living*, 144.
21. Clark, *Dyeing for a Living*, 139.
22. Clark, *Dyeing for a Living*, 132.
23. "The South in the Sixties," *New York Times*, April 24, 1960, E8.
24. William M. Freeman, "New Commerce Chief Pledges Research Step-Up," *New York Times*, February 2, 1961, 46.
25. Alex Sayf Cummings, "Of Sorcerers and Thought Leaders: Marketing the Information Revolution in the 1960s," *The Sixties: A Journal of History, Politics, and Culture* 9 (2016): 1–25.
26. "Suncoast Research Triangle," *St. Petersburg (FL) Times*, January 10, 1965.
27. *North Carolina: An Economic Profile*, Federal Reserve Bank of Richmond, November 1962, 8.
28. *North Carolina: An Economic Profile*, 10.

29. George H. Herbert, "Innovation in a Triangle," April 16, 1971, in RTF Papers, folder 3331: Research Triangle Institute: Promotional Materials (2 of 2), 2.
30. Herbert, "Innovation in a Triangle," 3.
31. Thomas C. Parramore, *Express Lanes and Country Roads: The Way We Lived in North Carolina, 1920–1970* (Chapel Hill, NC: University of North Carolina Press, 1983), 40.
32. Havlick and Kirsch, "Production Utopia," 266.
33. Albert N. Link, *Generosity of Spirit: The Early History of the Research Triangle Park* (Research Triangle Park, NC: Research Triangle Foundation, 1995), 83–84, 90; and note from Calvin Bryant, ca. June 23, 1969, in RTF Papers, folder 1191, Zoning: 1966–69, 1.
34. "Agenda for Executive Committee Meeting," October 15, 1959, in RTF Papers, folder 13, Research Triangle Foundation: General, 1.
35. "Obituary: Stanley Foster Reed, M&A's First Scribe," *M&A Advisor*, December 31, 2007; and Ralph A. Jackson to Romeo Guest, in RGP, box 10, Letters (Copies), 1953–54, 1.
36. "Research Staffs Being Beset By Problem of Where to Live," *New York Times*, June 16, 1962, 47.
37. "Research Park Development Begins," *New York Times*, November 17, 1957, AS9.
38. Moore, "The Research Triangle Park," 7; Mozingo, *Pastoral Capitalism*, 174–77.
39. *North Carolina: An Economic Profile*, 9.
40. *North Carolina: An Economic Profile*, 10.
41. Howard G. Clark, "The Camille Dreyfus Laboratory," in *Anton Peterlin, 1908–1993: His Life and Work* (Ljubljana, Slovenia: Institut Jozef Stefan, 2008), 381.
42. Clark, "Camille Dreyfus Laboratory," 383.
43. Tanja Peterlin, "Anton Peterlin and the Camille Dreyfus Laboratory (1961–1973)," in *Anton Peterlin, 1908–1993: His Life and Work* (Ljubljana, Slovenia: Institut Jozef Stefan, 2008), 389–90; and Clark, "Camille Dreyfus Laboratory," 383.
44. Tanja Peterlin, "Anton Peterlin," 390.
45. Clark, "Camille Dreyfus Laboratory," 384.
46. Petr Munk, "Streaming Birefringence," in *Anton Peterlin, 1908–1993: His Life and Work* (Ljubljana, Slovenia: Institut Jozef Stefan, 2008), 187–88.
47. Munk, "Streaming Birefringence," 193–94.
48. Tanja Peterlin, "Anton Peterlin," 391.
49. Interview with Buckley Crist Jr., April 21, 2014.
50. Anton Peterlin, "My Scientific Life," in *Anton Peterlin, 1908–1993: His Life and Work* (Ljubljana, Slovenia: Institut Jozef Stefan, 2008), 32.
51. Interview with Crist.
52. Tanja Peterlin, "Anton Peterlin," 397.
53. Peterlin, "My Scientific Life," 32.
54. Munk, "Streaming Birefringence," 188.
55. Iinterview with Crist.
56. Margaret Knox, "Should Science Have Limits?," *North Carolina Leader*, February 28, 1968, 2.
57. Peterlin, "My Scientific Life," 32; Munk, "Streaming Birefringence," 194.
58. Charles Landry, *The Creative City: A Toolkit for Urban Innovators*, 2nd ed. (London: Earthscan, 2008), xxiii.
59. "Rhine Announces Foundation Changes," June 21, 1965, in Parapsychology Laboratory Records Collection (hereafter cited as PLRC), Duke University, Durham, NC, folder 1965: Research Triangle Land, 1.
60. Governor's press release, November 11, 1964, in PLRC, folder News Items, 1963–66, 1–3.

61. "Research Triangle Institute Has Shown Remarkable Growth in Five-Year Period," *Lexington Dispatch*, November 13, 1964, 4.
62. Howard E. Covington and Marion A. Ellis, *Terry Sanford: Politics, Progress, and Outrageous* (Durham, NC: Duke University Press, 1999), 239–41; and "North Carolina May Win," *Dispatch* (Lexington, NC), November 1, 1963, 4.
63. "Carolina Shows How to Do It," *St. Petersburg (FL) Times*, January 8, 1965, 6A.
64. Terry Sanford press conference, January 6, 1965, in Terry Sanford Papers, 1946–93, Southern Historical Collecton, University of North Carolina at Chapel Hill, Chapel Hill, NC.
65. Evert Clark, "3 States to Get U.S. Science Sites," *New York Times*, January 7, 1965, 26; and Covington and Ellis, *Terry Sanford*, 348.
66. Link, *Generosity of Spirit*, 87–88.
67. Margaret Pugh O'Mara, *Cities of Knowledge: Cold War Science and the Search for the Next Silicon Valley* (Princeton, NJ: Princeton University Press, 2004), 36–45.
68. Marjorie Hunter, "North Carolina Strong Prospect for Giant U.S. Research Center," *New York Times*, December 22, 1964, 32.
69. J. W. Davis, "Getting New Industry for a City Can Be a Real Coup," *Herald-Tribune* (Sarasota), July 11, 1965, 10A; and "Triangle Research Center Is Among Top in Country," *Spartanburg Herald*, July 5, 1972, B1.
70. "'Research Triangle' Important," *The Bend Bulletin*, August 25, 1962, 4.
71. "Triangle," *Eugene Register-Guard*, October 23, 1962, 12A.
72. "'Research Triangle' Important," 4; "Research Triangle" (letter to the editor), *Eugene Register-Guard*, April 18, 1964, 4A.
73. "Research Triangle."
74. "Triangle."
75. "Suncoast Research Triangle," *St. Petersburg (FL) Times*, January 10, 1965.
76. "Suncoast Research Triangle."
77. Interview with Gordon Gray, *Eisenhower Administration Project: Oral History, 1962–1972* (New York: Columbia Center for Oral History), 175.
78. "University Complex Is Urged Upstate," *New York Times*, February 12, 1967, 71.
79. Ralph McGill, "Education, Economic Progress Inescapably Together," *Miami News*, May 31, 1964, 6A.
80. "Suncoast Research Triangle."
81. William M. Rohe, *The Research Triangle: From Tobacco Road to Global Prominence* (Philadelphia: University of Pennsylvania Press, 2011), 149.
82. J. B. Rhine letter to Worth Lutz, January 29, 1965, in PRLC, folder 1965: Research Triangle Land, 1–3.
83. George Akers Moore to J. B. Rhine, April 9, 1965, in PRLC, folder 1965: Research Triangle Land, 1–2.
84. J. B. Rhine to George Akers Moore, June 10, 1965, in PRLC, folder 1965: Research Triangle Land, 1.
85. "Electronics Firm to Open in RTP," *Durham Morning Herald*, January 22, 1965, 1.
86. "Technical Librarians: There's a Whole World of Opportunity in IBM's Technical Library Near Raleigh, N.C.," *New York Times*, December 8, 1968, 257; and "Technicians: Get in on the Ground Floor at IBM—North Carolina's Fastest Growing Big Company," *Spartanburg Herald-Journal*, January 8, 1967, C5.
87. "Research Triangle Progress," *Times-News* (Hendersonville, NC), November 2, 1964, 2.
88. Thomas O'Toole, "Computer to Aid Three Campuses," *New York Times*, February 15, 1966, 25.
89. "Cancer Research Asked," *Times-News* (Hendersonville, NC), December 6, 1967, 2.
90. Robert Fishman, "The End of Suburbia: A New Kind of City Is Emerging—The 'Technoburb,'" *Los Angeles Times*, August 2, 1987, http://articles.latimes.com/1987-08-02/magazine/tm-724_1_central-cities.

3. WELCOME TO PARKWOOD: NEWCOMERS FIND THEIR WAY IN THE EMERGING TRIANGLE

1. Jim Wise, interview with Mayor William "Bill" Bell, August 7, 2012, Durham County Library (hereafter cited as DCL), North Carolina Collection, 4–5.
2. "Enjoy a Home of Your Own in Parkwood (brochure)," ca. 1961, in DCL, Parkwood Subject File (hereafter cited as PSF), 1.
3. Wise, interview with Bell, 24.
4. William M. Rohe, *The Research Triangle: From Tobacco Road to Global Prominence* (Philadelphia: University of Pennsylvania Press, 2011), 181.
5. "Scientific City," in RGP, box 10, Newspaper Clippings, 1957, 2 of 2.
6. J. Fellig, "Research Department Trip Report," July 25, 1958, in RTF Papers, folder 4, Research Triangle Committee, Inc.: General, 1956–58, 1–2.
7. "Five Projects Cited in Builders' Contest," *New York Times*, February 6, 1949, R1.
8. Jim Wise, "Future of Beloved Community in Limbo," *Durham Herald-Sun*, December 22, 2002, E1, in DCL, Lowe's Grove Subject file.
9. Kim Darnofall, "Parkwood, 1960–1990" (Parkwood Association), in PSF, 5.
10. "Enjoy a Home of Your Own in Parkwood," 1.
11. Kathryn D. McPherson, "'Grand Mix of People' With Community Sense," *Durham Morning Herald*, December 2, 1979, 2A, in PSF; and "Historical Census of Housing Tables: Home Values," *Census of Housing*, June 6, 2012, https://www.census.gov/hhes/www/housing/census/historic/values.html.
12. Darnofall, "Parkwood," 5.
13. "Welcome to Parkwood," May 1965, 1, in Parkwood Homeowner's Association Archive (hereafter cited as PHA), Durham, North Carolina, Parkwood History folder.
14. "Prepare for School!" August 12, 1962, in PHA, Parkwood History folder, 1.
15. "Declaration of Restrictions Affecting 'Parkwood,' Property of Equitable Construction Company," August 15, 1960, in PHA, Parkwood History folder, 4.
16. Regular Monthly Meeting Minutes, July 10, 1969, in PHA, 1969-Minutes folder, 1.
17. John McDonald, "Where's the Ceiling on New Houses?," *Fortune*, June 1963, 130.
18. *Welcome to Parkwood* (Durham, NC: Parkwood Association, 1965), 9, in PHA, Parkwood History folder.
19. "Meeting Minutes," May 11, 1961, 3–4, in PHA, Parkwood History folder; and letter from Josephus D. Ferguson, December 9, 1963, in PHA, Parkwood Apartments-Related Documents folder, 1–3.
20. "Meeting Minutes," March 5, 1962, in PHA, Parkwood History folder, 1; and "Minutes of Annual Membership Meeting of Parkwood Association," June 6, 1966, in PHA, Minutes 1966 folder, 1.
21. "Durham County Planning Commission Minutes," November 12, 1973, and January 14, 1974, in PHA, Emerald Forest Apt-Related Documents folder; "Points of Agreement between Key Homes and Parkwood Homeowners Association," July 12, 1971; and "Contract between Parkwood Community Center, Inc. and Equitable Construction Company," September 22, 1971, in PHA, Parkwood Apartments-Related folder. For the broader trend, see Mark Obrinsky and Debra Stein, "Overcoming Opposition to Multifamily Rental Housing," *Joint Center for Housing Studies*, March 2017, http://www.jchs.harvard.edu/sites/jchs.harvard.edu/files/rr07-14_obrinsky_stein.pdf.
22. See the discussion of "septic-tank suburbia" in Adam Rome, *The Bulldozer in the Countryside: Suburban Sprawl and the Rise of American Environmentalism* (Cambridge: Cambridge University Press, 2001), 87–118.
23. "Meeting Minutes," September 13, 1962, 4, in PHA, Parkwood History folder.
24. Ida Kay Jordan, "Water Issue Muddied in Parkwood," *North Carolina Leader*, February 28, 1968, 6.

25. "Welcome to Parkwood," 7.
26. "Final Report on Survey," April 11, 1968, in PHA, Historical folder, Reports—Special, 1.
27. Interview with Buckley Crist Jr., April 21, 2014.
28. Interview with Al Alphin and Sol Ellis, May 29, 2014; and McPherson, "'Grand Mix of People,'" 1A.
29. Interview with Smita Patel, May 2, 2014. Rohe noted that the Asian and Hispanic populations in the overall Triangle metro remained vanishingly small in the 1970s and grew significantly only with the "robust job market" of the 1990s; Rohe, *Research Triangle*, 106–7.
30. Sherwood Ross, "Roll Out Red Carpet," *Chicago Defender*, February 8, 1964, 5.
31. Margaret Ruth Little, "Getting the American Dream for Themselves: Postwar Modern Subdivisions for African Americans in Raleigh, North Carolina," *Buildings & Landscapes: Journal of the Vernacular Architecture Forum* 19 (Spring 2012): 74.
32. Bill Surface, "The World of the Wealthy Negro," *New York Times*, July 23, 1967, 38–40.
33. John Drescher, *Triumph of Good Will: How Terry Sanford Beat a Champion of Segregation and Reshaped the South* (Jackson: University Press of Mississippi, 2000), 114, 132–34.
34. Jack K. Russell, "Supreme Court Refuses to Review Holt Case," *Raleigh News & Observer*, October 13, 1959, in North Carolina Collection (hereafter cited as NCC), University of North Carolina at Chapel Hill, folder 780, School Segregation, Terry Sanford Papers.
35. "A Promise—And a Warning," *Greensboro Daily News*, October 14, 1959, in NCC, folder 780, School Segregation, Terry Sanford Papers.
36. Jack Michael McElreath, "The Cost of Opportunity: School Desegregation and Changing Race Relations in the Triangle Since World War II" (PhD diss., University of North Carolina, 2002), 342.
37. Minutes of Parkwood Association Board of Directors, Special Meeting, April 22, 1968, 1–2, in PHA, folder 1968.
38. Board of Directors, letter to residents of Parkwood, May 13, 1968, 1, in PHA, 1960s folder.
39. Board of Directors, letter to residents of Parkwood, 1.
40. Minutes of Parkwood Association Board of Directors, Special Meeting, 1.
41. Hale Sweeny, Minutes of a Meeting of Concerned Parkwood Citizens, April 12, 1968, 5, in PHA, folder 1968.
42. Board of Directors, letter to residents of Parkwood, 1.
43. Board of Directors, letter to residents of Parkwood, 2.
44. Board of Directors, letter to residents of Parkwood, 2.
45. Board of Directors, letter to residents of Parkwood, 2.
46. Board of Directors, letter to residents of Parkwood, 2–3.
47. Board of Directors, letter to residents of Parkwood, 1.
48. Joseph High, letter to residents of Parkwood, May 17, 1968, in PHA, folder 1968, 1.
49. High, letter to residents of Parkwood, 2–3.
50. "Incorporation or Annexation?," January 10, 1969, in PHA, folder Historical, Reports—Special, 1.
51. Untitled report, in PHA, folder 1968, 1.
52. "Incorporation or Annexation?," 2.
53. Barbara Friedman, "Plants May Lose Sewer-Rate Break," *Durham Herald*, November 6, 1979, in PHA, Parkwood History Folder, PHA.
54. "Neighbors Harass, Threaten New Tenant, Family in N.C.," *Afro-American*, October 5, 1968, 3.
55. "Negro Family Moves from White Community; Say Lives Threatened," *Lexington Dispatch*, October 16, 1968, 7.
56. Harry Golden, "The Acquittal of James Lawing," *Chicago Defender*, April 12, 1969, 8.
57. E. W. Kenworthy, "An Uneasy Calm Returns to 3 Campuses," *New York Times*, March 16, 1969, 67; and Golden, "The Acquittal of James Lawing," 8.

58. Ann McColl, interview with Daniel H. Pollitt, Southern Oral History Program Collection, March 21–22, 1991, http://docsouth.unc.edu/sohp/L-0064-6/L-0064-6.html.
59. Martin Waldron, "Chapel Hill's New Negro Mayor Declares, 'I've Got to Be Good,'" *New York Times*, May 12, 1969, 41; and Howard N. Lee, *The Courage to Lead: One Man's Journey in Public Service* (Chapel Hill: Cotton Patch Press, 2008), 2, 9–10.
60. Oliver White, interview with Edwin Caldwell, Southern Oral History Program Collection, March 2, 2001, http://docsouth.unc.edu/sohp/playback.html?base_file=K-0202&duration=02:59:20.
61. White, interview with Caldwell.
62. Kathryn Nasstrom, interview with Anne Barnes, Southern Oral History Program Collection, January 30, 1989, http://docsouth.unc.edu/sohp/playback.html?base_file=C-0049&duration=01:28:45.
63. White, interview with Caldwell.
64. Lawrence van Gelder, "New Mayors, and Some Old Ones, to Run Big Cities," *New York Times*, November 8, 1973, 52.
65. Marian Houston and Terrele Schumake, "'73 Saw Plenty of Headlines," *Chicago Defender*, December 29, 1973, 4.
66. "Notebook Traps Mayor's Wife," *Chicago Defender*, December 24, 1974, 23.
67. Dewey Potter, Editorial, *Florida Sun*, November 30, 1973, in Voter Education Project Organizational Records (hereafter cited as VEP), Robert W. Woodruff Library of Atlanta University Center, Series VI Printed and Published Materials, Newsclippings: 1973, box 14, folder 11.
68. "New Trend Toward Political Coalitions," *Birmingham Times*, November 22, 1973, in VEP, Series VI, box 14, folder 11.
69. Little, "Getting the American Dream for Themselves," 75.
70. "Black Wins Mayoralty in Raleigh," *Charlotte Observer*, November 7, 1973, 1A, VEP, in Series VI, box 14 folder 2; Little, "Getting the American Dream for Themselves," 78–79.
71. Rob Christensen, "Precinct 39: Prototype of 'New Raleigh,'" *Raleigh News & Observer*, November 13, 1973, in VEP, Series VI Printed and Published Materials Newsclippings: 1973, Politics, North Carolina, box 14, folder 2.
72. Lee, *The Courage to Lead*, 135–40.
73. Louis Martin, "Lightner Got Short End of the Stick," *Chicago Defender*, October 18, 1975, 3; Mary R. Warner, "Harassment of Black Elected Officials Charged," *San Francisco Sun Reporter*, October 27, 1977, 14; and Kenyon C. Burke, "Black Officials Under Attack?," *San Francisco Sun Reporter*, June 8, 1978, 6.
74. "History of CMS," Charlotte-Mecklenburg Schools, https://www.wearecms.com/apps/pages/thehistoryofcms.
75. *Milliken v. Bradley*, 418 U.S. 717 (1974). For *Milliken*'s impact, see William L. Taylor, "Desegregating Urban School Systems After Milliken v. Bradley: The Supreme Court and Urban Reality: A Tactical Analysis of Milliken v. Bradley," *Wayne Law Review* 21, no. 3 (March 1975); and Robert A. Sedler, "The Profound Impact of Milliken v. Bradley," *Wayne Law Review* 33, no. 5 (1987): 1693.
76. "An Agenda for Merger," *Raleigh News & Observer*, February 5, 1995, 8; McElreath, "Cost of Opportunity," 383; Gerald Grant, *Hope and Despair in the American City: Why There Are No Bad Schools in Raleigh* (Cambridge, MA: Harvard University Press, 2009); and *A Community United: Celebrating 30 Years of Courageous Leadership* (Raleigh: Wake Education Partnership, 2006), 4–7.
77. Matthew D. Lassiter, *The Silent Majority: Suburban Politics in the Sunbelt South* (Princeton, NJ: Princeton University Press, 2006), 296.

78. McElreath, "The Cost of Opportunity," 13. On opposition to consolidation in Cary, see Lassiter, *Silent Majority*, 296; and Peggy Van Scoyoc, *Desegregating Cary, North Carolina* (Cary, NC: Passing Time Press, 2009).
79. Grant, *Hope and Despair in the American City.*

INTERLUDE: SWEET GUMS, TRAFFIC JAMS, AND CILANTRO

1. William M. Rohe, *The Research Triangle: From Tobacco Road to Global Prominence* (Philadelphia: University of Pennsylvania Press, 2011),74; Lawrence K. Altman, "Gertrude Elion, Drug Developer, Dies at 81," *New York Times*, February 23, 1999.
2. Katherine Bouton, "The Nobel Pair," *New York Times*, January 29, 1982, 87.
3. Email correspondence with author, January 27, 2015.
4. Wayne King, "A Research Center Flourishes in North Carolina," *New York Times*, February 4, 1977, 38
5. Interview with Tom Wenger, December 20, 2016.
6. Interview with Tom Wenger.
7. Interview with Tom Wenger.
8. Interview with Smita Patel, May 2, 2014.
9. Interview with Chuck Till, November 8, 2016.
10. Peter Range, "Chapel Hill: 'Capital of the Southern Mind,'" *Lakeland Ledger*, January 1, 1973, 3.
11. Wendell Rawls Jr., "The Good Life in North Carolina," *New York Times*, March 20, 1983, 67.

4. "THE GREATEST CONCENTRATION OF PhDs IN THE COUNTRY": THE IDEA ECONOMY COMES OF AGE IN THE TRIANGLE

1. William M. Rohe, *The Research Triangle: From Tobacco Road to Global Prominence* (Philadelphia: University of Pennsylvania Press, 2011), 94, 146.
2. *A Dynamic Concept for Research: The Research Triangle Park of North Carolina*, 1981, in DCL, Research Triangle Park subject file, n.p.
3. *A Dynamic Concept for Research.*
4. Rohe, *Research Triangle*, 74.
5. "Growing Computer Firm Plans New Plant," *Raleigh News & Observer*, October 1, 1979, special supplement, 24; Thomas C. Hayes, "Triangle Park: North Carolina's High-Tech Payoff," *New York Times*, April 26, 1987, F12; and Peter Range, "Chapel Hill: 'Capital of the Southern Mind,'" *Lakeland Ledger*, January 1, 1973, 6A.
6. Rohe, *Research Triangle*, 79.
7. For examples of the claim, see *A Dynamic Concept for Research*; Ruth Walker, "A Research Center Takes Root Among Pine and Possums," *Christian Science Monitor*, June 15, 1982, B2; Hayes, "Triangle Park," F12; and James Cobb, *The Selling of the South: The Southern Crusade for Industrial Development, 1936–1990* (Urbana-Champaign: University of Illinois Press, 1993), 175.
8. "Hodges Cites Research Plan," *Raleigh News & Observer*, March 26, 1955, in RGP, box 10, Research Triangle Correspondence, 1955.
9. Sources differ as to whether the Burroughs Wellcome building was officially completed in 1971 or 1972, but the preponderance suggest 1971. "Iconic Burroughs Wellcome Headquarters Open for Rare Public Tour," *NC Headlines*, October 9, 2012, https://www.ncheadlines.com

/releases/iconic-burroughs-wellcome-headquarters-open-for-rare-public-tour; and David Kroll, "Burroughs-Wellcome Elion-Hitchings Building Open for Public Tours October 20th Only," *Terra Sigillata* (blog), October 18, 2012, http://cenblog.org/terra-sigillata/2012/10/18/burroughs-wellcome-elion-hitchings-building-open-for-public-tours-october-20th-only/.

10. "Burroughs Wellcome Moving," *New York Times*, August 22, 1969, 2.
11. Mark Clark, *Dyeing for a Living: A History of the American Association of Textile Chemists and Colorists: 1921–1996* (Research Triangle Park: American Association of Textile Chemists and Colorists, 2001), 137–49.
12. "Burroughs Wellcome to Move Operations," *Wall Street Journal*, February 5, 1969, 2.
13. *History of the Burroughs Wellcome Fund* (Raleigh: Historic Preservation Foundation of North Carolina, 2005), 25.
14. Ajax [JB Jackson], "Living Outdoors with Mrs. Panther," *Landscape* 4, no. 2 (Winter 1954–55), 24–25.
15. Margaret Knox, " 'BW Mission Is to Help People,' " *North Carolina Leader*, August 20, 1971, 1.
16. "Burroughs Wellcome Sends Drugs to Moon," *Raleigh News & Observer*, October 1, 1979, 14.
17. D. Bruce Cohen, comment on Alex Sayf Cummings, "Into the Spaceship: A Visit to the Old Burroughs Wellcome Building," *Tropics of Meta*, October 17, 2016, https://tropicsofmeta.com/2016/06/13/into-the-spaceship-a-visit-to-the-old-burroughs-wellcome-building.
18. Luther J. Carter, "Research Triangle Park Succeeds Beyond Its Promoters' Expectations," *Science* 200 (June 30, 1978): 1470.
19. Richard McKenna, " 'Building Meaningfully': Burroughs Wellcome Corporate Headquarters, 1972," *We Are the Mutants*, July 25, 2019, https://wearethemutants.com/2019/07/25/building-with-meaning-burroughs-wellcome-corporate-headquarters-1972/.
20. Katherine Bouton, "The Nobel Pair," *New York Times*, January 29, 1982, 28.
21. David Kroll, "GSK to Sell Iconic Elion-Hitchings Building," *Terra Sigillata* (blog), April 18, 2011, http://cenblog.org/terra-sigillata/2011/04/18/gsk-to-sell-iconic-elion-hitchings-building/; and Sean Ekins, "Pharma Architecture and Informatics, Whiteboards as the Silo of Ideas, Symbol of Demise," *Collaborative Chemistry*, October 21, 2012, http://www.collabchem.com/2012/10/21/pharma-architecture-and-informatics-whiteboards-as-the-silo-of-ideas-symbol-of-demise/.
22. Cheapdadoo, "Inside the (Now-Deserted) Iconic Burroughs-Wellcome Building," *City Data*, October 8, 2016, http://www.city-data.com/forum/raleigh-durham-chapel-hill-cary/2657308-inside-now-deserted-iconic-burroughs-wellcome-2.html#post45905917.
23. Ekins, "Pharma Architecture and Informatics."
24. "Burroughs Wellcome Company Corporate Headquarters and Office and Dining Facility Addition, Research Triangle Park, NC, 1969–1972," *Paul Rudolph and His Architecture*, http://prudolph.lib.umassd.edu/node/4561; see also Paul Rudolph and Sibyl Moholy-Nagy, *The Architecture of Paul Rudolph* (New York: Praeger, 1970), 233.
25. McKenna, " 'Building Meaningfully.' "
26. David H. Schroeder, comment on Alex Sayf Cummings, "Into the Spaceship: A Visit to the Old Burroughs Wellcome Building," *Tropics of Meta*, October 8, 2016, https://tropicsofmeta.com/2016/06/13/into-the-spaceship-a-visit-to-the-old-burroughs-wellcome-building.
27. Interview with Tom Wenger.
28. Laura Oleniacz, "Smarter Way to Office," *Durham Herald Sun*, April 18, 2011, A1.
29. Nikil Saval, *Cubed: A Secret History of the Workplace* (New York: Doubleday, 2014), 183–255.
30. Jefferson Cowie and Joseph Heathcott, *Beyond the Ruins: The Meanings of Deindustrialization* (Ithaca, NY: ILR Press, 2003), 1–15; Cummings, *Democracy of Sound*, 209–211; and "Supporting Our Members' Vision for a Better Future," *Association of University Technology Managers*, 2018, https://autm.net/about-autm/mission-history.

31. Burton R. Clark, *Creating Entrepreneurial Universities* (Bingley, UK: Emerald Group, 1998); Sheila Slaughter and Gary Rhoades, "The Neo-Liberal University," *New Labor Forum* 6 (Spring-Summer 2000): 73–79; and Andrew Seal, "How the University Became Neoliberal," *Chronicle of Higher Education*, June 8, 2018, https://www.chronicle.com/article/How-the-University-Became/243622.
32. Carter, "Research Triangle Park Succeeds," 1469.
33. Rohe, *Research Triangle*, 74.
34. Carter, "Research Triangle Park Succeeds," 1469.
35. Albert N. Link, *Generosity of Spirit: The Early History of the Research Triangle Park* (Research Triangle Park, NC: Research Triangle Foundation, 1995), 92–93; and Rohe, *Research Triangle*, 75, 81.
36. "TUCASI," Research Triangle Park, https://www.rtp.org/tucasi/.
37. Carter, "Research Triangle Park Succeeds," 1470.
38. Peggy Schmidt, "The Greening of Research Parks," *New York Times*, October 14, 1984, NER37.
39. Charles W. Minshall, *An Overview of Trends in Science and High Technology Parks* (Columbus, OH: Battelle, 1983), 6.
40. Carter, "Research Triangle Park Succeeds," 1469.
41. Interview with Chuck Till, November 8, 2016.
42. "National Humanities Center Groundbreaking," *Digital Public Library of America*, April 1977, http://dc.lib.unc.edu/cdm/ref/collection/morton_highlights/id/1547.
43. Benjamin DeMott, "Are the Humanities Really Out of Style?," *New York Times*, October 26, 1975, 211.
44. "The National Humanities Center," *Bulletin of the American Academy of Arts and Sciences* 30 (April 1977): 6.
45. Michael Sterne, "Dream of Humanities Center About to Come True," *New York Times*, July 2, 1978, 34.
46. Sterne, "Dream," 34.
47. Sterne, "Dream," 34.
48. James Feron, "Columbia Service Eulogizes Frankel as Activist Thinker," *New York Times*, May 16, 1979, B10.
49. Sterne, "Dream," 34; "Scholars Discover Center for Humanities," *New York Times*, August 5, 1986, C7.
50. Interview with Robert Newman, December 14, 2015.
51. John Brinckerhoff Jackson, "The Almost Perfect Town," in *Landscape in Sight*, ed. Helen Lefkowitz Horowitz (New Haven, CT: Yale University Press, 1997), 107–17.
52. "The National Humanities Center," *Bulletin of the American Academy of Arts and Sciences* 30 (April 1977): 6.
53. Sterne, "Dream," 34.
54. "Humanists Find Happiness Amid the Pine Forest," *Christian Science Monitor*, June 15, 1982, B6.
55. Sterne, "Dream," 34.
56. Sterne, "Dream," 34.
57. Carter, "Research Triangle Park Succeeds," 1470.
58. "National Humanities Center," 7.
59. "Contact Staff," North Carolina Biotechnology Center, http://www.ncbiotech.org/about-us/staff-listing-dept/all; and e-mail correspondence with Karin J. Shank, April 10, 2018.
60. "Biotechnology," North Carolina in the Global Economy, http://www.ncglobaleconomy.com/biotechnology/overview.shtml.
61. John Hardin and Maryann Feldman, "North Carolina's Board of Science and Technology: A Model for Guiding Technology-Based Economic Development in the South," in *A Way Forward:*

Building a Globally Competitive South, ed. Daniel P. Gitterman and Peter A. Coclanis (Chapel Hill: University of North Carolina Press, 2011), 121.
62. Carter, "Research Triangle Park Succeeds," 1469.
63. *Durham: Where Visions Become Reality* (Atlanta: Riverbend Books, 2001), 9.
64. Wayne King, "A Research Center Flourishes in North Carolina," *New York Times*, February 4, 1977, 38.
65. King, "Research Center," 38.
66. Alexander L. Taylor, "Striking It Rich: A New Breed of Risk Takers Is Betting on the High-Technology Future," *Time*, February 15, 1982.
67. Manuel Castells, *The Informational City: Information Technology, Economic Restructuring, and the Urban-Regional Process* (Oxford: Blackwell, 1989).
68. Thomas C. Parramore, *Express Lanes and Country Roads: The Way We Lived in North Carolina, 1920–1970* (Chapel Hill: University of North Carolina Press, 1983), 40.
69. James Vickers, *Raleigh City of Oaks: An Illustrated History* (Sun Valley, CA: American Historical Press, 1994), 128.
70. Walker, "Research Center Takes Root," B1.
71. Ferrel Guillory, "New Infusion of State Funds Brightening Job Prospects," *New York Times*, March 28, 1982, 47.
72. Vickers, *Raleigh City of Oaks*, 135–36.
73. *A Dynamic Concept for Research*.
74. "Series on 'New' Cities," *Christian Science Monitor*, June 15, 1982, B2.
75. Ruth Walker, "Luring Companies with Pirouettes and a Symphony," *Christian Science Monitor*, June 15, 1982, B6.
76. Taylor, "Striking It Rich."
77. Michael I. Luger and Harvey A. Goldstein, *Technology in the Garden: Research Parks and Regional Economic Development* (Chapel Hill: University of North Carolina Press, 1991), 94.
78. Ruth Walker, "A North Carolina Renaissance Built on 'Idea' Industries," *Christian Science Monitor*, June 15, 1982, B8, in DCL, Research Triangle subject file.
79. Rohe, *Research Triangle*, 4.
80. Hayes, "Triangle Park," F12.
81. Luger and Goldstein, *Technology in the Garden*, 95; and William Graves and Christopher Woodey, "Risk, Finance and North Carolina's Post-Industrial Future," *Southeastern Geographer* 46 (2006): 245–58.
82. Hayes, "Triangle Park," F12.
83. Minshall, *Overview of Trends*, 1.
84. Minshall, *Overview of Trends*, 11.
85. Ferrell Guillory, "Raleigh," *New York Times*, October 22, 1989, 10.
86. "Luring Technology to Science Parks," *New York Times*, April 24, 1983, F9.
87. "Luring Technology to Science Parks," F9.

5. CARY, SAS, AND THE SEARCH FOR THE GOOD LIFE

1. Doug Marlette, *The Bridge* (New York: Harper Collins, 2002), 36.
2. "Cary, North Carolina," *City-Data*, http://www.city-data.com/city/Cary-North-Carolina.html; and "Gloria G. Guzman," "Household Income: 2016," *United States Census*, September 2017, https://www.census.gov/content/dam/Census/library/publications/2017/acs/acsbr16-02.pdf.
3. Tom Byrd and Jerry Miller, *Around and About Cary*, 2nd ed. (Ann Arbor, MI: Edwards Brothers, 1994), 160.
4. Gerald Grant, *Hope and Despair in the American City: Why There Are No Bad Schools in Raleigh* (Cambridge, MA: Harvard University Press, 2009); and "Dr. Goodnight to Speak at

Graduation," *Cary Academy*, December 7, 2016, https://www.caryacademy.org/page.cfm?p=9009&newsid=2555&ncat=24.

5. Byrd and Miller, *Around and About Cary*, 145.
6. For instance, signs could display only a handful of colors, with "the use of high intensity colors or fluorescent pigments . . . prohibited." Cary, NC Code of Ordinances and Land Development Ordinances, 9.8.3 Colors. Building codes also specify that neighborhood developments "should be built on a human scale and designed with a common, harmonious architectural vocabulary and landscaping to lend an intimate and personal feel to the streetscape. The intent should not be to create a uniform appearance, but rather a distinct sense of place." 8.53 (H) Relationship Between Building Types.
7. John Brinckerhoff Jackson, "The Almost Perfect Town," in *Landscape in Sight: Looking at America*, ed. Helen Lefkowitz Horowitz (New Haven, CT: Yale University Press, 1997), 31.
8. Matt Young, "Profile: Former Cary Mayor Koka Booth," *Cary Citizen*, June 30, 2010, http://carycitizen.com/2010/06/30/profile-former-cary-mayor-koka-booth/.
9. Town of Cary, *Cary Historic Preservation Master Plan*, n.d., http://www.townofcary.org/home/showdocument?id=9545,7–8.
10. Ella Arrington Williams-Vinson, *Both Sides of the Tracks II: Recollections of Cary, North Carolina 1860–2000* (West Columbia, SC: Wentworth Printing, 2001), 243–57.
11. Town of Cary, *Cary Historic Preservation Master Plan*, 9; Byrd and Miller, *Around and About Cary*, 61–62.
12. Byrd and Miller, *Around and About Cary*, 95.
13. Sherry Monahan, *Images of Cary* (Charleston, SC: Arcadia, 2011), 8.
14. Williams-Vinson, *Both Sides of the Tracks II*.
15. Byrd and Miller, *Around and About Cary*, 96, 124, 127.
16. Byrd and Miller, *Around and About Cary*, 133.
17. *U.S. News and World Report*, July 12, 1982; and Aaron Moody, "NC Towns Make Money Magazine's List of Best Places to Live in US. One Made the Top 5," *Raleigh News & Observer*, September 19, 2018.
18. Jim Wise, *Durham: A Bull City Story* (Charleston, SC: Arcadia, 2002), 138.
19. Hal Goodtree, "Cary Artist: Jerry Miller," *Cary Citizen*, March 12, 2010, http://carycitizen.com/2010/03/12/cary-artist-jerry-miller/; and interview with Jerry Miller, December 17, 2015.
20. Interview with Miller.
21. Byrd and Miller self-published the first edition in 1973, but an expanded and updated version was released in 1994. Interview with Miller.
22. Interview with Miller.
23. Byrd and Miller, *Around and About Cary*, 96.
24. Byrd and Miller, *Around and About Cary*, 96.
25. Tyler Gray Greene, "Farm to Factory: Secondary Road Building and the Rural Industrial Geography of Post-World War II North Carolina," *Journal of Southern History* 84 (2018): 277–310; and "Interstate 40," AA Roads, September 10, 2018, https://www.aaroads.com/guides/i-040-nc/. Meredith McCarroll offers a lyrical meditation on the ways in which the interstate shaped the contours of Tar Heels' lives across the state in her essay, "I-40," *The Bitter Southerner*, http://bittersoutherner.com/folklore-project/i-40/.
26. Byrd and Miller, *Around and About Cary*, 96.
27. Town of Cary, *Cary Historic Preservation Master Plan*, 14.
28. Byrd and Miller, *Around and About Cary*, 109.
29. Byrd and Miller, *Around and About Cary*, 110.
30. Byrd and Miller, *Around and About Cary*, 109.
31. Interview with Miller.

32. Jim Wise, "A Sense of Place," in *27 Views of Durham: The Bull City in Prose and Poetry* (Hillsborough, NC: Eno Publishers, 2012), 29–36.
33. Jack Michael McElreath, "The Cost of Opportunity: School Desegregation and Changing Race Relations in the Triangle Since World War II" (PhD diss., University of North Carolina, 2002), 281.
34. Byrd and Miller, *Around and About Cary*, 121.
35. Byrd and Miller, *Around and About Cary*, 122; see also the oral history accounts in Peggy Van Scoyoc, *Desegregating Cary, North Carolina* (Cary, NC: Passing Time Press, 2009).
36. Byrd and Miller, *Around and About Cary*, 122.
37. Byrd and Miller, *Around and About Cary*, 123; and McElreath, "Cost of Opportunity," 355–56.
38. McElreath, "Cost of Opportunity," 356.
39. Byrd and Miller, *Around and About Cary*, 122.
40. *A Community United: Celebrating 30 Years of Courageous Leadership* (Raleigh, NC: Wake Education Partnership, 2006), 4–7.
41. Drew Jackson, "Leader in Merger of Wake County and Raleigh Schools, Roy Tilley, Dies," *Raleigh News & Observer*, February 18, 2018; Byrd and Miller, *Around and About Cary*, 160; and Matthew D. Lassiter, *The Silent Majority: Suburban Politics in the Sunbelt South* (Princeton, NJ: Princeton University Press, 2006), 296–97.
42. Lassiter, *The Silent Majority*, 297; Grant, *Hope and Despair in the American City*; and Ansley Erickson, *Making the Unequal Metropolis: School Desegregation and Its Limits* (Chicago: University of Chicago Press, 2016).
43. Byrd and Miller, *Around and About Cary*, 106–7.
44. Byrd and Miller, *Around and About Cary*, 144.
45. Byrd and Miller, *Around and About Cary*, 144.
46. Byrd and Miller, *Around and About Cary*, 145. See also *Cary News*, November 2, 1977, p. 1.
47. David Carlton, "The Revolution from Above: The National Market and the Beginnings of Industrialization in North Carolina," *Journal of American History* 77, no. 2 (1990): 445–75.
48. Byrd and Miller, *Around and About Cary*, 147–48; and Town of Cary, *Cary Historic Preservation Master Plan*, 17–18.
49. Ralph McGill, "Education, Economic Progress Inescapably Together," *Miami News*, May 31, 1964, 6A.
50. Byrd and Miller, *Around and About Cary*, 129; Steve Kichen, "The Biggest Privately Held Tech Companies," *Forbes*, November 14, 2006, https://www.forbes.com/2006/11/13/private-technology-companies-pf-ii-cx_sk_1113sf.html#2dfeac9e6a9d; and Steve Lohr, "At a Software Powerhouse, the Good Life Is Under Siege," *New York Times*, November 21, 2009.
51. Randall Lane, "Pampering the Customers, Pampering the Employees," *Forbes*, October 14, 1996, 74.
52. Byrd and Miller, *Around and About Cary*, 151–52.
53. Jim Goodnight, "A Selectric Made Me Do It," *New York Times*, October 20, 2002, B14.
54. Paul Nowell, "Software Company SAS Institute Evolving Along with Its Customers," *Spartanburg Herald Journal*, June 15, 1997, E2.
55. Lane, "Pampering the Customers, 74–80; and Joseph Mosnier, interview with Jim Goodnight, Southern Oral History Program Collection, http://docsouth.unc.edu/sohp/html_use/I-0073.html, July 22, 1999, 16.
56. Interview with Goodnight, 29.
57. Interview with Goodnight, 28.
58. "From the College to the Pros," *Beaver County Times*, July 8, 1992, B6.
59. Lane, "Pampering the Customers," 76.

60. Steven Eisenstadt, "SAS: A Hard-to-Define Product but Simple Success," *Raleigh News & Observer*, July 21, 1996, https://web.archive.org/web/20170427065637/https://biostat.wustl.edu/~phil/stuff/si.html.
61. "SAS Institute . . . Setting the Pace," advertisement, *Gainesville Sun*, December 4, 1983, 8F.
62. Paul Nowell, "Cary Software Firm Handles Growth Without Losing Human Touch," *Wilmington Star-News*, June 28, 1992, 5E.
63. Lane, "Pampering the Customers," 74.
64. Madeline Hutcheson, "The Best First Jobs," *Schenectady Gazette*, May 12, 1989, 55.
65. Louise A. Mozingo, *Pastoral Capitalism: A History of Suburban Corporate Landscapes* (Cambridge, MA: MIT Press, 2011).
66. Kristina Shevory, "The Workplace as Clubhouse," *Wall Street Journal*, February 16, 2008, C5.
67. Karen V. de Asis, "Creating Great Brands by Caring for People First," *Philippine Daily Enquirer*, May 14, 2004, B4.
68. Leslie Kaufman, "Some Companies Derail the 'Burnout' Track," *New York Times*, May 4, 1999, A1, C8.
69. "Right Up There as #3 on Fortune's '100 Best,'" advertisement, *New York Times*, August 1, 1999, BU16.
70. Emery P. Dalesio, "Little-Known Software Giant to Raise Its Profile," *The Hour*, May 5, 2001, B7.
71. Interview with Goodnight, 29. On welfare capitalism, see Lizabeth Cohen, *Making a New Deal: Industrial Workers in Chicago, 1919–1939* (New York: Cambridge University Press, 1990), 161–62.
72. Interview with Goodnight, 28.
73. Lane, "Pampering the Customers," 78.
74. Timothy D. Schellhardt, "An Idyllic Workplace Under a Tycoon's Thumb," *Wall Street Journal*, November 23, 1998, B1.
75. Joann S. Lublin, "Nurturing Innovation," *Wall Street Journal*, March 20, 2006, B1.
76. Andrew J. Wefald and Ronald G. Downey, "Job Engagement in Organizations? Fad, Fashion, or Folderol," *Journal of Organizational Behavior* 30 (2009): 141–45.
77. Shevory, "Workplace as Clubhouse," C5.
78. Peter F. Drucker, *Management Challenges for the 21st Century* (New York: Harper Collins, 1999), 159.
79. Nowell, "Software Company SAS Institute Evolving," E2.
80. Nancy Holt, "Workspaces," *Wall Street Journal*, November 5, 2003, B8.
81. "SAS—The Royal Treatment," *60 Minutes*, https://www.youtube.com/watch?v=lvsIcwHavOs; and Rebecca Leung, "Working the Good Life," *CBS News*, April 18, 2003, https://www.cbsnews.com/news/working-the-good-life/.
82. Lublin, "Nurturing Innovation," B1.
83. Schellhardt, "An Idyllic Workplace," B1.
84. Christina Dyrness, "James Goodnight, the Ultimate Programmer," *Raleigh News & Observer*, n.d., quoted in Williams-Vinson, *Both Sides of the Tracks II*, 110.
85. Lane, "Pampering the Customers."
86. David Streitfeld, "Welcome to Zucktown. Where Everything Is Just Zucky," *New York Times*, March 21, 2018; and "The YIMBY Failing Project Feat. Shanti Singh," *Chapo Trapo House* (podcast), March 28, 2018, https://soundcloud.com/chapo-trap-house/unlocked-episode-197-the-yimby-failing-project-feat-shanti-singh-32818.
87. Schellhardt, "An Idyllic Workplace," B1.
88. Kaufman, "Some Companies Derail," A1.

89. Nikil Saval, *Cubed: A Secret History of the Workplace* (New York: Doubleday, 2014), 6. See also Douglas Coupland's influential fiction portrayal of the tech workplace in *Microserfs* (New York: Harper-Collins, 1995).
90. "From the College to the Pros," B6.
91. "SAS—The Royal Treatment."
92. "SAS—The Royal Treatment."
93. Dalesio, "Little-Known Software Giant," B7.
94. Kelly Crow, "Executive In-Baskets Meant for a Park Picnic," *New York Times*, June 30, 2002, CY5.
95. Williams-Vinson, *Both Sides of the Tracks II*, 110.
96. Interview with Miller.
97. Lily Geismer, "Good Neighbors for Fair Housing: Suburban Liberalism and Racial Inequality in Metropolitan Boston," *Journal of Urban History* 39 (2013): 454–77; and Rachel Guberman, "The Real Silent Majority: Denver and the Realignment of American Politics After the Sixties" (PhD diss., University of Pennsylvania, 2015).
98. "Past as Prologue? Presidential Election Results by Precinct," *Environmental Systems Research Institute*, http://storymaps.esri.com/stories/2012/precincts-2008/, indicates that Cary's precincts recorded lopsided margins for Barack Obama in 2008.
99. Amy Harmon, "Backers of Linux Say System Is Basis for Revolutionizing Computer Business," *New York Times*, September 28, 1998, C1.
100. Memo to Phyllis Branch, November 5, 1954, in RGP, 1925–87, and undated (RGP), Think Up/Start Up Era, Advertising and Related Correspondence, 1954, box 10, 1.
101. Maryann Feldman and Nichola Lowe, "Triangulating Regional Economies: Realizing the Promise of Digital Data," *Research Policy* 44 (2015): 1791.
102. Feldman and Lowe, "Triangulating Regional Economies," 1791.
103. Joel Kotkin, "The U.S.' Biggest Brain Magnets," *Forbes*, February 10, 2001, https://www.forbes.com/2011/02/10/smart-cities-new-orleans-austin-contributors-joel-kotkin.html#2426d1c577dc.
104. "Cary, NC," *CNN Money*, July 6, 2006, http://money.cnn.com/blogs/bplive/2006/07/cary-nc.html.
105. E-mail correspondence with Ben Drasin, April 7, 2016.
106. Interview with Sarah Taber, March 29, 2018.
107. David Havlick and Scott Kirsch, "A Production Utopia: RTP and the North Carolina Research Triangle," *Southeastern Geographer* 44, no. 2 (2004): 263–77.
108. Edward Relph, *Place and Placelessness* (London: Academic Press, 1976).
109. Alex Sayf Cummings, "'We Think a Lot': From Square to Hip in North Carolina's Research Triangle," in *The Bohemian South: Creating Countercultures, from Poe to Punk*, ed. Shawn Bingham and Lindsey Freeman (Chapel Hill: University of North Carolina Press, 2017), 242–63.

INTERLUDE: THE ISLAMIC SCHOOL IN PARKWOOD

1. Nazeeh Z. Abdul-Hakeem, *The Athaan in the Bull City: Building Durham's Islamic Community* (Morrisville, NC: Lulu, 2015), 4–5.
2. Abdul-Hakeem, *Athaan in the Bull City*.
3. Abdul-Hakeem, *Athaan in the Bull City*, 95–101.
4. Sol and Helen Ellis to Keith Edmonds, July 23, 1997, in PHA collection, Annexation file; John Stevenson, "Judge Weighs Arguments Over Parkwood Plans," *Durham Herald-Sun*, March 28, 1995; and "Parkwood Annexation Fight Shifts to Assembly," *Durham Herald-Sun*, April 12, 1995, A1–A2.
5. Photo in PHA, Annexation file.

6. Christopher Kirkpatrick, "Annexation-Reversing Bill Given One Last Shot, Then Dies Without Vote," in PHA, Annexation file.
7. U.S. Census Data for Durham, North Carolina Census Tract 20.13. U.S. Census Bureau, *Census of Population and Housing, 1990: Summary Tape File 1 on CD-ROM*, 1991; U.S. Census Bureau, *2000 Census of Population and Housing, Summary File 1: Technical Documentation*, 2001; U.S. Census Bureau, *2011–2015 American Community Survey 5-Year Estimates*, December 6, 2016.
8. Mike Davis, *Magical Urbanism: Latinos Reinvent the U.S. City* (New York: Verso, 2000); Wendy Cheng, *The Changs Next Door to the Diazes: Remapping Race in Suburban California* (Minneapolis: University of Minnesota Press, 2013); and Stanley Thangaraj, *Desi Hoop Dreams: Pickup Basketball and the Making of Asian American Masculinity* (New York: New York University Press, 2015).
9. Hannah Gill, *The Latino Migration Experience in North Carolina: New Roots in the Old North State* (Chapel Hill: University of North Carolina Press, 2010); and Sarah Mayorga-Gallo, *Behind the White Picket Fence: Power and Privilege in a Multiethnic City* (Chapel Hill: University of North Carolina Press, 2014).
10. William M. Rohe, *The Research Triangle: From Tobacco Road to Global Prominence* (Philadelphia: University of Pennsylvania Press, 2011), 106–7. See "Raleigh, North Carolina: Census 2010 and 2000 Interactive Map," Census Viewer, http://censusviewer.com/city/NC/Raleigh, http://censusviewer.com/state/NC, and http://censusviewer.com/city/NC/Morrisville.

6. "WE THINK A LOT": THE TRIANGLE IN THE AGE OF GENTRIFICATION

1. Faith No More, *We Care a Lot* (San Francisco: Mordam Records, 1985).
2. Sarah Willets, "Mayor Bill Bell Has Overseen a Bull City Renaissance. So Why Has Durham's Poverty Rate Gone Up on His Watch?," *Indy Week*, June 14, 2017, 11.
3. Willets, "Mayor Bill Bell," 11.
4. Stephen Heyman, "Raleigh-Durham: North Carolina's Axis of Cool," *New York Times*, November 19, 2010, http://www.nytimes.com/interactive/2010/11/19/t-magazine/21remix-scene.html?_r=0.
5. Margaret Pugh O'Mara, *Cities of Knowledge: Cold War Science and the Search for the Next Silicon Valley* (Princeton, NJ: Princeton University Press, 2005); and Lily Geismer, *Don't Blame Us: Suburban Liberals and the Transformation of the Democratic Party* (Princeton, NJ: Princeton University Press, 2015).
6. Marko Maunula, *Guten Tag, Y'all: Globalization and the South Carolina Piedmont, 1950–2000* (Athens: University of Georgia Press, 2009).
7. Albert N. Link and John T. Scott, "The Growth of Research Triangle Park," *Small Business Economics* 20 (2003): 167–75.
8. "Startup accelerators support early-stage, growth-driven companies through education, mentorship, and financing in a fixed-period, cohort-based setting," economist Ian Hathaway has explained. "While they are often grouped with other early-stage support and investing organizations, such as incubators, angel investors, seed-stage venture capitalists, and even co-working spaces, these are all distinct things." In the twenty-first century, the Triangle expanded its strength in each of these areas. Ian Hathaway, "Accelerating Growth: Startup Accelerator Programs in the United States," Brookings Institution, February 17, 2016, https://www.brookings.edu/research/accelerating-growth-startup-accelerator-programs-in-the-united-states/; and Nichola Lowe, "Lessons from the American Underground," *Planning* 83 (2017): 24–31.

9. Center for Entrepreneurial Development, "2014 Innovators Report: Tracking North Carolina's Entrepreneurial Activity," https://cednc.org/sites/default/files/cednc-innoreport-030215.pdf; interview with Jay Bigelow, August 15, 2016; "North Carolina's Research Triangle Is Ready for Its Startups to Go Big," *Red Herring*, January 6, 2017, https://www.redherring.com/startups/north-carolinas-research-triange-ready-startups-go-big/; and Zachary Eanes, "North Carolina Startups Raise More than $347 Million in First Quarter of 2017," *Raleigh News & Observer*, May 16, 2017, http://www.newsobserver.com/news/business/article150750687.html.
10. Christopher M. Cirillo, "Birth of an Idea: The Creation of Research Triangle Park and Its Sustained Economic Impact on the Research Triangle Area," *Urban Economics*, April 28, 2013, https://sites.duke.edu/urbaneconomics/?p=899.
11. "Hodges Cites Research Plan," *Raleigh News & Observer*, March 26, 1955, in RGP, Think Up/Start Up Era, box 10, Research Triangle Correspondence, 1955.
12. "School Merger Chronology," in DCL, School Merger subject file, DCL; and "Back to the Classroom," *Raleigh News & Observer*, February 5, 1995, 1A–9A. Sociologist Gerald Grant tells the story in *Hope and Despair in the American City: Why There Are No Bad Schools in Raleigh* (Cambridge, MA: Harvard University Press, 2009), and Jack Michael McElreath provides a finer grain of detail in "The Cost of Opportunity: School Desegregation and Changing Race Relations in the Triangle Since World War II" (PhD diss., University of Pennsylvania, 2002).
13. Interview with Jerry Miller, December 17, 2015, 10.
14. "Cancer Research Asked," *Times-News* (Hendersonville, NC), December 6, 1967, 2.
15. Kim Lachance Shandrow, "How Durham's Health Tech Startups Are Changing the City—and Future—of Medicine," *Free Enterprise*, June 8, 2017, https://www.freeenterprise.com/how-durham-health-tech-startups-are-changing-future-of-medicine/; Research Triangle Regional Partnership, "Durham County," 2019, https://researchtriangle.org/counties/Durham; and interview with Bigelow, 6–10.
16. Sociologist Sarah Mayorga-Gallo observed that some local white residents in a Durham community actually cheer gentrification in their communities; in Mayorga-Gallo, *Behind the White Picket Fence: Power and Privilege in a Multiethnic Neighborhood* (Chapel Hill: University of North Carolina Press, 2014), 53. See also Gavin Mueller, "Liberalism and Gentrification," *Jacobin*, September 26, 2014, https://www.jacobinmag.com/2014/09/liberalism-and-gentrification/.
17. Derek Hyra, *Race, Class, and Politics in the Cappuccino City* (Chicago: University of Chicago Press, 2017).
18. Early on, planners even worked out ratios of how many scientists and technicians the park would need, "assuming that a new laboratory moves in and imports into the area all of its scientists and half of its technicians and assuming that the balance of workers are home folk consisting of mechanics, office personnel, maintenance people and all other supporting personnel." See "Estimate of Personnel for the Research Triangle Park," January 22, 1958, in RGP.
19. Suzanne Haire, "London Home Buyers Fear Gazumping," *New York Times*, July 2, 1972, R1.
20. Ruth Rejniz, "'Back to City' Conference Set," *New York Times*, August 25, 1974, 453.
21. Eileen Segrest, "Inman Park: A Case Study in Neighborhood Revitalization," *Georgia Historical Quarterly* 63 (Spring 1979): 109–17; and Tyrell G. Moore and Gerald L. Ingalls, "A Place for Old Mills in a New Economy: Textile Mill Reuse in Charlotte," in *Charlotte, NC: The Global Evolution of a New South City*, ed. William Graves and Heather Smith (Athens: University of Georgia Press, 2010), 123.
22. "General Characteristics: North Carolina," U.S. Census 1950, 35–36, 126–31; *United States Summary: 2010, Population and Housing Unit Counts*, U.S. Census 2010, 78–80.
23. See U.S. Census Bureau, "QuickFacts: Orange County, North Carolina; Wake County, North Carolina; Durham County, North Carolina; North Carolina," https://www.census.gov/quickfacts/fact/table/orangecountynorthcarolina,wakecountynorthcarolina,durhamcountynorthcarolina,NC/EDU635216.

24. See U.S. Census Bureau, *American Fact Finder*, https://factfinder.census.gov/faces/nav/jsf/pages/index.xhtml#.
25. Reema Khrais, "In North Carolina, Clinton Hopes to Win Over White, Educated Voters," Marketplace, October 19, 2016, https://www.marketplace.org/2016/10/19/business/how-hillary-clinton-closing-educated-voter-gap.
26. Willets, "Mayor Bill Bell," 12, 14.
27. Thomas Sugrue, *The Origins of the Urban Crisis: Race and Inequality in Postwar Detroit* (Princeton, NJ: Princeton University Press, 1996).
28. Willets, "Mayor Bill Bell," 13.
29. Interview with Tyran Hill, July 12, 2017.
30. Henry Gargan, "Neighbors Oppose Habitat for Humanity's Plan to Build in Cary. If Not Here, Then Where?," *Raleigh News & Observer*, May 8, 2017, https://www.newsobserver.com/news/local/counties/wake-county/article149262379.html.
31. Interview with Hill.
32. Sarah Willets, "Durham's $429 Million Budget Raises Taxes to Fund Affordable Housing, Additional Firefighters," *Indy Week*, June 20, 2017, https://indyweek.com/news/archives/durham-s-429-million-budget-raises-taxes-fund-affordable-housing-additional-firefighters/; and Tammy Grubb, "Chapel Hill Wants $10 Million for Affordable Housing. Here's Where the Money Would Go," *Raleigh News & Observer*, October 17, 2018, https://www.newsobserver.com/news/local/counties/orange-county/article219677125.html.
33. W. Fitzhugh Brundage, *The Southern Past: A Clash of Race and Memory* (Cambridge, MA: Harvard University Press, 2005), 227–69; Jean Bradley Anderson, *Durham County: A History of Durham County, North Carolina* (Durham: Duke University Press, 2011); Leoneda Inge, "The Search for Affordable Housing in Durham," North Carolina Public Radio, July 17, 2017, http://wunc.org/post/search-affordable-housing-durham; Gillian White, "The Downside of Durham's Rebirth," *Atlantic*, March 31, 2016, https://www.theatlantic.com/business/archive/2016/03/the-downside-of-durhams-rebirth/476277/; and Mayorga-Gallo, *Behind the White Picket Fence*, 144–45, 148–54.
34. Thomas Piketty, *Capital in the Twenty-First Century* (Cambridge, MA: Harvard University Press, 2014).
35. Karin Fischer, "The 2 North Carolinas: Higher Education Transformed the State's Economy, but It Left Some Residents Behind," *Chronicle of Higher Education*, March 31, 2017, A16–A20.
36. Rose Haban, "NC Infant Mortality Rate Remains Stubbornly High," *North Carolina Health News*, October 21, 2016, https://www.northcarolinahealthnews.org/2016/10/21/nc-infant-mortality-rate-remains-stubbornly-high/; and Marian F. MacDorman and Elizabeth C. W. Gregory, "Fetal and Perinatal Mortality, United States, 2013," *National Vital Statistics Reports* 64 (July 2015), 1.
37. Sandy Grady, "To Jesse Helms: You're In. Why Not Help Your State?," *Pittsburgh Press*, November 9, 1990, D3.
38. Peter A. Coclanis, "Down Highway 52: Globalization, Higher Education, and the Future of the American South," *Journal of the Historical Society* 3 (2005): 334.
39. Interview with Chuck Till, November 8, 2016.
40. Bryant Simon, *The Hamlet Fire: A Tragic Story of Cheap Food, Cheap Government, and Cheap Lives* (New York: New Press, 2017).
41. Graves and Middleton have highlighted the shortcomings of Greensboro and its greater Triad metro area in an unpublished policy proposal. William Graves and Jon Middleton, "The Greensboro Innovation Hub: SC2 Challenge Proposal," n.d., 9.
42. Marla Frederick, "North Carolina: A Southerner Mines the Meaning of Progress," *Religion and Politics*, September, 2012, https://religionandpolitics.org/2012/09/04/north-carolina-a-southerner-mines-the-meaning-of-progress/.

43. Paul Luebke, *Tar Heel Politics 2000* (Chapel Hill: University of North Carolina Press, 1998), vii–ix; and Mac McCorkle, "History and the 'New Economy' Narrative: The Case of Research Triangle Park and North Carolina's Economic Development," *Journal of the Historical Society* 12 (December 2012): 483.
44. Shandrow, "How Durham's Health Tech Startups."
45. This claim is not to imply that past North Carolina leaders, notably Governors Terry Sanford (1961–65) and Jim Hunt (1977–85 and 1993–2001), did not pursue policies that promoted education and training more broadly. They enacted such measures as the School of Science and Mathematics, a residential high school for gifted students in Winston-Salem founded in 1980, and the state's extensive community college system. These actions have resulted in measurable, if modest, gains for ordinary North Carolinians. See Nichola Lowe, "Job Creation and the Knowledge Economy: Lessons from North Carolina's Life Science Manufacturing Initiative," *Economic Development Quarterly* 21 (2007): 339–53.
46. "About CED," Center for Entrepreneurial Development, https://cednc.org/about.
47. For an assessment of the Triangle's progress in patent registration, venture capital, and initial public offerings in the 1990s, see Michael E. Porter, *Research Triangle: Clusters of Innovation Initiative* (Washington, DC: Council on Competitiveness, 2001).
48. William Graves, "The Southern Culture of Risk Capital: The Path Dependence of Entrepreneurial Finance," *Southeastern Geographer* 51 (2011): 49–68.
49. Susan Walcott, "Growing Global: Learning Locations in the Life Sciences," *Growth and Change* 32 (Fall 2001): 527–28.
50. Albert N. Link, *Generosity of Spirit: The Early History of the Research Triangle Park* (Research Triangle Park, NC: Research Triangle Foundation, 1995), 70.
51. Interview with Bigelow.
52. Memo to Phyllis Branch, November 5, 1954, in RGP, 1925–87 and undated, Think Up/Start Up Era, Advertising and Related Correspondence, 1954, box 10, 1.
53. Sharon Zukin, *Loft Living: Culture and Capital in Urban Change* (New Brunswick, NJ: Rutgers University Press, 1982); and Charles Landry, *The Creative City: A Toolkit for Urban Innovators* (New York: Earthscan, 2000).
54. On the idea of hegemony, see Michael Hardt and Antonio Negri, *Multitude: War and Democracy in the Age of Empire* (New York: Penguin, 2004), xv, 107.
55. Skeptical views of Florida's development ethos and sociological vision are not in short supply. Geographer Jamie Peck offered one of the most trenchant critiques in "Struggling with the Creative Class," *International Journal of Urban and Regional Research* 29 (December 2005): 740–70. Historian Andrew T. Simpson also has cast doubt on the fiscal implications of a creative-class-oriented approach to development in " 'We Will Gladly Join You in Partnership in Harrisburg or We Will See You in Court': The Growth of Large Not-for-Profits and Consequences of the 'Eds and Meds' Renaissance in the New Pittsburgh," *Journal of Urban History* 42 (2016): 306–22.
56. Peck, "Struggling with the Creative Class," 747–49.
57. Sociologist Derek Hyra provided one of the most salient analyses of the "back to the city" movement and gentrification in "The Back-to-the-City Movement: Neighbourhood Redevelopment and Processes of Political and Cultural Displacement," *Urban Studies* 52 (2015): 1753–73. See also Richard Lloyd, *Neo-Bohemia: Art and Commerce in the Postindustrial City* (New York: Routledge, 2005).
58. Rohe, *Research Triangle*, 191.
59. "Brightleaf Square: History," n.d., https://historicbrightleaf.com/history/; "The New American Tobacco Campus Takes Shape," *North Carolina Department of Natural and Cultural Resources*,

https://www.ncdcr.gov/blog/2015/06/24/the-new-american-tobacco-campus-takes-shape-2004; Rohe, *Research Triangle*, 196–97; Jean Bradley Anderson, *Durham County: A History of Durham County, North Carolina* (Durham, NC: Duke University Press, 2011); Joe DePriest, "Gastonia's Historic Loray Mill's Renovation Brings Secrets, Memories," *Charlotte Observer*, March 7, 2014, https://www.charlotteobserver.com/news/local/article9102536.html.

60. Albert N. Link, *From Seed to Harvest: The Growth of the Research Triangle Park* (Research Triangle Park, NC: Research Triangle Foundation, 2002), 23–4.
61. Florida, *Rise of the Creative Class* (first edition), 285.
62. Richard Florida, "America's Brainiest Cities," *The Daily Beast*, August 27, 2010, https://www.thedailybeast.com/americas-brainiest-cities.
63. Joel Kotkin, *The Next Hundred Million: America in 2050* (New York: Penguin, 2010), 56; see also Joel Kotkin, "How the South Will Rise to Power Again," *Forbes*, January 31, 2013, https://www.forbes.com/sites/joelkotkin/2013/01/31/how-the-south-will-rise-to-power-again/#4b72515f5b86; and Joshua Keating, "Urban Warfare: Joel Kotkin vs. Richard Florida on Cities and the Creative Class," *Foreign Policy*, March 22, 2013, http://foreignpolicy.com/2013/03/22/urban-warfare-joel-kotkin-vs-richard-florida-on-cities-and-the-creative-class/.
64. For the paradigmatic case of the metropole in a globalizing capitalism, see Saskia Sassen, *The Global City: New York, London, Tokyo* (Princeton, NJ: Princeton University Press, 2001); on mulitethnic suburbia, see Mike Davis, *Magical Urbanism: Latinos Reinvent the U.S. City* (London: Verso, 2000), Wendy Cheng, *The Changs Next Door to the Diazes: Remapping Race in Suburban California* (Minneapolis: University of Minnesota Press, 2013), and Willow Lung-Amam, *Trespassers? Asian Americans and the Battle for Suburbia* (Berkeley: University of California Press, 2017).
65. Kotkin, *Next Hundred Million*, 56.
66. J. J. Goode, "36 Hours in Research Triangle, N.C.," *New York Times*, June 14, 2009.
67. William M. Rohe, *The Research Triangle: From Tobacco Road to Global Prominence* (Philadelphia: University of Pennsylvania Press, 2011), 2–6; and Smart Growth America, *Measuring Sprawl 2014* (Washington, DC: Smart Growth America, 2014), 7, 19.
68. David Brooks, *Bobos in Paradise: The New Upper Class and How They Got There* (New York: Simon & Schuster, 2000), 31–48.
69. Peter Drucker is widely regarded as coining the term "knowledge worker," edging close to the concept with his discussion of "knowledge jobs" in *Landmarks of Tomorrow: A Report on the New "Post Modern" World* (New York: Harper & Row, 1959).
70. "The VICE Guide to Killing Your Parents," *VICE*, December 3, 2005, https://www.vice.com/en_us/article/exagmm/the-vice-v12n8.
71. Rick Smith, "IBM Layoff Total Surges Past 2,500 across 22 Work Groups, Union Reports," *WRAL Tech Wire*, March 1, 2010, https://www.wraltechwire.com/2010/03/01/ibm-layoff-total-surges-past-2500-across-22-work-groups-union-reports/.
72. Jane Jacobs was probably the main avatar of a movement that wanted to sustain and rebuild density in American cities since the 1960s, best exemplified by her seminal book *The Death and Life of Great American Cities* (New York: Random House, 1961). See also Ilse Helbrecht and Peter Dirksmeier, *New Urbanism: Life, Work, and Space in the New Downtown* (Surrey, UK: Ashgate, 2011).
73. Interview with Bob Geolas, January 13, 2016.
74. Interview with Kristie VanAuken, November 13, 2018.
75. Lisa Sorg, "The Frontier Launches New Way of Working at Research Triangle Park," *Indy Week*, January 16, 2015, https://indyweek.com/news/archives/frontier-launches-new-way-working-research-triangle-park/.

76. Jeffrey C. Billman, "Why Is Research Triangle Park Building Its Own Mini-City?," *Indy Week*, October 7, 2015, https://www.indyweek.com/indyweek/why-is-research-triangle-park-building-its-own-mini-city/Content?oid=4794379.
77. Interview with Geolas; and Billman, "Why Is Research Triangle Park Building Its Own Mini-City?"
78. Rohe, *Research Triangle*, 4.
79. Interview with Kristie VanAuken.
80. Stefano Lucarelli and Carlo Vercellone, "The Thesis of Cognitive Capitalism," *Knowledge Cultures* 1 (2013); and Dillon Mahmoudi and Anthony Levenda, "Beyond the Screen: Uneven Geographies, Digital Labour, and the City of Cognitive-Cultural Capitalism," *Open Access Journal for a Global Sustainable Information Society* 14 (2016), 99–120. For a wider-ranging discussion of informational capitalism, see Michael Hardt and Antonio Negri, *Empire* (Cambridge, MA: Harvard University Press, 2000), 280–303.
81. As Hardt and Negri observed, summarizing the influential work of economist Robert Reich: "Reich calls the kind of immaterial labor involved in computer and communication work 'symbolic-analytical services'—tasks that involve 'problem-solving, problem-identifying, and strategic brokering activities.' This type of labor claims the highest value, and thus Reich identifies it as the key to competition in the new global economy." Hardt and Negri, *Empire*, 291.
82. Robert E. Scott, "The Manufacturing Footprint and the Importance of U.S. Manufacturing Jobs," Economic Policy Institute, January 22, 2015, http://www.epi.org/publication/the-manufacturing-footprint-and-the-importance-of-u-s-manufacturing-jobs/.
83. Legendary Austin booster Pike Powers put it this way: "I think we've changed in a very constructive, futuristic way, to be more connected with research, science, the stuff that matters. The universities played a huge role in helping to drive that equation. . . . The Chamber of Commerce decided in the fairly early days that we were not going to take on companies or groups that polluted the air or the water." Interview with Pike Powers, *We Are Austin Tech*, July 10, 2012, https://www.youtube.com/watch?v=UKz3zzkF7VQ. For a full treatment of Austin's postindustrial development, see Eliot M. Tretter, *Shadows of a Sunbelt City: The Environment, Racism, and the Knowledge Economy in Austin* (Athens: University of Georgia Press, 2016).
84. V. O. Key, *Southern Politics in State and Nation* (New York: Knopf, 1949), 205; and Dan T. Carter, "North Carolina: A State of Shock," *Southern Spaces*, September 24, 2013, https://southernspaces.org/2013/north-carolina-state-shock.
85. Glenna Matthews, *Silicon Valley, Women, and the California Dream: Gender, Class, and Opportunity in the Twentieth Century* (Stanford, CA: Stanford University Press, 2002); Stephen J. Pitti, *The Devil in Silicon Valley: Northern California, Race, and Mexican Americans* (Princeton, NJ: Princeton University Press, 2003); and Brentin Mock, "When It Comes to Tech, Racial Disparities Are Far Worse than Gender Disparities," *CityLab*, October 5, 2017, https://www.citylab.com/equity/2017/10/when-it-comes-to-tech-racial-disparities-are-far-worse-than-gender-disparities/542013/.
86. Sean Hollister, "Protesters Block Silicon Valley Buses, Smash Google Bus Window," *Verge*, December 20, 2013, https://www.theverge.com/2013/12/20/5231758/protesters-target-silicon-valley-shuttles-smash-google-bus-window; David Meyer, "Apple and Google Are Rerouting Their Employee Buses as Attacks Resume," *Fortune*, January 18, 2018, http://fortune.com/2018/01/18/apple-google-bus-attacks/; and Min Li Chan, "The Google Bus," *The Point* 14 (2017), https://thepointmag.com/2017/examined-life/the-google-bus.
87. Marisa Kendall, "Income Inequality: Where Is the Gap Largest," *Mercury News*, February 15, 2018, https://www.mercurynews.com/2018/02/15/income-inequality-in-the-bay-area-is-among-nations-highest/.

EPILOGUE

The third epigraph is from Rob Sullivan, *Geography Speaks: Performative Aspects of Geography* (New York: Routledge, 2016), 78; the original citation is in Raymond Williams, *The Country and the City* (New York: Oxford University Press, 1973), 124.

1. John Freeman, "More's Place in 'No Place': The Self-Fashioning Transaction in Utopia," *Texas Studies in Literature and Language* 34 (1992): 192–217.
2. Stephen Kotkin, *Magnetic Mountain: Stalinism as a Civilization* (Berkeley: University of California Press, 1995); and Kate Brown, *Plutopia: Nuclear Families, Atomic Cities, and the Great Soviet and American Plutonium Disasters* (New York: Oxford University Press, 2013).
3. Adrienne Rich, *The Dream of a Common Language, Poems 1974–1977* (New York: Norton, 1987).
4. For the classic statement of the concept of "placelessness," see Edward Relph, *Place and Placelessness* (London: Academic Press, 1976).
5. Judith Stein, *Pivotal Decade: How the United States Traded Factories for Finance in the Seventies* (New Haven, CT: Yale University Press, 2011); and Alex Sayf Cummings, *Democracy of Sound: Music Piracy and the Remaking of Copyright in the Twentieth Century* (New York: Oxford University Press, 2013).
6. Lisa McGirr, *Suburban Warriors: e Origins of the New Right* (Princeton, NJ: Princeton University Press, 2001); Margaret Pugh O'Mara, *Cities of Knowledge: Cold War Science and the Search for the Next Silicon Valley* (Princeton, NJ: Princeton University Press, 2004); Rachel Guberman, "The Real Silent Majority: Denver and the Realignment of American Politics After the Sixties" (Ph.D. diss., University of Pennsylvania, 2015); and Lily Geismer, *Don't Blame Us: Suburban Liberals and the Transformation of the Democratic Party* (Princeton, NJ: Princeton University Press, 2015).
7. For uses of the concept, see Ann Markusen and Anne Gadwa, *Creative Placemaking* (Washington, DC: National Endowment for the Arts, 2010), https://www.arts.gov/sites/default/files/CreativePlacemaking-Paper.pdf; Cynthia G. Falk and Marta Gutman, "Editors' Introduction," *Buildings & Landscapes: Journal of the Vernacular Architecture Forum* 20 (Fall 2013): v–x; and Ann Markusen and Alan Brown, "From Audience to Participants: New Thinking for the Performing Arts," *Análise Social* 49 (2014): 866–83.
8. William Rankin, "The Epistemology of the Suburbs: Knowledge, Production, and Corporate Laboratory Design," *Critical Inquiry* (Summer 2010): 771–806.
9. Richard Florida, "America's Brainiest Cities," *Atlantic*, August 27, 2010, https://www.thedailybeast.com/americas-brainiest-cities; and Eliot M. Tretter, *Shadows of a Sunbelt City: The Environment, Racism, and the Knowledge Economy in Austin* (Athens: University of Georgia Press, 2016).
10. Steve Lohr, "At a Software Powerhouse, the Good Life Is Under Siege," *New York Times*, November 21, 2009.
11. Richard Florida, *The Rise of the Creative Class: And How It's Transforming Work, Leisure, Community, and Everyday Life* (New York: Basic Books, 2002), 133.
12. Paul Starr, *The Creation of the Media: Political Origins of Modern Communications* (New York: Basic Books, 2004).
13. "Letter from John Adams to Abigail Adams," May 12, 1780, Massachussetts Historical Society, https://www.masshist.org/digitaladams/archive/doc?id=L17800512jasecond.
14. Alex Sayf Cummings, "On Creativity, Knowledge, and Epistocracy," *Tropics of Meta*, October 18, 2016, https://tropicsofmeta.wordpress.com/2016/10/18/on-creativity-knowledge-and-epistocracy/.

15. Jamie Cohen-Cole, *The Open Mind: Cold War Politics and the Sciences of Human Nature* (Chicago: University of Chicago Press, 2014).
16. Robert E. Scott, "The Manufacturing Footprint and the Importance of U.S. Manufacturing Jobs," *Economic Policy Institute*, January 22, 2015, http://www.epi.org/publication/the-manufacturing-footprint-and-the-importance-of-u-s-manufacturing-jobs/.
17. Dan Kopf, "The Future of American Jobs Is Taking Care of the Elderly," *Quartz*, November 2, 2017, https://qz.com/1114615/the-future-of-american-jobs-is-taking-care-of-the-elderly/; Nichole Gracely, "'Being Homeless Is Better than Working for Amazon,'" *Guardian*, November 28, 2014, https://www.theguardian.com/money/2014/nov/28/being-homeless-is-better-than-working-for-amazon; and David Barboza, "In Chinese Factories, Lost Fingers and Low Pay," *New York Times*, January 5, 2008.
18. Anne Krishnan, "Big Blue's Red-letter Day," *Durham Herald-Sun*, September 19, 2005, A1; and Rob Shapard, "Triangle Research: CTRL+ALT+DELETE, Bacteria in Water," *Durham Herald-Sun*, April 28, 2007.
19. Sam Kriss, "The Long, Slow, Rotten March of Progress," *The Outline*, May 31, 2017, https://theoutline.com/post/1611/the-long-slow-rotten-march-of-progress?zd=1&zi=jhyxvi2b.

Index